Russia in Flux

Russia in Flux

The Political and Social Consequences of Reform

Edited by

David Lane

Reader in Sociology
Cambridge University

Edward Elgar

Published by
Edward Elgar Publishing Limited
Gower House
Croft Road
Aldershot
Hants GU11 3HR
England

Edward Elgar Publishing Company
Old Post Road
Brookfield
Vermont 05036
USA

A CIP catalogue record for this book
is available from the British Library

A CIP catalogue record for this book
is available from the US Library of Congress

ISBN 1 85278 680 9
      1 85278 713 9 (paperback)

Phototypeset in 10 point Times by Intype, London
Printed and bound in Great Britain by
Biddles Ltd, Guildford and King's Lynn

Contents

List of Figures and Tables   vii
List of Contributors   ix
Preface   xiii

PART I   THE CHANGING STRUCTURE OF LEADERSHIP

1. Soviet Elites, Monolithic or Polyarchic?   3
   David Lane
2. The Top Leadership: from Soviet Elite to Republican
   Leadership   24
   Alexander Rahr
   Appendix: Biographies of Major Politicians   38
3. Political Elites and Politics in the Republics   41
   Darrell Slider
4. Social Groups, Party Elites and Russia's New Democrats   62
   Sergei Mitrokhin and Michael E. Urban

PART II   CIVIL SOCIETY

5. Professionalization   85
   Anthony Jones
6. The Role of Journalists and the Media in Changing
   Soviet Society   101
   Vera Tolz
7. Manual Workers and the Workforce   114
   Elizabeth Teague
8. The Emergence of New Family Farmers: The
   Countryside of Estonia in Transition   133
   Ray Abrahams
9. Soviet Youth   149
   Jim Riordan
10. *Perestroika* and Female Politicization   166
    Genia Browning and Armorer Wason

PART III   NEW INEQUALITIES
11. The New Business Elite   185
     Olga Kryshtanovskaya
12. Poverty and Underprivileged Groups   196
     Alastair McAuley
13. Housing Reform and Social Conflict   210
     Greg Andrusz

Index   239

Figures and Tables

FIGURES

1.1	Central Committee Membership, 1917–90	9
1.2	Politburo, 1919–90	10
1.3	Types of elite structure	15
1.4	Political stability/instability	19
2.1	USSR political system before and after the putsch	35
4.1	Income stratification of the Russian population and the Party elites (DPR/SDPR combined)	68

TABLES

1.1	Growth of ministries, USSR, 1924–87	6
1.2	Growth in number of state employees in USSR, 1922–80	7
1.3	Work background of top Soviet government administrators	14
3.1	Percentage of women elected to republic parliaments	43
3.2	Composition of new parliaments in selected republics, by occupation	44
3.3	Percentage representation of the largest ethnic groups in the republic parliaments	46
3.4	Communist Party membership of deputies in republic parliaments at the time of the elections	49
3.5	Elections to top posts in the republics	52
4.1	Education levels in the Soviet population and among Party elites	66
4.2	Per capita monthly income levels in Russia and individual income of DPR and SDPR elites	67
4.3	Occupational structures of the USSR (1987) and the DPR and SDPR	69
4.4	Levels of educational attainment of Party elites (DPR/SDPR combined) by occupational group	70
4.5	Levels of income of Party elites (DPR/SDPR combined) by occupational group	70
4.6	Education of DPR and SDPR elites	73

4.7 Age structure of DPR and SDPR elites 74
4.8 Date of entry into politics, DPR and SDPR elites 75
12.1 Distribution of the population by per capital total
income in 1988 and 1989 199
12.2 Geographical distribution of the poor, USSR, 1988 200

Contributors

RAY ABRAHAMS is a Fellow of Churchill College and Lecturer in Social Anthropology at the University of Cambridge, UK. His publications include *The Nyamwezi Today* (1981) and *A Place of Their Own: Farming Families in Eastern Finland* (1991).

GREG ANDRUSZ is Principal Lecturer in the School of Sociology, Faculty of Social Science at Middlesex Polytechnic, UK. His publications include *Housing and Urban Development in the USSR* (1984), and 'Housing Policy in the Soviet Union' in J. Sillince (ed.), *Housing Policies in Eastern Europe and the Soviet Union* (1990). He is currently working on an ESRC project, 'The Causes and Consequences of Homelessness in the USSR and Bulgaria'.

GENIA BROWNING is the author of *Women and Politics in the USSR, Consciousness Raising and Soviet Women's Groups* (1987). She lived in Moscow for three years: two years working at Radio Moscow and one year studying at Moscow State University. She is now Access Co-ordinator and Sociology Lecturer at Woolwich FE College.

ANTHONY JONES is Associate Professor of Sociology at Northeastern University and a Fellow of the Russian Research Center at Harvard University, US. His recent publications include *KO-OPS: The Rebirth of Entrepreneurship in the Soviet Union* (with W. Moskoff); *Professions and the State: Expertise and Autonomy in the Soviet Union and Eastern Europe* (ed.); and *Soviet Social Problems* (ed. with W. Connor and D. Powell).

OLGA KRYSHTANOVSKAYA is a senior research fellow of the Institute of Sociology of the Russian Academy of Sciences, Moscow. She is head of a project on 'The Administrative System and its Personnel' and has recently completed a study of the new rich in Moscow.

DAVID LANE is Reader is Sociology at Cambridge University, UK and a Fellow of Emmanuel College. His most recent book is *Soviet*

Society Under Perestroika (revised edition 1992). He is currently working on the evolution of elites.

ALASTAIR MCAULEY is Reader in Economics at the University of Essex, UK. He has written numerous articles and books on the subject of inequality and poverty under socialism including *Economic Welfare in the Soviet Union*. He is at present engaged on a study of poverty in Russia.

SERGEI MITROKHIN is a research associate at the Institute for Humanist-Political Research in Moscow. His articles on party formation and youth subculture politics have appeared in Russia and in Germany.

ALEXANDER RAHR is a senior research analyst at Radio Free Europe/Radio Liberty Research Institute, Munich. He is the author of *Biographical Directory of 100 Leading Soviet Officials* (five editions) and other papers on Soviet elites and politics.

JIM RIORDAN is Professor of Russian Studies and Head of the Department of Linguistic and International Studies at the University of Surrey, UK. Recent publications include *Soviet Youth Culture* (ed., 1990); *Sport, Politics and Communism* (1991); (ed., 1991); and *Sex and Soviet Society* (ed. with Igor Kon, 1992).

DARRELL SLIDER is Associate Professor of Government and International Affairs at the University of South Florida (Tampa), US and has published a number of articles on political and economic reform in the Soviet Union in journals including *Soviet Studies, The Journal of Politics, Comparative Politics, The British Journal of Political Science, Electoral Studies* and *The Journal of Soviet Nationalities*. He is editor of, and a contributor to, the forthcoming book, *Elections and Political Change in the Soviet Republic*.

ELIZABETH TEAGUE is a senior research analyst with the Radio Free Europe/Radio Liberty Research Institute in Munich. She has written widely on Soviet affairs and particularly on the problems of labour.

VERA TOLZ is a senior research analyst at the Radio Free Europe/Radio Liberty Research Institute in Munich and a doctoral student at the Centre for Russian and East European Studies at the University of Birmingham, UK. She is the author of *The USSR's Emerging Multiparty System* (1990).

MICHAEL E. URBAN is Associate Professor of Politics at the University of California at Santa Cruz, US. His recent books include *Ideology and System Change in the Soviet Union and East Europe* (1992); *More Power to the Soviets: The Democratic Revolution in the USSR* (1990) and *An Algebra of Soviet Power* (1989).

ARMORER WASON is a freelance researcher and translator currently researching a BBC documentary project on the present work of the Russian state security service and editor of the forthcoming book, *We Won't Let You Use Our Silence.*

Preface

Until the rise of the reform leadership of Mikhail Gorbachev in 1985, the Soviet Union and the bloc of East European states constituted a stable and enduring political entity. The leaders of the socialist bloc claimed a monolithic unity in their goal of moving to a communist society: Marxism-Leninism legitimated central planning and a full-employment economy; centralized political leadership under the Communist Party presided over a redistributive welfare state. In Eastern Europe and China reform had led to piecemeal changes in the economy, including the rise of market elements; politically the dominant communists were under pressure – particularly so in Poland – but nowhere did the viability of the economic and political system appear to be under threat.

From the assumption of power by Gorbachev as General Secretary of the Communist Party of the Soviet Union (CPSU) in March 1985, the system of state socialism began to crumble. The policies of *perestroika* (restructuring), *glasnost* (openness), democratization and economic accountability undermined the foundations of the old order. In foreign affairs the USSR relinquished control in Eastern Europe: Poland elected a non-communist government in August 1989; in December the Berlin Wall was broken down and the German Democratic Republic was absorbed into the Federal Republic of Germany. In February 1990 the monopoly of leadership of the CPSU was abolished; in March Lithuania declared its independence; in June Eltsin became leader of the Parliament of the Russian Republic and declared its laws to have precedence over those of the USSR. In the next year similar announcements were made in the other republics of the USSR. In August 1991, in an attempt to halt the disintegration of the Soviet system and to restore the role of the Party and central control, the leaders of the government – including the deputy president, the prime minister and the chiefs of the armed forces and state security – declared a state of emergency and attempted to oust Gorbachev and assert control. Their attempted coup failed.

Consequently, the reform movement entered a new stage. The Communist Party was outlawed. Its property was seized. Marxism-Leninism

xiii

was repudiated. New political parties and groups flourished in a reconstituted civil society. Economic and social policy became radicalized. As organizing principles, the market, privatization and competition took the place of planning, state property and political control. Symbolically, on Christmas Day 1991, the hammer and sickle Red Flag was hauled down from the Kremlin. In its place rose the tricolour of the Russian Republic. Gorbachev resigned. The USSR was disbanded. In its place came the Commonwealth of Independent States.

The chapters in this book study both the background and the impact of these developments in the former areas of the USSR. The book is in three parts, addressing the changing structures of political leadership, the development of civil society and a new pattern of inequalities, and hopes to capture the essential developments which characterize the reforms which have taken place under Gorbachev and the immediate post-coup period.

In the first chapter David Lane outlines the growth of the Soviet bureaucracy and suggests that Gorbachev was confronted by a segmented power elite structure with closed recruitment legitimated by a single ideology. Gorbachev, in weakening the role of the Party, undermining the consensus among the elites and destroying the dominant ideology of Marxism-Leninism, created the conditions for elite instability and a volatile confrontational political structure. In Chapter 2 Alexander Rahr details the ensuing changes in the political structures and in the personnel of the political leadership. He describes the faction associated with the disintegration of the Union and the unsuccessful attempts under Gorbachev to maintain the Soviet Union. He charts the rise of Eltsin following the unsuccessful coup of August 1991. Darrell Slider focuses in Chapter 3 on the transformed legislatures of the republics and their influence on the formation of new political elites. He considers the changing social and ethnic background of the elected deputies and details the rise of the new anti-communist elites in the republics which led to the rise of independent states. The rapid decline of the Communist Party of the Soviet Union under Gorbachev was accompanied by the rise of new political groups and parties. Chapter 4, by Sergei Mitrokhin and Michael E. Urban, is based on original research in Russia on the rise of two new major political parties: the Democratic Party of Russia (DPR) and the Social Democratic Party of Russia (SDPR). They profile the origins of these parties, their social composition, their leaders, support and emergent programmes.

In the second part of the book we turn from elite politics to developments in civil society. First Anthony Jones considers the intelligentsia from the point of view of the professionalization of occupations and relates developments to patterns in market societies where professions have autonomy and are self-governing bodies. The author considers the position of physicians, lawyers, scientists and journalists and shows how the conditions which arose under the reform leadership of Gorbachev strengthened these groups and how in turn they participated in the evolving democratic structures. As the media have been so important in the process of change, Vera Tolz, in Chapter 6, appraises the role of journalists. She brings out the importance of *glasnost* and the rise of an independent culture from the 1960s and shows how the intelligentsia provided a base for the democratization pursued under Gorbachev. In Chapter 7 Elizabeth Teague studies the largest single group in the workforce, the manual working class. She considers its growth and differentiation from the time of Khrushchev. She shows both its greater assertiveness and the ways in which it is likely to suffer adverse effects from market reform. The third major occupational stratum are the farmers. Here Ray Abrahams, on the basis of the field work in Estonian villages, describes the emergence of new family farmers. He shows in detail how the process of privatization in farming is taking place and the kinds of future developments that are likely.

Two other important social groupings are discussed: youth, by Jim Riordan (Chapter 9) and women, by Genia Browning and Armorer Wason (Chapter 10). In the former chapter is described the disillusionment of youth under the traditional system of Soviet communism and the degeneration of the Youth Communist League (the Komsomol). The author documents the rise of a spontaneous youth culture since the 1960s which was rejected by the official youth movement. Consequently youth has been a major support in the reform movement and also in informal gangs. The chapter on women contrasts their position before and after *perestroika*. It is concluded that the rising political parties are less likely than the CPSU to champion women's equality. Women's groups in the early post-*perestroika* period have a diverse political consciousness, some rejecting 'equality' and others presenting a potential challenge to male dominance in politics.

The final part of the book is concerned with the impact of the evolving system on social inequality. Chapter 11, by Olga Kryshtanovskaya, considers the new business elite and its privileges. Using original research in Moscow she profiles the social background of the new entrepreneurs in Russia's capital. She shows that this new class is recruited both from members of the old administrative elite and from people who had previously been either peripheral or working in the shadow economy. Alastair McAuley turns in Chapter 12 to the other end of the scale of income distribution: the poor. He outlines the problems connected with the definition and extent of poverty. He concludes that the rapid inflation and collapse of the traditional system of distribution have exacerbated the position of the poor. In addition to the customary groups of the poor – pensioners, single-parent families – reform will threaten unemployment, with many unskilled middle-aged people who may not be able to adjust to the new conditions. Finally Greg Andrusz appraises the distributive effects of social policy, with particular respect to housing. After describing many of the problems inherited by the reformers, he outlines the policies being pursued by the reform leadership. He argues that rent reform and privatization will undermine previous forms of inequality but will create new ones and probably greater differentiation in the housing market.

The book is the outcome of a conference held in Cambridge. In addition to the above authors, the conference was enlivened by the presence of David Anderson, John Barber, A. Beruchashvili, Otto Cappelli, Peter Frank, Ernest Gellner, George Kolankiewicz, Christopher Hann, Max Haller, Tatyana Menshikova, Catherine Meridale, Felicity O'Dell, John Scott, Vinayak Srivastava and Jacek Wasilewski. I would like to thank the Master of Emmanuel College, Lord St John of Fawsley, for opening the conference and the Governing Body of the College for their support and the use of College premises. Finally I am indebted to the Ford Foundation, the Nuffield Foundation and the ESRC, without whose assistance the conference would not have been possible.

David Lane

PART I

The Changing Structure of Leadership

1. Soviet Elites, Monolithic or Polyarchic?

David Lane

Most influential writers on Soviet elites, ranging politically from Alfred Meyer through T. H. Rigby to Hillel Ticktin, assume that the elite structure is monolithic, totalitarian and that the Party working through its control of the Politburo is dominant. Alfred Meyer has described the USSR as 'a modern corporation writ large'[1] and Rigby in one of his earlier works, in similar vein, asserts that in modern industrial society it has 'become technically possible to run a large nation as a single corporation'.[2] More recently 'mono-organisational socialism' he has defined as 'the running of all aspects of social life through official bureaucracies, coordinated by the party apparatus and under the arbitrary direction of a personal dictator or tiny oligarchy'.[3] These assertions raise a number of questions: how do we define the elite (or elites) and evaluate its power? How is coordination and domination achieved by a mono-organizational elite?

In this chapter the above approach is criticized. The growth and complexity of the government bureaucracy is outlined: it is argued that the traditional system was characterized by an evolving autonomy of elites which was not subject to autocratic Party control. A consequence of this elite structure was a corporatist segmented power elite under Brezhnev enclosed in a Marxist-Leninist framework. The stable and consensual political order was dependent on its political environment: positive-sum political outcomes, a dominant ideology and a pluralist but closed elite structure. This framework was destroyed by the reformers under Gorbachev and replaced by pluralistic elites lacking ideological and political consensus.

The development of elites is linked to the formation of bureaucratic structures. Scale and complexity entail organization, specialized knowledge and division of authority. The nature of bureaucratic organization necessitates elite formation and the incumbents of elite positions form a directing group with authority over the resources of an organization. Despite formal controls over political elites seeking to make them

3

accountable to a wider constituency (shareholders and parliamentary bodies in the West, soviets and the Party under traditional state social-ism) in practice, bureaucratic politics entails the accretion of political power to elites. It is an assumption of this chapter that Soviet society has been and is characterized by segmented oligarchic bureaucratic rule: hierarchical bureaucratic organizations accumulate relative politi-cal autonomy. This autonomy in turn is conditioned by the ideological environment and by the form of recruitment of the elites. The relation-ship and balance between the various organizational structures is a potent factor in the dynamics of political change.

THE EVOLUTION OF THE STRUCTURE OF SOVIET POLITICAL ELITES

Prior to *perestroika*, there were four spheres of political interest articu-lation in the USSR: the Communist Party, the government executive, the elected system of soviets and voluntary organizations. The Com-munist Party has provided the political leadership of the Soviet state. From the early days of the Party's formation, a central committee has been the major forum of political authority; the Party elite in the body of the Politburo has been formed from it (from 1918 until 1952 an Orgburo also existed for internal party affairs: it will be ignored in this chapter). The Soviet government (*pravitel'stvo*) had executive powers: it directed and controlled the economy and provided the administrative apparatus of the state. After the revolution it was called the *Sovet narodnykh komissarov* (Sovnarkom), Council of People's Commissars, though from 1946 the name reverted to its pre-revolution-ary title: *Sovet Ministrov*, Council of Ministers. During the later period of Stalin's rule, a Presidium of this body was formed and from the 1970s it had a constitutional status and was composed of the economic members of the Council of Ministers. A formal legislature having executive functions, the soviets, has served as a mass representative body at local and higher levels. Its elite was originally called the Presidium of the Central Executive committee of the Congress of Soviets (VTsII). Since 1936 it has been called the Presidium of the Supreme Soviet of the USSR. Finally there are a number of voluntary organizations, such as trade unions, women's councils, friendship societies and sports clubs which were organizationally distinct from the other three bodies. They were unsatisfactorily defined as 'volun-tary' because they were not part of the Party-government complex of organizations. This basic scheme of elite power – Party, government and soviets – continued right down to the Gorbachev period and the changes introduced under Gorbachev.

As far as the structure of elite political power is concerned, before 1989 only two of these constituencies of politics may be considered as major components: the Council of Ministers and the Communist Party of the Soviet Union. The soviets have been ineffective bodies of interest aggregation, though they have performed other important administrative and representational roles. Voluntary organizations, the essence of Western civil society, have also been subject to penetration and control by Party and government agencies and have had little autonomous authority. There has been a 'closed' elite structure in the sense that autonomous groupings outside the state have either been denied the rights of formation or have been excluded from access to political power. The crucial problems of elite politics have been the process of interaction between the various departments, and between institutions of Party and government.

To indicate the changing structure of elite positions of the USSR, we may consider two indexes: first, the changes which have occurred in the number of institutions forming the government of the USSR and the size of the organizations (measured by the number of dependent employees);[4] second, the size of the top USSR Party bodies. These data will bring out the growing mass and complexity of the all-union elite structure and indicate the scope of bureaucratic politics. We shall then proceed to discuss the interconnection between the government and Party apparatus and to consider the changes which occurred under Gorbachev.

THE GROWTH OF THE GOVERNMENT BUREAUCRACY

In the early period of Soviet rule, the number of ministries and committees directing the activity of the USSR was relatively small, being only 10 in 1924. (See Table 1.1 for data for 1924 to 1987; 1991 is considered in Chapter 2.) At this time the size of the economy was relatively modest and undeveloped.

Following the rapid industrialization and investment in social infra-structure of the 1930s the economy became much more complex. The number of ministries mushroomed to 59 in 1947 and coordinating committees on planning, supply and prices were formed. The number of ministries was reduced to 25 following amalgamations after the death of Stalin,[5] but this consolidation did not last as it was found to be too unwieldy for efficient administration: by 1956 the number

The Changing Structure of Leadership

Table 1.1   Growth of ministries, USSR, 1924–87[6]

	1924[7]	1936	1947	1949	1952	1953	1954 (Apr)	1956 (Jan)
All-Union mins	5	8	36	28	30	12		
Union-Repub mins	5	10	23	20	21	13		
Total mins/comms	10	18	59	48	51	25	46	56
Non-voting members[8]	8[9]	14[10]						
TOTAL	18	32						

	1962	1966	1971	1977	1984	1987
All-Union mins	5	22	27	30	31	38
Union-Repub mins	10	25	31	32	31	19
Committees/commissions	31	9	9	19	19	33
Total mins/comms	46	56	67	81	81	90
Non-voting members[11]	34	32	39	52	51	41
TOTAL	80	88	106	133	132	131

increased to 56. The ousting of Khrushchev led to the reinstatement of the centralized ministerial system and to its steady growth. By the mid–1980s the Council of Ministers was composed of over 130 members: 81 ministries and state committees, 15 representatives of republican Councils of Ministers and an inner circle, composed of the Presidium of the Council, of 14 Chairs, Vice Chairs and Deputy Chairs.

GROWTH IN NUMBER OF EMPLOYEES IN THE GOVERNMENT SECTOR

These economic and political elites are only the apex of large complex organizations. The number of people employed may be used as an index of their size.[12] The numbers in paid work (excluding collective farmers) rose from 6.235 million in 1922 to 33.9 million in 1940, 76.9 million in 1965, 112.498 million in 1980 and 117.798 million in 1985). (See Table 1.2.) This spawned a vast bureaucracy: in 1922 in the government apparatus (including administration of cooperatives) 700 000 personnel were employed; the figure rose to 1.837 million in 1940 and to 2.495 million in 1980.[13] This bureaucratic apparatus was in charge of massive sectors of the economy: by 1981 there were over 37 million employees in industry, over 11 million in building and 10.4 million in education and culture. For detailed growth see Table 1.2.

Table 1.2   *Growth in number of state employees in USSR, 1922–80 (selected sectors, 000s)*

	1922	1940	1965	1970	1980
Industry	1 900	13 079	27 447	31 593	36 891
Transport	1 020	3 525	7 252	7 985	10 324
Building	102	1 993	7 301	9 052	11 240
Education and culture	500	2 678	6 600	8 070	10 456
Administration (apparat)	700	1 837	1 460	1 838	2 495
TOTAL	6 235	33 926	76 915	90 186	112 498

Source: *Narodnoe Khoziaystvo SSSR 1922–1982*, Moscow, 1982.

By functional division the government apparatuses giving rise to elites in the post-Khrushchev period could be grouped[14] as follows:

Non-economic administrative organs: culture, defence, health, interior, justice, state security; education – higher and secondary (ministry), vocational and technical education (state committee); external relations – external economic relations (state committee), foreign affairs; media – communications, cinematography, publishing/printing/ books, television and broadcasting.

Economic committees: state bank, statistical administration, finance, administration of Council of Ministers, inventions and discoveries, labour and social, material and technical supply, material resources, people's control, state planning, prices, science and technology, standards, trade, hydrometeorology and environmental control.

Industrial ministries (37 in all) with the following important subdivisions: (1) defence:[15] aviation, defence, electronics, general machine building, machine building, medium machine building, radio, shipbuilding; (2)energy: coal, gas, oil, oil refining, electric power development; (3) food: fish, fruit and vegetables, meal and milk; (4) machine tools: chemical and oil, construction and highways, heavy transport, animal husbandry and fodder, light/food/household appliances, machine tool and tool building, power, agricultural; (5) general industrial: motors, chemicals, communication equipment, construction materials, electrical equipment, iron and steel, geology, instrument building/automation, light industry, medical industry, non-ferrous industry, timber/paper/wood processing; and (6) agriculture: forestry, agriculture, land reclamation, fertilizer production, products procurement, supply of production equipment for agriculture.

Building: building (ministry), building (state committee), Far East and Transbaikal, heavy industry enterprises, petroleum and gas, industrial construction, installation and special construction work, agricultural enterprises, transport.

Transport: civil aviation, merchant marine, railways.

The major political problem facing the leadership of the Soviet state has been how to control and to decide who is to control this large, complex, differentiated administrative structure. The vast size of the Soviet Union led to the growth of Union-Republican ministries in which devolution from the centre to the republics occurred. This developed under Gorbachev into a major political division in which the elites in the republics, having a local power base, sought and eventually contrived to extend their power at the expense of the centre.

THE PARTY AS AN AGENCY OF POLITICAL COHESION AND CONTROL

The Communist Party (until 1989) and the soviets (particularly since 1989) are institutions which should provide coherence and control over the bureaucratic structures. This is achieved through control of personnel (the *nomenklatura*), through ideology (Marxism-Leninism) and through policy formation. The political institutions of the Politburo and the Central Committee attempted to legitimate and aggregate interests through the cooption of various members of functional groups from the state bureaucracy.

Unlike the government apparatus, which in the early years was patterned on and had bureaucratic procedures inherited from the Tsarist political order, the Party had a relatively primitive organization. In the immediate post-revolutionary period, the Central Committee of the Party had no full-time executive. While an apparatus in the form of a Politburo, Orgburo and secretariat was in place by 1920, the Central Committee of 19 under Lenin's leadership constituted the Party elite. As the party grew in size and leadership became more complex, the Politburo and Orgburo became the executive bodies. Total membership of the Party grew from some 350 000 in October 1917 to 528 354 in 1922, 1.080 million in 1926, 1.678 million in 1930, 3.400 million in 1940, 6.340 million in 1950, 8.709 million in 1960, 14.012 million in 1970, 17.082 million in 1980 and 19.84 million in 1989.

Figure 1.1   Central Committee Membership, 1917–90

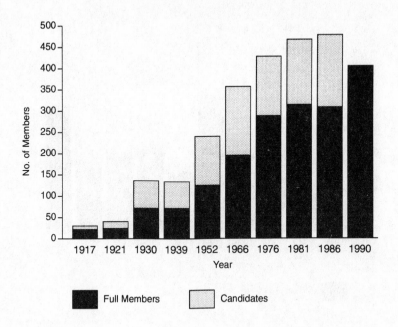

Full Members ☐ Candidates

The growth of the membership of the Central Committee is indicated in Figure 1.1.[16]

The Central Committee's expansion parallels that of the state apparatus, the top membership of which (for example, government ministers, heads of state committees) is represented in the central committee. From the mid–1920s, the Politburo (called the Presidium of the Central Committee, 1952–66) became the chief deliberative and decision-making body of the Party. Its membership increased in size, as indicated by Figure 1.2.[17] Since the mid–1950s it has remained fairly constant, with about a dozen members constituting the party elite though overlapping with membership of the Council of Ministers and the Supreme Soviet.

Effectively subordinate to the Politburo (though technically it was responsible to the Central Committee) was the Party secretariat. This body was the administrative arm of the Party constituting its apparat. Its departments parallel those of the government: in 1978 they included the Administrative Organs Department, Agriculture, Cadres, Chemical Industry, Building, Culture, Defence Industry, Economic Collaboration with Foreign Countries, General, Heavy Industry, Information, International, Liaison with Communist and Workers' Parties of Social-

Figure 1.2   Politburo, 1919–90

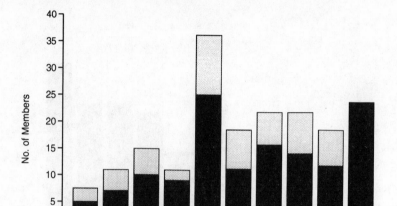

ist Countries, Light and Food Industry, Machine building, Organizational Party Work, Planning and Finance Organs, Propaganda,
Science and Educational institutions, Trade and Domestic Services,
Transport and Communications and Main Political Directorate of
Soviet Army and Navy. Other organizations coming under its jurisdiction were the Party Control Committee, Academy of Sciences, Institute of Scientific Atheism, Higher Party School, Higher Party Correspondence School, Institute for Raising the Qualifications of Leading
Party and Soviet Cadres of the Higher Party School, Institute of
Marxism-Leninism and Institute of Social Sciences; also the chief editors of the newspapers and journals of the Central Committee.[18]

ELITE COHERENCE AND INTEGRATION

By the early 1920s the Party's coordinating body was the Politburo.
It is important to note, however, that this body had no executive
powers: the executive positions of its leading voting members were in
the government – Lenin was the Chair of Sovnarkom and the Labour
and Defence Council; Trotsky was Commissar for War and Chair of
the Revolutionary-Military Council and Stalin was People's Commissar

for Nationalities and for Worker-Peasant Inspection (the other two full members, Kamenev and Zinoviev, were respectively Chairs of the Moscow and Petrograd Soviets); the Party Secretariat was represented on the Politburo by Molotov, who was a candidate member.

It should be questioned whether the Politburo and the Central Committee could control the operation of the government bureaucracy; considerable autonomy remained with government departments, though the Politburo could influence the main directions of internal and external policy. The Politburo was also a conduit for ministerial interests and for the aggregation of demands articulated by the government bureaucracy.

This overlap of Party and government positions (though in different proportions at different times) continued up to the time of Gorbachev. By the end of the Stalin period, the government bureaucracy dominated the Politburo: of its 11 members in 1951, 10 had senior government posts (including Stalin, who was Chair of the Council of Ministers); Malenkov held a second post as Secretary of the Central Committee, and only Khrushchev remained solely in that Party post. In practice, 'The Politburo had ceased to operate as a regular decision-making body, and membership in these and other top executive bodies had become little more than a register of standing within the leader's entourage and a reflection of the administrative duties assigned by him.' In this context, Rigby voices the received wisdom that 'Stalin's authority was absolute.'[19] But 'absolute authority' excludes consideration of the origins of decisions, recommendations and influences on the leader, and here the ministerial apparatus must have been the major source. Authority involves legitimacy, not the enforcement of decisions.

There can be no doubt that the state administration was the dominant political body under Stalin. The de jure controls by the elected soviets and political influence by the Party were ineffective. As the administration of the economy and the welfare agencies exploded during the late Khrushchev and Brezhnev period, the power of centrifugal forces increased and bureaucratic autarchy became dominant. Khrushchev recognized the weakness of the Party machine: by the end of 1957 he had reversed the representation in the Presidium of the Party (that is, the Politburo) – 10 of its 15 members were Party secretaries and only two representatives of the government Presidium remained (Mikoyan and Bulganin). In 1958 Khrushchev assumed the Chair of the Council of Ministers.

LOCALISM AND DEPARTMENTALISM

The centre (defined as the Politburo and the Party Secretariat) has been confronted with the twin countervailing forces of localism and departmentalism. By the latter we mean the assertion of autonomy by the ministerial apparat; localism is the practice of units identifying with and maximizing local interests spatially constituted. It is from these sources that demands for regional autonomy came and led to claims for sovereignty and independence in the early 1990s.

The problem of control of the massive state bureaucracy led Khrushchev to experiment with a cumbersome decentralization scheme in 1957 which led to the abolition of most of the industrial ministries and the creation of 105 regional economic councils (*sovnarkhozy*), later reduced to 40 in 1962. In that year, however, there were 46 institutions[20] represented in the USSR Council of Ministers (in addition to its Chair, two First Vice Chairs, and nine Vice Chairs).

Following the dismissal of Khrushchev in 1964, the Brezhnev-Podgorny-Kosygin leadership initially strengthened ministerial participation in the Politburo and reinstated the ministerial system. By 1978, only five voting members out of 14 of the Politburo had government posts: Andropov (KGB), Gromyko (Foreign Affairs), Kosygin (Chair), Mazurov (First Deputy Chair) and Ustinov (Defence). This balance continued into the early years of Gorbachev's rule. In 1985, for instance, seven out of 18 full members were in government posts: Ligachev (Deputy Chair), Chebrikov (KGB), Ryzhkov (Chair), Shevardnadze (Foreign Affairs), Demichev (Culture), Sokolov (Defence) and Talyzin (Gosplan). As noted above, the Presidium of the Council of Ministers was mainly concerned with economic matters.

This brief outline of the institutional structure of elite power in the USSR indicates an intricate and labyrinthine network of organizational structures.

MONO-ORGANIZATIONAL SOCIALISM?

What is the relationship between these institutions and how can one characterize the make-up of elite rule? There are a number of theoretical and empirical objections that may be made to the notion of 'mono-organizational socialism' described above. Firstly, such analysts adopt a reputational standpoint: essentially observers believe that the Politburo and its leader are dominant. There is no appeal to the decision-making and enforcement process. Clearly for many periods of Soviet history the Politburo has 'taken' the major decisions, but has it 'made' them? The inclusion of major actors from the government bureaucracy in the Politburo might make the latter an agent of the former and packing the Politburo with Party secretaries only makes control of the bureaucracy more difficult.

Secondly, as noted above, for much of the period of Soviet rule the Politburo has not been the dominant body but has been displaced by the rule of cliques. Thirdly, attempts by reformers to displace the government apparatus have failed either completely or partially. Khrushchev's decentralization of the administration did not succeed in breaking the power of the ministries. Brezhnev[21] adapted to the government bureaucracy and consequently various forms of corruption and self-interest developed which weakened central control: 'departmentalism' has characterized Soviet government administration. Gorbachev was unable to manage the structure; he sought to replace it in the early period with greater central control and after the late 1980s with a market orientation.

Fourthly, the 'mono-organizational society' approach[22] cannot explain the changes which came about under Gorbachev. If, as Rigby has put it, 'command is a relationship in which one party is active and the other is passive in the determination of what is done',[23] how could the Politburo abolish the sovereignty of the Party? Is it conceivable that the Party ruling elite would abdicate its political power? The measures of control of the Soviet leaders to modernize society have been confused with a propensity on their part to maintain themselves in power. Finally, such models ignore the context in which the elites operate and the style of leadership. What might be attributed to the monopolistic rule of the Party elite, might be conditions which have favoured the evolution of consensual elites.

It is more realistic to consider the government structure as a network of bureaucratic elites. The diversity and differentiation of functions of the bureaucracy noted above give rise to heterogeneity of elites rather than to a monopolistic unitary elite. The government apparatus is largely internally recruited, giving rise to a strong organizational consciousness and to the definition of independent goals and interests. Study of the work histories of government ministers shows a long career in a given sector. A study by Ryavec[24] of 121 obituaries of higher national-level Soviet government civilian leaders who died between October 1964 and the spring of 1979 examines their work experience in the Party apparatus and government bodies. His results are shown in Table 1.3. At the level of Minister 73 per cent, Deputy Minister 62 per cent and First Deputy Minister 50 per cent had no previous work in the Party apparatus. When they had it had often been at an early stage of their careers. These conclusions are confirmed by study of the internal mobility within the government apparatuses in the 1980s: self-recruitment in the Council of Ministers was 75 per cent in 1989 and 73 per cent in 1980.[25] It seems unlikely that early service in the Party apparat or the placement of Party plenipotentiaries in posts of Deputy Minister is likely to be very effective as a means of securing Party control.

Table 1.3 Work background of top Soviet government administrators

Worked in Party apparatus	Minister N=26	First Deputy Minister N=8	Deputy Minister N=34
Yes	27%	50%	32%
No	73%	50%	62%
Not known			6%

Source: Ryavec

THE MOVE TO PLURALISTIC ELITES UNDER GORBACHEV

Figure 1.3 illustrates the conditions determining different kinds of elite structures. It is defined in terms of

- Institutional formation: unitary (with a single dominant institution, such as a hegemonic Party or army command, or where there is a fusion under a ruling class of major constituencies); pluralistic (political, economic or military institutions having relative autonomy).
- Recruitment of elites: 'closed' being when counter-elites or potential elites are excluded from competing for entry to positions of power – for instance, when the formation of economic enterprises, or political parties is banned.
- Ideology: this distinguishes between a monopoly (which excludes the articulation of any other), dominant ideology shared by the elites or elite, such as that of traditional Marxism-Leninism, or capitalism and where counter-ideologies are marginalized and insignificant, and a situation with competing ideologies – such as between capitalism, socialism and anarchism.

Box 1 illustrates the conditions for a mono-organizational bureaucratic power elite, as conceived by Rigby (closed recruitment, unitary institutional structures, and a single value system). Box 3 allows for

Figure 1.3   Types of elite structure

INSTITUTIONAL FORMATION

RECRUITMENT	Unitary	Pluralistic	IDEOLOGY
Closed	1. Monopolistic power elite	2. Segmented power elites	Monopoly
Open	3. Meritocratic power elites	4. Consensual elites	Dominant
Open		5. Pluralistic elites	Pluralist

open recruitment through a circulation of elites. It illustrates C. W. Mills's power elite – an institutional bloc of the hypothesized military-industrial complex – and indicates a dominant ideology as postulated by the Marxist idea of a dominant ideological apparatus. Elite positions are 'open' in the sense that (bourgeois) parties and economic enterprises compete to occupy the elite positions.

Box 4, consensual elites, signifies the formation of stable Western democratic societies. These have open recruitment, a pluralistic form (of competing parties, private business and trade unions) but a dominant ideology: the elites are agreed about fundamentals of the political and economic system and respect the law. The important conditioning factor is the presence of 'loyal' oppositions.

Box 2 is my own version of the power structure under Brezhnev: a power elite with segmented constituencies, with closed recruitment (in the sense of an absence of political competition) and a single legitimating value system (Marxism-Leninism). They were largely self-governing elites, formed along the lines of segmented functional division outlined above, administering their own affairs. What was considered to be a growing 'pluralism' and democratization under Brezhnev involved greater functional specialization and autonomy to the elite segments. As Hough pointed out in 1979:

The definition of goals formally remains the responsibility of the party leadership, but except for ensuring that the Marxist goals in social policy are pursued, the leadership . . . should follow the advice of specialist 'complexes' or 'whirlpools' in their respective areas, limiting itself to a mediation of the conflicts that arise among them. In practice, policy-making power informally comes to be delegated to these complexes.[26]

The segmentation of elites is based on the division of bureaucratic institutions: police/security, foreign affairs, economic and political organs – as defined in the functional divisions above. Hence 'departmentalism' and corruption stemmed from the operational independence of these functional groups. And what was originally operational independence led to strategic independence in the sense that the ministries were able to write their own plans and make their own policies.

The appearance of monolithic unity through Party control is derived from the environment in which the elites operated. Marxism-Leninism has provided an ideological legitimation not only for state ownership and control through planning but also for the integration of regional elites into an All-Union one; it has prevented the aggregation of an alternative conception of ways of doing things and has thwarted the formation of counter-elites. Membership of positions within the elite structures has been closed and pressures have been exerted to secure loyalty of incumbents to the system. The elite has been agreed about relations to property, the distribution of resources, the legitimacy of the system and its institutions of interest aggregation (the Party) and enforcement (the KGB). In this sense the segmented elites have constituted a power elite: they have sought to maintain their position and to exclude contending groups.

This system has worked fairly well when political outcomes have been positive-sum: members of the ruling bureaucracies have enjoyed security and stability and non-elites have shared in the results of economic growth. This stable corporatist elite brought about its own downfall: Marxism-Leninism as an ideology failed to contain the materialist and ideal aspirations of younger generations – indeed Soviet leaders, in claiming the superiority of socialism over capitalism, had fuelled consumerist expectations. The more articulate and highly educated population became critical of the closed nature of the elites and the declining rates of growth increasingly made positive-sum political outcomes problematic. Intra-elite conflict (within the parameters of the existing system) destroyed the political compact of the Brezhnev period.

CHANGE UNDER GORBACHEV

The Gorbachev leadership undermined the traditional elite structure by pulling away its major ideological and political supports: the legitimacy of Marxism-Leninism, the hegemony of the Party and the destruction of the apparat of the central committee. Under pressure from the forces unleashed by *perestroika*, the Communist Party of the Soviet Union was confronted with competing political parties and groups. In the Russian Federation alone in 1991 there were over 100 parties and political groups.[27] From 1986, it had lost its traditional raison d'être: its discipline, organization and ideology provided a shell to the Soviet political order. In 1991, even before the attempted August coup, it had disintegrated into a number of heterogeneous groups and interests; many of its former leaders had broken away and formed other parties. Its Politburo was impotent when its General Secretary was held under house arrest by the ill-fated State Committee for the State of Emergency led by other senior Party members. The elites under Gorbachev lacked coherence and authority, which ensured that the coup failed.

There has been a shift of organizing principles away from planning to the market in both politics and economics. Self-interest has led to the legitimacy of counter-elites both on a geographical basis (national and ethnic) and functional (work-based collectivities, such as workers and professionals); the market has stimulated a class awareness on the part of an ascendant entrepreneurial class and a belief among many others of the advantages of a market-type system with private ownership.

Under Gorbachev there was a movement towards a more pluralistic system in ideology and the institutional formation and, as a result of a more open political arena, recruitment has become open. Before the attempted coup of August 1991, Soviet society was moving in the direction of a pluralistic elites structure (box 5), though there were important qualifications which become evident when one considers the institutional arrangements created under presidential power (Cabinet, Federation Council, Security Council – this is discussed below in Chapter 2).

The real political threat to the established USSR elites was over control of the resources then managed by the All-Union ministries located in the republics. It is here that the legitimacy of markets and privatization on the part of the republican governments may overlap and lead to class divisions. ('Class' is used here in the sense of ownership and control of productive assets and the extraction of surplus value.) Conflict between the centre and periphery is not only due to ethnic differentiation but has a base in control over productive assets (by different ethnic and social groups). A consequence of declarations of sovereignty in many of the republics has been a claim to All-Union assets located in the republics, and a decree to this effect was enacted by Eltsin during the state of emergency in August 1991 – subsequently endorsed by Gorbachev. This gave legitimacy to the republican governments and the banning of the Communist Party further led to the weakening of the All-Union state.

POLITICAL STABILITY/INSTABILITY

An analysis of political stability and instability is made in Figure 1.4. Here four variables are considered:

- Elite structures are of the power elite type, consensual or confrontational.
- Ideologies are dominant/monopolistic (a single ideology legitimating the political order and accepted by the masses – traditional Marxism-Leninism), consensual (a number of different ideologies, each with distinctive features but capable of coexistence – Christian democracy, democratic socialism, liberal capitalism) or antagonistic (world views which are incompatible one with another, such as communism and capitalism).
- Political organization is described in terms of interests (as defined above) or social blocs – such as classes, nations or ethnic groups.
- Political outcomes are defined as positive-sum or zero-sum.

The conditions for political stability and instability are shown in the various boxes. The combination of power elite and dominant ideology ensures stability whatever the political outcome or political organization. Even where political organizations are formed from social blocs (such as ethnic groups in the USA) the combination of elite unity and a dominant ideology secures a stable regime, even when outcomes are zero-sum. A consensual elite structure coupled to a positive-sum political outcome and an interest-type form of political organization within conditions of pluralistic ideologies also secure equilibrium. When linked to a zero-sum outcome and social bloc-type political organization, governments are unstable, as are confrontational elite structures matched to positive-sum outcomes, interest-type political organization and antagonistic ideologies. Governments are confronted with serious problems when conditions of box 6 develop: confrontational elite struc-

Figure 1.4   Political stability/instability

ELITE STRUCTURES

POLITICAL OUTCOMES	Power elites	Consensual	Confrontational	POLITICAL ORGANIZATION
Positive-sum	1. Stable	2. Stable	3. Unstable	Interests
Zero-sum	4. Stable	5. Unstable	6. Volatile	Social blocs
	Dominant/ monopolistic	Consensual	Antagonistic	

IDEOLOGY

tures, social bloc-type political organizations, zero-sum political out-comes and antagonistic ideologies.

The consequences of *perestroika* have been a move towards class and ethnic blocs, to open elite access and to a pluralism of values: communism, social democracy, monarchism, anarchism, capitalism and Christianity are now articulated by political associations. Elites have become confrontational. Since August 1991 the political structure is characterized by heterogeneous conflicting elites. There is a duality of power: the elected government institutions (the soviets) espouse a democratic order based on popular sovereignty; the economic units operate either on the basis of administrative control or increasingly private ownership exerted through the 'hidden hand' of the market. Unlike the pre-*perestroika* situation, when Marxism-Leninism provided a shell of ideological stability and elite legitimation, now in contrast there is a pluralistic value system and, given the sharp drop in gross national product and the rise of income differentials, political out-comes are zero-sum (that is, some players lose out to others).

The elite structure is confrontational. The control of assets is cur-rently a site of conflict between the administrative incumbents seeking to preserve power by a mixture of administrative controls or privatiz-ation (the transfer of ownership of assets to themselves) and new entrepreneurial classes originating from outside the old elites – from people in lower administrative positions, from the alternative economy and from the professionals. Engels, in discussing the basis of revolution, asserted: 'All revolutions until now have been revolutions for the protection of one kind of property against another kind of property. They cannot protect one kind without violating another.'[28]

Control over assets is the basis of the cleavage between the major actors in the class structure. On the one hand are those supporting and represented by the leaders of the coup of August 1991 – groups within the military industrial complex, members of the security apparatus and their backers in the state (including Party) apparatus. These groups, like Gorbachev, sought renewal within the administrative-command economy. They sought to reconstitute their power through quasi-state corporations, on the model of the nationalized British industries. They were confronted by a liberal-democratic opposition composed of people seeking a system based on private property and market. Some are disaffected members of the old structures: people who have 'jumped ship', as it were, used their authority and connections to further their ownership of assets. A second group is composed of others who have made money legally and illegally under the Brezhnev regime and who are able to buy assets following privatization. They are the basis of the cooperative movement and provide financial support for the new political parties and movements which have played an important role in bringing down the Communists. Thirdly there are farmers who have made profits out of their private plots and kolkhoz surplus produce. A fourth stratum originates from the middle and lower-level managerial strata previously employed in state industry. Fifthly there is a section of the 'intelligentsia' (physicians, lawyers, engineers) who see their professional advancement linked to their ability to maximize their skills on the market. All these groups have an elective affinity between their material interest which they may exploit on the market and the ideology of a free enterprise system. They constitute a revolutionary social bloc.

The lack of an ideology of class and national unity has led to the rise of national elites which have undermined the coherence of the pre-*perestroika* segmented power elite: this is witnessed by the declaration of independence or sovereignty by the leaders of these new political groups in the republics and other units (such as certain autonomous republics). It is the formation of regional blocs and elites which provides the strongest element of pluralism in the political structure and at the same time the greatest threat to stability. Western liberal democratic societies secure stability through a consensus of elites: they share a dominant ideology which is expressed in the acceptance of the political rules of the game, the sanctity of private property, limited state involvement and a respect for law. This is not the case in the post-*perestroika* politics of the USSR – and of course it is not characteristic of most market societies outside Western Europe and the USA and Canada.

As long as the combination of factors described in box 6 continues, systemic volatility is ensured. Gorbachev appeared weak and vacillating because he was unable to break out of this environment. The leaders of the State Committee for the State Emergency and Boris Eltsin were agreed that political stability could not be achieved under conditions of elite confrontation, social blocs and antagonistic ideologies. The strategy of both sides has been to secure conditions as in boxes 4 and 1 in Figure 1.2: to create a power elite structure, a single ideology, to move from social blocs to interests (by destroying class opposition) and to close recruitment to elite position. Here they parted company with Gorbachev, who advocated decisions based on compromise and consensus. Aided by the collapse of the traditional elites, Eltsin and the liberal supporters have succeeded where their opponents failed.

NOTES AND REFERENCES

1. Alfred G. Meyer, *The Soviet Political System*, Random House, New York, 1965, ch. 22.
2. T. H. Rigby, 'Traditional, Market and Organisational Societies and the USSR', *World Politics*, 1964, vol. 16, p.545.
3. T. H. Rigby, 'Gorbachev and Mono-organisational Socialism', *The Changing Soviet System*, Edward Elgar, Aldershot, 1990, p.233. For a detailed discussion see ch. 7, 'Political Legitimacy under Mono-organisational Socialism', pp.155–82.
4. In the republics there were also bureaucratic organizations; these have to be ignored here.
5. There were: Foreign Affairs, Internal Affairs, Defence, Internal and Foreign Trade, Agriculture, Culture, Light and Food Industry, Metallurgy, Machine Building, Transport and Heavy Machine Building, Electric Power Stations and Electrical Industry, Coal, Oil, Chemicals, Defence Industry, Building Materials Industry, Timber and Paper, Construction of Heavy Industry and Machine-Building Plants, Transport, Communications, Sea and River Transport, Health, Justice, Finance, State Control.
6. For the post-Second World War period, positions were not defined and hence there are blanks in this table where I have not been able to find sources which detail the non-voting members. However it is likely that a similar pattern persists as for the previous year shown. Membership of these institutions is continually changing (both in number of posts and personnel); the main sources used include, for period to 1962: Merle Fainsod, *How Russia is Ruled*, Harvard University Press, Cambridge, Mass., 1963, pp.392–402, R. W. Davies *et al.*, *Soviet Government Officials 1922–41: a Handlist*, Birmingham, 1989); for the earlier period sources are inexact but are good enough for the purposes of this article. For post–1952: data cited in D. Lane, *Politics in the USSR* (various editions), *State and Politics in the USSR*; for December 1987: H. Kraus and A. Rahr, *The Government of the USSR*, Munich: RL 514/87.

7. The composition of the Council of People's Commissars in 1924 was: Food Supply, Foreign Affairs, Chair of Supreme Council of National Economy, Internal Trade, Worker Peasant Inspection, Transport, Labour, Posts and Telegraph, Finance, Army and Navy, Chair of Gosplan. It was not until 1925 that republican representatives were added to the Council. In 1924 attached councils were: Labour and Defence, Administration.

8. Including Chairs, Vice-chairs and representatives of various committees and commissions.

9. Including Gosplan.

10. Including Gosplan in year 1935; in 1936 there were seven republican representatives attached to the Council: Tadzhik, Belorussian, Russian Republic, Transcaucasian, two from the Ukraine and Turkmen (source: Davies *et al.*, *Soviet Government Officials*, pp.17, 21.

11. These include Chairs of the Union-republic Councils of Ministers (five in 1961, *Ezhegodnik 1961*, and 15 in 1987) and other leading officials.

12. *Narodnoe khoziaystvo SSSR: 1922–82*, Moscow, 1982, p.399.

13. *Trud v SSSR*, Moscow, 1988, pp.30–1.

14. The following refer to ministries or state committees.

15. These following are the eight main 'defence industrial ministries; in addition there were the State Commission for Military-Industrial Activites and the State Committee for Computer Technology and Information Technology. It should be emphasized, however, that until relatively recently the defence industry was spread throughout the whole economy. Western analysts in the late 1970s and early 1980s estimated that some 40 per cent of the Soviet economy was linked in some way to the defence sector. See Z. K. Brzezinski in E. P. Hoffmann and F. J. Fleron (eds), *The Conduct of Soviet Foreign Policy*, Aldine, New York, 1980, p.322; and Karl F. Spielman, 'Defense Industrialists in the USSR', *Problems of Communism*, Sept-Oct. 1976, vol. 25, no.5, pp.52–69. John McDonnell, 'The Soviet Defense Industry as a Pressure Group', in Michael McGwire *et al.*, (eds), *Soviet Naval Policy*, Praeger, New York, 1975, pp.87–122.

16. A listing and analysis of the Central Committee between 1918 and 1961 is given in T. H. Rigby, 'The CPSU Elite: Turnover and Rejuvenation from Lenin to Khrushchev', *Australian Journal of Politics and History*, vol. 16, no.1, pp.11–23. See his list of membership, p.14. The data here are taken from the listing of the membership given by Ewan Mawdsley, 'The Central Committees of the CPSU since 1917', *Lorton Paper*, 2, University of Glasgow, 1991.

17. Based on entries collected by S. White, 'The Soviet Leadership: Politburo, Organisations and Secretariat of the CPSU, 1919–1990', *Lorton Paper*, 3, University of Glasgow, 1991.

18. The internal organization of the CPSU was before *perestroika* a private affair and no data on it were published. This list was derived from Radio Liberty Research (Munich) 9/1978. For an earlier and more comprehensive account see Abdurakhman Avtorkhanov, *The Communist Party Apparat*, Meridian Books, Cleveland and New York, 1966.

19. T. H. Rigby, 'The Soviet Political Executive 1917–1985', in Archie Brown (ed.), *Political Leadership in the Soviet Union*, Macmillan, London, 1989.

20. The Council included five All-Union ministries, ten Union-republican ministries and 31 committees, commissions, councils and adminstrations. See M. Fainsod, *How Russia is Ruled*, p.398.

21. Particularly under Brezhnev political honours were bestowed on the top bureaucrats: of Ryavec's sample, 66 held the Order of Lenin and 39 per cent held more than one honour; many held military honours for service in the defence sector: Karl W. Ryavec, 'The Soviet Bureaucratic Elite from 1964 to 1979: A Research Note', *Soviet Union*, 1985, vol.12, no.3, p.339.

22. T. H. Rigby, 'Political Legitimacy under Mono-organisational Socialism', *The Changing Soviet System*, pp.155–82.

23. 'Traditional, Market and Organisational Societies', p.539.
24. Karl W. Ryavec, 'Soviet Bureaucratic Elite', pp.322–45. See Table, p.338.
25. Eberhard Schneider, *Kaderpolitik in der sowjetischen Führung: eine sozialstatisti-sche Untersuchung des Elitenwechsels von Breschnew zu Gorbatschow*; Berichte des Bundesinstituts für ostwissenschaftliche und internationale Studien, 44–1989, p.40.
26. J. F. Hough and M. Fainsod, *How the Soviet Union is Governed*, Harvard University Press, Cambridge, Mass., 1979, p.526.
27. See listing, for instance, in *Slovar' oppozitsii*, nos 4/5, Postfaktum, Moscow, 1991. Other lists of new parties and opposition groups in the republics have been published in *Izvestia Ts. K. KPSS* in 1990 and 1991.
28. F. Engels, 'The Origin of the Family, Private Property and the State', *Selected Works*, Moscow, 1951, p.224.

2. The Top Leadership: from Soviet Elite to Republican Leadership

Alexander Rahr

WITHER THE CENTRAL STRUCTURES

In the first chapter of this book we discussed the lack of elite coherence. In December 1990 Gorbachev asked the USSR Congress of People's Deputies to grant him additional powers to prevent the disintegration of the Soviet Union. The Congress agreed to further strengthen his presidency by supplementing it with four powerful institutions: the vice presidency, a revamped Council of the Federation, the Cabinet of Ministers and the Security Council.[1] But in August 1991 three of these four institutions staged the coup against Gorbachev and had to be dissolved in the aftermath – at the Extraordinary USSR Congress of People's Deputies in September 1991. As a result of the abortive coup, Gorbachev lost his entire political power base, while Eltsin and other republican leaders enhanced their authority. The Council of the Federation was subsequently transformed by the USSR Congress into the USSR State Council, which became the top All-Union decision-making body, and Gorbachev was made almost completely subordinate to it.

The collapse of the Soviet Union, which had been accelerated by the August putsch, started in 1990, when the republican leaders, strengthened through popular elections, began to resist the policy of the centre. After the election of Boris Eltsin as chairman of the Russian parliament in the summer of 1990, the major republic of the Union – Russia – joined the Baltic and other republics in their demands for more independence from the centre. At that time Gorbachev was not willing to grant republics greater autonomy. Instead of seeking cooperation and compromise with the republican leaders and parliaments, he adopted a confrontational stance towards demands for secession.

Mikhail Gorbachev lost his struggle for the preservation of the Soviet Union. On 21 December 1991 the leaders of the Soviet republics agreed during a historical meeting in Alma Ata to disband the

Soviet central state and form a Commonwealth of Independent States. Gorbachev was left without a job and had no other choice than to resign peacefully.

The Council of the Federation had been created by Gorbachev as early as March 1990. The expectation was that it would bring republican leaders closer to his presidency and bind them to his policy of preserving the Union. It never did become an obedient body, however. Whereas all the members of the Presidential Council had been selected by Gorbachev personally, the Council of the Federation included, ex officio, the presidents or parliamentary chairmen of the 15 Union republics – each of whom had his own political agenda. The new constitutional amendments, adopted in 1990, granted membership of the council to the leaders of the autonomous republics as well. Top state officials from autonomous oblasts and okrugs were entitled to participate in meetings of the council 'with the right to a vote on questions affecting their interests'.[2]

Under growing pressure from the republics to restructure the Soviet political system on genuine federative principles, Gorbachev agreed at the end of 1990 to upgrade the Council of the Federation from a consultative to a policy-making body. Together with the institutions of the presidency and the Cabinet of Ministers, the Council of the Federation was supposed to constitute the executive branch of the future Soviet federation. The Council of the Federation became a collective decision-making body in which decisions were adopted on the basis of a two-thirds majority and enacted by presidential decrees. The USSR president had only one vote in the council and could theoretically be overruled by other members.[3]

But the Council of the Federation never worked in the manner prescribed by the constitutional amendments. One major reason for this was the continual absence of one or other of its key members. Eltsin, for example, in protest against the centre, preferred to send his deputy, Ruslan Khasbulatov, to the meetings of the council. The three Baltic republics declared from the beginning that they would maintain only observer status in the Council of the Federation.

The Security Council not only 'swallowed the functions'[4] of the defunct Presidential Council but had, at the same time, received broader powers as 'a consultative organ under the president'. Six members of the Security Council became ex officio members, and two – Vadim Bakatin and Evgenii Primakov – full-time members. Bakatin was appointed in charge of domestic security affairs, and Primakov dealt with questions of economic security.[5] Unlike the Council of the

Federation, the Security Council did not receive constitutionally granted authority to adopt independent decisions.

At the beginning of March 1991 the USSR Supreme Soviet approved eight of the nine candidates for membership of the Security Council proposed by Gorbachev.[6] Foreign Minister Aleksandr Bessmertnykh was unanimously approved, Kryuchkov received 339 votes, Prime Minister Valentin Pavlov 320, Defence Minister Dmitrii Yazov 310, Vice-President Gennadii Yanaev 304, Interior Minister Boris Pugo 296 and former Interior Minister Bakatin 279. Foreign policy specialist Primakov was confirmed in a second round of voting, but the head of Gorbachev's staff, Valerii Boldin, failed to gain the necessary number of votes, even in the second round. Liberals in the parliament criticized Boldin's conservatism, while hard-liners disliked his decade-long association with Gorbachev. Gorbachev told the parliament that he intended nevertheless to entrust Boldin with organizational matters for the Security Council.

KGB Chairman Kryuchkov started to play a leading role in the Security Council. Of all the members of that body, Kryuchkov was (with the exception of Gorbachev) the only person with past experience both as a full member of the Politburo and as a member of the Presidential Council. In his present capacity he had been expected to deal with a wide range of security issues. The KGB, besides handling state security and matters relating to 'economic sabotage', expanded its activities into the area of environmental protection.

Conflicts between the Security Council and the Council of the Federation became virtually unavoidable, and prospects for fruitful cooperation between the two institutions did not appear bright from the beginning. The majority of the members of the Security Council held conservative views and regarded the possible disintegration of the Soviet Union with alarm. In sharp contrast to the former Presidential Council, which included several reform-oriented politicians and scientists, the Security Council had the only known liberal, former Interior Minister Bakatin. A major task of the Security Council was the supervision of the work of the Defence Council. Chaired by Gorbachev, the Defence Council consisted of Kryuchkov, Pavlov, Bessmertnykh, Yazov, two of Yazov's First Deputies, and a number of representatives of the military-industrial complex – those figures who staged the coup against Gorbachev.

The USSR Congress also adopted a decision in December 1990 to abolish the Council of Ministers and replace it with a Cabinet of Ministers, with a slightly reduced ministerial structure. The idea was to make the government directly subordinate to the president. Gorbachev intended to downgrade the office of prime minister to the level of a chief aide to the president with responsibility for organizing, but not presiding over, the day-to-day activities of the government.[8]

The functions of the central government comprised several key areas of All-Union significance and execution of its resolutions and ordinances as mandatory throughout the USSR. These key areas included defence, security, foreign policy, finance, justice, ecology, energy, transport and communications. Responsibility for broader economic issues, such as construction, machine building and trade, has been, at least on paper, delegated to the republics. The abolition of the State Planning Committee (Gosplan) seemed not to have been the major step it appeared at first: its place was immediately taken by a new Ministry of Economics and Forecasting. Gorbachev was apparently acceding to some of the demands of the old-style bureaucracy.

The Cabinet of Ministers was planned to consist of the prime minister, his deputies, and USSR ministers. Heads of the republican (and autonomous republican) governments could participate in the sessions of the cabinet and received the right to vote. Contrary to Gorbachev's promises to the republican leaders, the new cabinet included few representatives of the non-Russian nationalities. In fact the Council of the Federation seemed not to have been fully consulted during the nomination of the candidates, as it should have been under the new constitutional amendments. It may have wanted, for example, a greater turnover of ministers, but more than half of the former ministers and state committee chairmen kept their jobs. They include Nikolai Konarev, who was first appointed minister of railways under Yurii Andropov in 1982 and who had since then done little to improve the country's railway system. Gorbachev failed to appoint specialists in economic reform or representatives of the democratic wing, even though there were some in the former Ryzhkov government.[9]

Responding to what he then saw as Gorbachev's determination to reinstate the old bureaucracy and his rejection of democratic appointees, Eltsin publicly declared war on Gorbachev and said the main difference between them was that Gorbachev wanted to retain the centralized system while he – Eltsin – sought to 'destroy' it.[10] In a live interview on Soviet television, he demanded that the presidency be eliminated and supreme power transferred to the Council of the Federation, in which he, as Russian Soviet Federated Socialist Republic leader, would be *primus inter pares*.[11]

THE NOVO-OGAREVO PROCESS AND THE GORBACHEV-ELTSIN ALLIANCE

On 23 April 1991 Gorbachev summoned the leaders of the nine Union republics that had not refused to participate in the work of the Council of the Federation to a meeting outside the Kremlin at a dacha in Novo-Ogarevo. Eltsin, until then rarely a participant in the meetings of the Council of the Federation, was also present with Gorbachev and the other republican leaders. The leaders of the USSR and nine Union republics agreed to join forces to halt the disintegration of the Soviet Union at the republican level and to turn the Soviet Union into a federation of sovereign states. From that point the alliance between republican leaders and Gorbachev became genuine. An alliance of this sort, the basis of the Shatalin/Yavlinsky economic plan, almost succeeded in the summer of 1990. But, in November, Gorbachev balked at radical change – probably because, at that time, the reformers were still poorly organized and had no real power base. Hard-liners in the Communist Party and the military bluntly warned Gorbachev that he would lose their support if he joined the reformers. For six months – from November until April 1991 – Gorbachev tried to preserve the middle ground that he tended to favour, only to find that the gap between the two sides was too wide to bridge.

In the first months of 1991, conservative forces almost managed to stop the reform process at the All-Union level, but democratization at the republican level proceeded at a great pace. No opposition from hard-liners could prevent Eltsin from building his authority in the Russian Federation. Gorbachev again decided to switch sides and allied himself with the republics. As a result he lost a tremendous amount of support in his traditional power base in the centre and indirectly provoked the coup against him. Since the beginning of the Novo-Ogarevo process, Gorbachev had become dependent on the republican leaders and, as he came increasingly under attack from Communist Party hard-liners, he found that his best means of staying in power was to form an alliance with Eltsin.

Who were the winners and the losers in the nine-plus-one agreement? Eltsin and other republican leaders won from Gorbachev recognition of the sovereignty of their republics. Gorbachev recognized, with some exceptions, the supremacy of republican law over All-Union legislation. He agreed to transfer most of the functions of the central government to the republics. He also agreed to new elections to all representative central organs, which meant that the conservatives would be swept out of power. Through the agreement, Gorbachev opened the way for the closest participation by the republics in the Kremlin's political decision-making process.

Gorbachev's main achievement was to win the recognition by the republics of the legitimacy of the centre, and particularly of his presidency. The strongest instrument left at Gorbachev's disposal was the Soviet armed forces: the republics' leaders agreed that the USSR president should remain in charge of a centralized army. Gorbachev also succeeded – obviously with the support of the leaders of the Central Asian republics – in preserving the RSFSR as the economic backbone of the future federation. The leaders of Kazakhstan, Uzbekistan and Tajikistan were among the first to praise the nine-plus-one agreement as the beginning of a process of political and economic stabilization.

The main result of the agreement, the provisions of which were never disclosed in full, was the weakening of the centre's powers to legislate and govern.[12] The treaty envisaged limiting the centre's functions to defence, coordination of the foreign policy of the republics, coordination of finances and foreign economic relations of the republics, and control over national communications and the atomic energy industry. The new Union treaty was to be signed between the republics and Gorbachev himself and the USSR legislature would have played only a secondary role. In order to hold on to power, Gorbachev seemed prepared to sacrifice the unitary state structures. In doing so, he put his fate completely in the hands of the leaders of the republics.

Eltsin won six critical victories in the first quarter of 1991. This feat has earned him respect inside and outside the Soviet Union and made Gorbachev rethink his strategy towards recognition of the democratic movement and towards sharing power with Eltsin. The first victory was achieved during the period of the conservative backlash in Soviet politics. Eltsin managed to secure a quadrilateral agreement involving the republican leaders of Ukraine, Belorussia and Kazakhstan, which demonstrated firm resistance to the Kremlin's attempts to preserve its hegemony by force. Second was the referendum of 17 March 1991 in which an impressive 70 per cent of the Russian electorate gave their support to Eltsin's proposal that the powerful post of RSFSR president be instituted. Third, at the end of March, Eltsin defeated the conservative Communist faction at the RSFSR Congress of People's Deputies (which had tried to strip him of power) and won parliament's approval for his plans for the RSFSR presidency. Fourth, on 23 April Eltsin, in an alliance with other republican leaders, won important political concessions from Gorbachev on the future, reconstituted USSR at the meeting in Novo-Ogarevo where the nine-plus-one agreement was hammered out. Fifth, he was elected RSFSR president in the first round, with an impressive share of the vote: nearly 60 per cent. Finally Eltsin was received by US President George Bush in the White House immediately after his election, which tended to detract from the importance of Gorbachev's meeting with Bush scheduled to take place in London after the Group of Seven leading industrialized nations summit between 15 and 17 July.

What did Eltsin's victory in the presidential elections signify before the putsch? In reality, Gorbachev remained the nominal head of the Soviet Union. He was still in charge of the country's nuclear weapons and controlled the budget, the military, and the KGB. But the leader of the RSFSR – the republic that encompasses three-quarters of the land mass of the USSR – had read his election and the nine-plus-one agreement as meaning a radical transfer of power from the centre to the republics.

Eltsin took several steps towards achieving his goal. In July 1991 he brought the RSFSR's coal mines under his jurisdiction and later did the same with other sectors of the economy on the territory of the RSFSR. Eltsin demanded control of military plants on Russian territory and, also in July 1991, issued a decree outlawing Party cells in the KGB, armed forces, police and state enterprises in the RSFSR. This goal from the beginning was to bring the KGB structures on Russian territory under his firm control, to participate in all decisions concerning the military, to replace USSR law with Russian legislation and to exercise an independent Russian foreign policy. He also demanded the power of veto over the use of nuclear weapons, full control over the republic's finances and retention by the RSFSR of the exclusive right to collect taxes on the territory of the republic and to decide what percentage would be handed over to the centre.

Eltsin has completely distanced himself from communism and described Marxism-Leninism as an 'experiment' that was unfortunately attempted in Russia instead of 'some African country'.[13] In his view, communism was to blame for the destruction of Russian traditions and religion. His aim was to form a coalition of democratic, Western-oriented political forces and moderate Russian nationalists. He wants to revive Russian traditional values – now almost forgotten – not in order to isolate Russia from the rest of the world, but to return it to civilization.

During his visit to the United States after his election, Eltsin promised to dismantle the communist system in Russia and stressed that he would oppose Gorbachev again if the latter delayed reform. Concerning foreign relations, Eltsin rejected a policy based on power. He emphasized that 'Russia has become very independent, in foreign policy as well', and he said that he favoured eliminating all foreign aid to Cuba and Afghanistan. While in the United States, Eltsin also stated that, under his leadership, Russia was going to become 'a stabilizing factor' in world politics.[14]

If Eltsin's victory shocked the established All-Union power elite, they must have been even more alarmed at Gorbachev's expressions of support for Eltsin. Fearing that a Gorbachev-Eltsin alliance could deny them power, they made an attempt to curtail Gorbachev's powers and have Prime Minister Valentin Pavlov run the country. While Eltsin was on his visit to the United States, Pavlov appealed to the USSR Supreme Soviet for additional authority and asked that the USSR President be subordinated to the parliament. Pavlov's proposal was supported in the parliament by the heads of the armed forces, the interior ministry and the KGB – precisely those officials who, two months later, staged the coup.

Gorbachev took several steps to demonstrate his firm commitment to the new alliance with Eltsin following the nine-plus-one agreement of 23 April. From that time on, he started to ignore the central legislature and government. The political decision-making process shifted from the central institutions to the regular meetings of the Council of the Federation.

PRESIDENTIAL SYSTEM SET UP IN RUSSIA

In anticipation of the signing of the Union treaty and the subsequent devolution of many of the centre's powers to the republics, RSFSR President Boris Eltsin had begun even before the putsch to establish a presidential system in Russia capable of absorbing that power and, above all, of executing presidential policy in the RSFSR more effectively than at the All-Union level. Eltsin's main concern in creating the new presidential apparatus was to avoid Gorbachev's mistake of continuing to rely heavily on the communist-dominated government structures. In the light of this, the hard-liners' coup against Gorbachev one day before the Union treaty was due to be signed was a last-ditch attempt by the conservatives to wrest power back to the centre just as Eltsin was poised to achieve broad powers in the RSFSR.

Eltsin wanted to avoid the critical mistake made by Gorbachev, who, after becoming USSR President in March 1990, failed to create an executive apparatus capable of implementing his decisions. In fact a functioning presidential system has never been established in the Soviet Union: neither the USSR Presidential Council nor the USSR

Security Council ever assumed real power in the country, mainly because Gorbachev failed to provide these institutions with the appropriate structures. The Soviet leader continued to rely on the All-Union parliament and the communist-dominated Soviet government, which resisted reform. This resulted in a confrontation with the republics, the collapse of central power and the disintegration of the Soviet Union.

In November 1991 Eltsin signed a decree appointing himself Chairman of the Russian government. He divided his government into four sections. The first comprised the Ministries of Foreign Affairs, Press and Mass Media, and Justice; the second, 13 economic ministries charged with implementing Eltsin's radical reform programme; the third, five ministries responsible for social policy; and the fourth, which was the most sensitive, the Ministries of Internal Affairs and Defence and the RSFSR KGB. Supervision over the first section was given to First Deputy Chairman of the RSFSR Government, Gennadii Burbulis, the second to Deputy Chairman and Russian economic overlord, Egor Gaidar, and the third to Aleksandr Shokhin, who was also made a Deputy Chairman of the government. The fourth section went to Eltsin's legal advisor, Sergei Shakhrai. Burbulis became the second most powerful politician in Russia. He won a number of functions that would normally have fallen within the purview of the premier. Indeed the position was made so powerful in order to relieve Eltsin of some of his responsibilities as head of government and give him time to perform his duties as President. Burbulis's tasks include coordinating the work of the entire government, and he received the right to sign government decrees in the absence of Eltsin.

A further instrument of presidential power is the appointed presidential representatives (envoys) at the regional level, or, as Eltsin described them, 'the eyes and ears of the head of state'. The idea of sending presidential envoys to control local politics did not originate with Eltsin. It was widely discussed in 1990 by Gorbachev's advisors. Conservative Party apparatchiks, such as the Leningrad Party boss, Boris Gidaspov, as well as leaders of the democratic movement, such as the mayor of Leningrad, Anatolii Sobchak, had appealed to Gorbachev to appoint personal envoys to various regions of the country in order to bring the situation in some regions under control. Gorbachev rejected the idea, presumably because at that time the introduction of direct presidential rule by the Kremlin would have been interpreted as the first step towards a new kind of dictatorship and, in a situation where the republics had just proclaimed their sovereignty, could have led to unpredictable developments.

The envoys will be elected in their regional constituencies in the winter of 1992 and, armed with a popular mandate, will gain the authority they need to combat the resistance of opponents of reform. In the meantime, they will be appointed by the RSFSR president. Their task is to watch over the implementation of Eltsin's policy on the periphery. During the first stage, the appointed envoys do not have the right to interfere directly in local decision making but will be entitled to demand information about a given region. The idea is to make the elected envoys heads of local presidential administrations and thus heads of the executive at the periphery.

The officials that Eltsin has appointed to leading positions in the new presidential apparatus may be divided into three distinctive groups. The first consists of former Party apparatchiks from Sverdlovsk, the region where Eltsin once held the post of regional Party leader. Three leading members of 'the Sverdlovsk mafia' – Yurii Petrov, Viktor Ilyushin and Aleksei Tsaregorodtsev – were recently appointed heads of the Administration of the RSFSR President, the Secretariat of the RSFSR President, and the Secretariat of the RSFSR Vice President, respectively. The second group includes such officials as Chairman of the RSFSR Supreme Soviet Committee for Defence Konstantin Kobets. They are all highly qualified specialists from the country's military-industrial complex and, unlike many leaders of the present democratic movement, are capable administrators in their own areas of responsibility. In the third group are members of the democratic movement who have developed political skills either in parliamentary work or in administration. The main representatives of that group are Burbulis – a former philosophy professor at a Sverdlovsk institute and now RSFSR state secretary; Sergei Shakhrai – a young lawyer who has been appointed state councillor for legal affairs after performing brilliantly in the capacity of Chairman of the RSFSR Supreme Soviet Committee for Legislation in the first year of the existence of the Russian parliament; Sergei Stankevich – who switched from the post of First Deputy Chairman of the Moscow City Soviet to become state councillor with responsibility for cooperation with social organizations; and the ecologist and cofounder of the Interregional Group of USSR deputies, Aleksei Yablokov, who is now RSFSR State Councillor for science, education and culture.

While Gorbachev hesitated to take bold decisions after becoming USSR president, Eltsin, following his popular election, immediately declared war on the CPSU by issuing the decree on depoliticization. After the putsch he went even further and temporarily banned all CP activities in Russia. He seeks to prevent the old Party bureaucracy from reorganizing itself in the new political and economic structures in Russia after the actual transfer of power from the centre to the republics. Eltsin also seems to be determined to use all his powers to implement radical reform in the economy of the RSFSR, including privatization, the distribution of state property and handing over land to the peasants. Finally Eltsin has shown remarkable tactical skills in the formation of the new institutions of presidential power.

THE USSR AFTER THE FAILED PUTSCH

As a result of the coup, Gorbachev lost the Communist Party apparatus and the Cabinet of Ministers. The majority of the members of the USSR Security Council and the USSR Defence Council betrayed him and were imprisoned. On the second day of the coup, Eltsin appointed himself Commander-in-Chief of all Soviet armed forces on Russian territory.[15] A major agreement was reached about the Soviet Union's nuclear arsenals. A joint control mechanism was introduced according to which strategic weapons cannot be used without the consent of both the RSFSR and the USSR presidents.[16] Eltsin also issued a decree placing all central Soviet organs of executive power in Russia under his control. He refused to hand back the reins to Gorbachev. By the end of 1991 Eltsin had practically placed all USSR ministries under Russian jurisdiction and seized all political and economic initiative from the centre. The central structures fell apart, and in an attempt to rescue their careers thousands of former Soviet bureaucrats switched to the new Russian state institutions, in the hope that Russia at least could pay their salaries.

Eltsin demonstrated his control of nuclear weapons in the meeting with the Soviet military leaders on the eve of Gorbachev's resignation, when he urged the marshals and generals to support his plea for a Commonwealth of Independent States (CIS), dominated by Russia, against Gorbachev's attempts to preserve the Union. Eltsin's control over approximately 80 per cent of the Soviet Union's nuclear arsenal became his major bargaining chip in the struggle for Russia to inherit superpower status from the Soviet Union. The republics had to promise to relocate their nuclear weapons to Russia.

Eltsin insisted on the appointment of Air Force head Colonel General Evgenii Shaposhnikov as the new Soviet defence minister and later to the post of Commander-in-chief of the armed forces of the CIS. Shaposhnikov's First Deputy, Lieutenant General Pavel Grachev, who formerly commanded the Airborne Troops, is also a Eltsin appointee. Both men were promoted because of their resistance to

Figure 2.1 USSR political system before and after the putsch

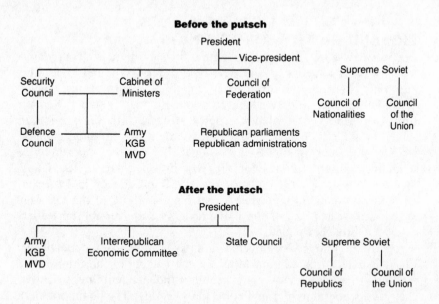

the coup. Grachev has also been made Chairman of the newly created RSFSR State Committee for Defence Questions, which is the equivalent of a republican defence ministry.[17] The All-Union military chain of command will, therefore, be firmly under the control of the RSFSR; ultimately, the Soviet army may become the Russian army. Figure 2.1 shows the transformation in the political system brought about by the putsch.

Eltsin also pressed Gorbachev to hand over to him Soviet government communication lines previously run by the KGB. Moreover, Eltsin was directly involved in breaking up the monopoly of the central KGB organization.[18] Most of the powers of the All-Union KGB were taken over by the RSFSR KGB. The newly formed USSR State Council lacked sufficient power and legitimacy to implement policy at the all-Union level. It consisted of Gorbachev and the leaders of those republics who regarded the newly created State Council from the beginning as an institution that should oversee the dismantling of the Soviet empire rather than strengthening it. Most of the republican leaders participated in the sessions of the State Council not in order to work out a common strategy for the preservation of the Union but rather to make sure they did not lose out in the process of redistributing the powers and functions of the old Union among the republics.

THE END OF THE SOVIET UNION

Gorbachev was intent on preserving the Soviet Union as a confederative state with a strong presidency, but he received support for this idea only from the Central Asian republics, which were strongly dependent on the Union for their economic survival. In mid-November 1991 Gorbachev entered into a fierce struggle with the republican leaders in the USSR State Council for the right to hold direct popular elections for the post of USSR President. He had the opportunity to stand in popular elections for the post of Chairman of the USSR Supreme Soviet in 1989, and for the USSR presidency in 1990; but on both occasions he preferred to put his popularity to the test only in the narrow confines of the parliament. But the republican leaders rejected Gorbachev's plea.

After the Ukraine voted overwhelmingly in favour of independence, Eltsin initiated a meeting in Minsk of the leaders of the three Slavic republics to establish a Commonwealth of Independent States. Gorbachev was deliberately not invited to that meeting. The commonwealth accord became an attractive alternative to Gorbachev's plan for a new Union treaty; the other republics could now choose between becoming part of a confederative state under Gorbachev and joining the Commonwealth as fully sovereign states. The republics chose the second option. Gorbachev's plan failed and he was forced to resign at the end of December 1991. Thus ended the Soviet Union.

NOTES AND REFERENCES

1. See Stephan Kux, *Soviet Federalism: A Comparative Perspective*, Institute for East-West Security Studies, New York, 1990, pp. 84–9.
2. *Pravda*, 27 December 1990.
3. *Pravitelstvennyi vestnik*, 1991 no. 3. See also the Constitutional Amendments Law published in *Pravda*, 27 December 1990.
4. See Gorbachev's speech in *Izvestia*, 27 December 1990.
5. Bakatin revealed this during a press conference he gave on 26 March (Radio Moscow) that day.
6. *Izvestia*, 9 March 1991.
7. See the interview with the chairman of the RSFSR Supreme Soviet subcommission for servicemen's issues, Sergei Stepashin, in *Rossiya*, 15 February 1991.
8. See Shakhnazarov's interview in *Pravitelstvennyi vestnik*, 1991 No. 1.
9. *Interfax* 25 February 1991.
10. *AP*, 14 March 1991.
11. Central Television, 20 February, 1991.
12. *Kommersant*, on 29 April 1991, mentioned a secret memorandum signed at the

meeting in which Gorbachev reportedly agreed to transfer many of the centre's powers to the republics.

13. Radio Rossii, 1 June 1991.
14. *Reuters*, 19 June 1991.
15. Radio Moscow, 20 August 1991.
16. See press conference given by Aleksandr Rutskoi, *Reuters*, 26 August 1991).
17. *TASS*, 28 August 1991.
18. *TASS*, 24 August, 1991.

BIOGRAPHIES OF MAJOR POLITICIANS

Bakatin, Vadim Viktorovich: born 1937, Russian. Graduated from Novosibirsk Institute of Construction Engineering and CC CPSU Academy of Social Sciences; worked in Kemerovo Party apparatus; 1987–8 First Secretary, Kirov Oblast Party Committee; 1988–90 USSR Minister of Internal Affairs; 1990–1 Member, USSR Presidential Council; 1991 Member, USSR Security Council; 1991 Chairman, USSR KGB.

Burbulis, Gennadii Eduardovich: born 1945, Russian. Graduated from A. M. Gorkii Ural State University, Sverdlovsk (Ekaterinburg); candidate of philosophical sciences; until 1989 lecturer on Marxism – Leninism at Sverdlovsk institutes; 1989–91 deputy, USSR Congress of People's Deputies; member, USSR Supreme Soviet Committee for Soviet of People's Deputies, Management and Self-Management Development; 1990–1 Plenipotentiary Representative of the chairman of the RSFSR Supreme Soviet-department head, RSFSR Supreme Soviet; 1991 RSFSR State Secretary; 1991 – First Deputy Chairman, Russian Government (responsible for Foreign Affairs).

Gorbachev, Mikhail Sergeevich: born 1931, Russian. Graduated from Law Faculty, Moscow State University; worked in Stavropol Party apparatus; 1970–8 First Secretary, Stavropol Oblast Party Committee; 1978–85 Secretary, CC CPSU; 1979–80 Candidate Member, Politburo, CC CPSU; 1980–91 Full Member, Politburo, CC CPSU; 1985–91 General Secretary, CC CPSU; 1988–9 Chairman, Presidium, USSR Supreme Soviet; 1989–90 Chairman, USSR Supreme Soviet; 1990–91 USSR President; 1991 – President of International Foundation For Social, Economic and Political Research.

Kryuchkov, Vladimir Aleksandrovich: born 1924, Russian. Graduated from All-Union Juridicial Institute, Moscow; 1955–9 diplomatic service in Hungary; 1959–67 worked under Yu. Andropov in CC CPSU apparatus; 1967–71 Chief, USSR KGB Secretariat; 1974–88 Chief, First Main Administration, USSR KGB; 1988–91 Chairman, USSR KGB; 1989–90 Full Member, Politburo, CC CPSU; 1990–1 Member, USSR Presidential Council; 1991 Member, USSR Security Council; 1991 Member, State Emergency Committee (GKChP).

Silaev, Ivan Stepanovich: born 1930, Russian. Graduated from Kazan Aviation Institute; 1980–5 USSR Minister of Machine-Tool and Tool-

Building Industries, USSR Minister of Aviation Industry; 1985–90 Deputy Chairman, USSR Council of Ministers; 1990–1 Chairman, RSFSR Council of Ministers; 1991 Chairman, Interrepublican Economic Committee, 1991 – Representative of Russian Government at European Community (EC).

Stankevich, Sergei Borisovich: born 1954, Ukrainian. Graduated from V.I. Lenin State Pedagogical Institute, Moscow; candidate of historical sciences; 1989–91 Deputy, USSR Congress of People's Deputies, Member, USSR Supreme Soviet Committee on Legislation; since 1990 First Deputy Chairman, Moscow City Council; 1991–92 RSFSR State Counsellor on Cooperation with social organizations (parties); 1992 Russian State Counsellor on Political Questions.

Eltsin, Boris Nikolaevich: born 1931, Russian. Graduated from S. M. Kirov Ural Polytechnical Institute, Sverdlovsk; worked in Sverdlovsk Party apparatus; 1976–85 First Secretary, Sverdlovsk Oblast Party Committee; 1985–7 Secretary, CC CPSU for construction, then First Secretary, Moscow City Party Committee; 1987–9 First Deputy Chairman, USSR State Committee for Construction; 1989–91 Deputy, USSR Congress of People's Deputies; 1989–90 Deputy, USSR Supreme Soviet; 1989–90 Co-chairman, Interregional Deputies Group of USSR Congress of People's Deputies; 1990–1 Chairman, RSFSR Supreme Soviet; since 1991 RSFSR President, RSFSR Prime Minister.

Gaidar, Egor Timurovich: born 1956, Russian. Graduated in 1979 from Economics Faculty, Moscow State University; Candidate of Economic Sciences (1981); Doctor of Economic Sciences (1988); 1981–87 Researcher Analyst, Economic Faculty, Moscow State University; Senior Researcher Analyst, All-Union Scientific-Research Institute of Systems Studies; Leading Researcher Analyst, Institute for Economy and Forecast of Scientific-Technological Progress, USSR Academy of Sciences; 1987–90 Editor, Department of Political Economy and Economic Policy, journal *Kommunist*; Member, Editorial Board, *Kommunist*; 1990 Editor, Department of Economic Policy, *Pravda*; Member, Editorial Board, *Pravda*; 1990–91 Director, Institute of Economic Policy, USSR Academy of Economic Management; 1991 Deputy Chairman, RSFSR Government in charge of economy; 1991–92 RSFSR Minister of Economics and Finances; 1992 – RSFSR Minister of Finances.

Rutskoi Aleksandr Vladimirovich: born 1947, Russian. Graduated in

1979 from Economics Faculty, father and grandfather were military officers. Graduated from Air Force High School in Barnaul, Altai Krai; from Air Force Gagarin Academy in Moscow; and from Academy of the General Staff of the USSR Armed Forces (1990), Moscow. 1964 Fitter, aviation plant, Kursk Oblast; 1965 – in the Soviet Army, at one time stationed as military pilot in Group of Soviet Troops in Germany (GDR); 1985–86 Commander of an air force regiment, 40th Army (Afghanistan); 1987–88 Deputy Chief, Air Force Pilot Combat Training Center, Lipetsk; 1988 Deputy Commander, Air Force, 40th Army (Afghanistan); 1989 Deputy Chairman, Moscow branch, *Otechestvo* (Society for Rebirth of Russia); 1990 Chief, Air Force Pilot Combat Training Center, Lipetsk; 1990–91 Deputy, RSFSR Congress of People's Deputies; Member, Council of Nationalities, RSFSR Supreme Soviet; Chairman, Committee for Invalids' and Afghanistan War Veterans' Affairs and Social Protection of Army Servicemen and their Family Members, RSFSR Supreme Soviet; Member, Presidium, RSFSR Supreme Soviet; 1990 Deputy Chairman, Deputies Group of Representatives of Armed Forces, KGB and Officers of Reserve, RSFSR Congress of People's Deputies; 1990–91 Member, CC RSFSR CP; 1991 Chairman, Deputies Group 'Communists for Democracy' RSFSR Congress of People's Deputies; 1991 Expelled from CPSU; 1991 – Vice-President of the Russian Federation; 1991 – Major General; 1991 – Chairman, Democratic Party of Communists of Russia (renamed People's Party of Free Russia).

3. Political Elites and Politics in the Republics

Darrell Slider

The shift from Communist Party institutions to parliamentary bodies and the simultaneous shift in power from central political institutions to the republics gave new importance to political structures and the elites at the republic level. In some cases elections resulted in no change – the Communist Party retained its dominance over political life and the communist elite remained the political elite of the republic. In other republics elite changes were revolutionary in their significance. Here new political forces began to dominate parliamentary deliberations and they quickly set their republics on the path to greater sovereignty and eventual independence.

The years of Soviet power had attempted to suppress nationalist feelings in all republics. Influential elites in virtually all republics believed that the result of past membership of the USSR was economic sacrifice and the neglect of national cultural values. No doubt Mikhail Gorbachev imperfectly understood the depth of these sentiments, particularly in those republics incorporated into the Soviet Union after the Second World War (Latvia, Lithuania, Estonia and Moldavia).* Gorbachev was himself, of course, a Russian, who had spent virtually his entire life in the southern Russian province of Stavropol and in Moscow. There was little in his experience that would have prepared him for the explosion of nationalist feeling that was to come.

Gorbachev began the democratization process at the national level in 1989 with the elections to the Congress of People's Deputies. All of the Soviet republics held elections to republic Supreme Soviets in 1990 (to a Congress of People's Deputies in the Russian republic, which in turn chose deputies for the Russian Supreme Soviet from among its members). The composition of the parliaments elected in 1990 and the leaders who emerged from them constitute the single most important reflection or indicator of the increasing political diversity among the republics. The new parliaments and the leaders they selected set in motion a series of events that produced full independence for several republics in 1991 and reduced the union to a loose confederation.

THE CHANGING DEMOGRAPHY OF THE NEW PARLIAMENTS

One of the most striking changes that resulted from a competitive nomination and election system was the practical elimination of women, workers and peasants from most of the republic legislatures. In previous Soviet elections, the 'representativeness' of parliamentary bodies was guaranteed by nominating candidates in part on the basis of their demographic characteristics. In fact, of course, the formal role played by Supreme Soviets in the policy process rendered the composition of parliament meaningless. The 1990 elections, by comparison, led to parliaments that were more important politically, but in which women and other social groups were significantly under-represented in numerical terms. This, of course, brought the representation of such groups down to a level comparable with that of Western parliaments.

In most republics the under-representation of women was apparent as early as the nomination stage. Women made up only 7.5 per cent of the candidates registered in the Ukraine and 7.6 per cent in the RSFSR, for example.[1] In no republic did the number of women elected to parliament exceed 12 per cent. As is demonstrated in Table 3.1, women were represented in greater numbers in the most authoritarian republics of Central Asia and Kazakhstan, where the nomination process was as tightly controlled as in the past. Communist Party leaders arranged the nomination process so that women were paired to run against women, for example. An exception was Tajikistan, where (as is shown in Table 3.2) places in the parliament were assigned overwhelmingly to party and state officials as well as managers of farms and enterprises, who were mostly male. In one of the most democratic republics, Lithuania, women were also represented at levels slightly above average.

Another difference in the new parliaments elected in the republics is apparent in the occupational background of deputies. In the past, workers and peasants (collective farm workers) were always represented in large numbers in an attempt to demonstrate that the Supreme Soviets reflected the views of these groups in the population. In the new Supreme Soviets, workers and peasants (Table 3.2) formed a large percentage of the deputy body only in the Central Asian

Table 3.1   Percentage of women elected to republic parliaments

Uzbekistan	11.4
Turkmenistan	11.0
Lithuania	8.5
Kyrgyzstan	8.0
Kazakhstan	7.4
Georgia	7.0
Estonia	6.7
Latvia	5.5
Russia	5.3
Tajikistan	3.9
Moldavia	3.5
Belorussia	3.2
Ukraine	2.9

Sources: Baltic republics: Rain Taagepera, 'The Baltic States', *Electoral Studies*, vol. 9, no. 4, December 1990, pp. 303–11; *Sovetskaia Kirgiziia*, 11 April 1990 (based only on data for 342 of 350 deputies); Information Centre of the Georgian parliament; Belorussia, based on first 317 deputies elected: *Belorusskaia tribuna*, no. 4, 1990; Uzbekistan (data for first 368 elected): *Pravda vostoka*, 22 February 1990; Moldavia (of first 369 elected) *Sovetskaia Moldavia*, 17 March 1990; Russia: Regina Smyth, 'Ideological vs Regional Cleavages: Do the Radicals Control the RSFSR Parliament?', *Journal of Soviet Nationalities*, vol. 1, no. 3, Fall 1990, pp. 112–57; Kazakhstan (of first 338 elected): *Kazakhstanskaia pravda*, 4 April and 18 April 1990; Tajikistan: William Reisinger; Turkmenistan: Therese Zimmer; Ukraine: Bohdan Harasymiw.
Note: citations of individual scholars refer to chapters in the volume edited by Darrell Slider, *Elections and Political Change in the Soviet Republics*, published in 1992.

republics of Turkmenistan, Uzbekistan, Kyrgyzstan and Kazakhstan. Two Western republics where the Communist Party continued to play an important role, Belorussia and Ukraine, also had a somewhat larger share of worker and peasant deputies.

In all republics at the time of the elections, the continuing role of the Communist Party meant that, as in the past, a significant proportion of the deputies would be party and state officials. Of all the republics, Tajikistan stood out as a case where party leaders took advantage of their position to give the edge to candidates from the party and state apparatus – candidates from the *nomenklatura*, in other words. Together managers of farms and enterprises and party and state officials comprised fully 80 per cent of the deputies to the Tajikistan Supreme Soviet.

An important change in the new parliaments was the increasing representation of the intelligentsia. This was particularly true in republics marked by resurgent nationalism. Years of Russification in many

Table 3.2   Composition of new parliaments in selected republics, by
occupation (percentage)

	Intelligentsia	Worker peasant	Party/state	Managers
Turkmenistan	na	33	24 (a)	na
Uzbekistan	na	20	na	na
Kazakhstan	na	19	na	na
Kyrgyzstan	16	19	31	22
Belorussia	na	13	na	na
Ukraine	20	12	31	13
Moldavia	22	9	30	25
Russia	17	6	22	21
Azerbaijan	13	4	54 (b)	
Tajikistan	na	4	41	39
Estonia	na	na	30	na
Georgia	23	1	17	25
Latvia	23	na	24	na

a includes only Party officials.
b includes both Party/state officials and managers.
Sources: Azerbaijan: *Bakinskii rabochii*, 12 October 1990 (based on first 240 deputies);
Kyrgyzstan: *Sovetskaia Kirgiziia*, 1990, April 11; Estonia: Cynthia Kaplan; Latvia:
Juris Dreifelds; Russia: recalculated from Regina Smith; Tajikistan: William Reisinger;
Ukraine: B. Harasymiw; Georgia: Information centre, Georgian Supreme Soviet;
Moldavia: William Crowther; Turkmenistan: Therese Zimmer; Belorussia: (of first
317 deputies) *Belorusskaia tribuna*, no 4, 1990; Kazakhstan (of first 338 elected):
Kazakhstanskaia pravda, 4 April and 18 April 1990; Uzbekistan (of first 368 deputies)
Pravda vostoka, 22 February 1990.

areas of life in the republics meant that one of the few repositories
of nationalism was research institutes and museums connected with
language, literature, music and culture in general. In Belorussia, one
of the most thoroughly Russified republics, the cultural intelligentsia
was one of the few categories of the intelligentsia that remained fluent
in Belorussian.[2] Sometimes the impact of this group was felt even in
the composition of the new top leadership of the republics. It is no
accident that Landsbergis in Lithuania, Ter-Petrosian in Armenia and
Gamsakhurdia in Georgia were drawn from the cultural intelligentsia
– Landsbergis was a musicologist, Ter-Petrosian and Gamsakhurdia
both linguists. In the Russian republic as well, universities and institutes were centres of radical and reformist thought, and leading scholars often became political activists. Journalists, often highly visible
reformers who benefited from the policy of *glasnost* were also well
represented among deputies in many republics.[3]

Another of the emerging forces that sought a voice in political life was the new cooperatives. Created after 1987, cooperatives were in essence the first legal private enterprises in the Soviet Union since the Stalin period. Government policy toward cooperatives was contradictory. On the one hand, legislation encouraged their development and fostered an explosive growth in cooperative enterprises. On the other hand, ministries introduced a wide range of restrictions designed to preserve their monopoly status in many fields of activity. Public attitudes toward cooperatives were often negative, as old conceptions of 'exploitation' and 'speculation' coloured the perception of their activities. Despite this prevailing attitude, in Russia, Ukraine, Moldavia and Uzbekistan heads of cooperatives or their associations were elected to republic legislatures, thus giving private entrepreneurs their first direct voice in Soviet political life.[4]

Representation of ethnic minorities and the chief nationality in each republic was always a feature of pre-reform parliaments and typically minority groups were over-represented in these bodies. The 1990 elections produced a somewhat different result. In all republics except Belorussia and Russia, the dominant nationality is relatively over-represented among the deputies elected to parliaments. In the Russian republic many small ethnic groups are over-represented, in part a function of attempts to create special districts for 'national-territorial' units. In Belorussia the over-representation of Russians may reflect their concentration in large cities. Also the integration of Russians into Belorussian society is probably greater than in any other republic, though even here there are conflicts arising from the links between reformism and nationalism.

There are some difficulties in interpreting Soviet ethnic data, however. One problem with the 1989 census presented in Table 3.3 (the most recent data available) is that by the time of the elections it had already ceased to reflect the true ethnic mix in several republics: significant out-migration occurred of Armenians from Azerbaijan and Azeris from Armenia, for example, and many Russians had already emigrated from Central Asia.

Beyond these general problems of interpretation, there are special problems in evaluating ethnic representation in republic parliaments. In considering the results presented in Table 3.3, one should guard against assuming that the under-representation of minorities is, on the face of it, evidence of prejudice or political discrimination.[5] The regional distribution of ethnic groups and voting rules are crucial. If the ethnic factor was important in voters' choices and a single-member district, majority-voting system was in place, one would expect minorities to win only in those districts where they formed a local majority.

Table 3.3　Percentage representation of the largest ethnic groups in the republic parliaments

	Population	Deputies elected in 1990
RSFSR		
Russians	81.5	78.1
Tatars	3.8	2.6
Ukrainians	3.0	4.3
Jews	0.4	1.6
Kyrgyzstan		
Kyrgyz	52.3	64.3
Russians	21.5	18.8
*Uzbeks	12.9	8.0
Turkmenistan		
Turkmen	71.9	74.3
Russians	9.8	14.8
Uzbeks	9.0	6.8
Kazakhstan		
Kazakhs	39.7	54.2
*Russians	37.8	28.8
Ukrainians	2.9	6.7
Germans	5.8	3.9
Latvia		
Latvians	51.8	70.1
*Russians	33.8	21.3
Ukrainians	3.4	4.0
Estonia		
Estonians	61.2	76.2
*Russians	30.2	20.8
Lithuania		
Lithuanians	79.6	87.8
*Russians	9.4	3.8
Poles	7.0	7.1
Moldavia		
Moldavians	63.9	69.2
Russians	12.8	15.5
*Ukrainians	14.2	9.6
Gagauz	3.5	3.3
Ukraine		
Ukrainians	72.7	75.1
Russians	22.1	22.3
Tajikistan		
Tajiks	62.2	73.7
*Uzbeks	23.5	15.2
Russians	7.6	8.5
Uzbekistan		
Uzbeks	71.3	77.7
Russians	8.3	8.6

Table 3.3   continued

	Population	Deputies elected in 1990
*Tajiks	4.7	2.6
Belorussia		
Belorussians	77.8	73.5
Russians	13.3	19.5
Poles	4.1	3.5
Georgia		
Georgians	70.1	na
*Armenians	8.1	na
*Russians	6.3	na
*Azeris	5.7	na
Armenia		
Armenians	93.4	na
*Azeris	2.6	na
*Russians	1.6	na
Azerbaijan		
Azeris	82.7	na
*Russians	5.6	na
*Armenians	5.6	na

* indicates most significant cases of under-representation

Sources: Population figures based on 1989 census data; republic parliament data of Moldavia: William Crowther; Ukraine: Bohdan Harasymiw; Tajikistan: William Reisinger; Lithuania, Latvia and Estonia: Rein Taagepera. Other republics: Valery Tishkov, 'Ethnicity and Power in the Republics of the USSR', *Journal of Soviet Nationalities*, vol. 1, no. 3, fall 1990, pp. 33–66.

If a minority was widely dispersed across a republic, winning even one seat would be difficult. If instead a proportional voting scheme was employed, then minorities voting for 'their' candidates would tend to be better represented.

A proportional voting scheme was used in the Georgian elections, but rules about which parties would be eligible to put forward a party list prevented regional parties from registering. The Georgian election law only allowed the registration of republic-wide political organizations, and no minority-based parties could claim such a following. In Georgia the ethnic mix of deputies – in particular the under-representation of Abkhaz and Ossetian groups – was also a result of the decision by local elites to prevent the election being held in their regions or to urge voters to boycott the elections. The Abkhaz and Ossetians are the two ethnic groups that have most frequently been at odds with the Georgian population, and soviets in the autonomous territories set up for each group sought independence outside Georgia. The combination of the boycott and voting rules meant that the only

minority candidates elected were on the Communist Party list. The
list put forward by the bloc that won the elections, the Round Table,
was comprised entirely of Georgians.[6]

The political consequences of the ethnic mix of deputies are potentially serious. One implication is that parliaments at the republic level,
with the exception of Russia, may not give due consideration to the
interests of minorities living in the republics, if only because their
deputies are not needed to form a majority within the parliament.
Most ethnic minorities can hope for little more than a voice in parliamentary debates since, even if they were to ally themselves with other
minority deputies, the resulting bloc would be too small to influence
legislation.

In parliaments of Lithuania, Estonia and Moldavia ethnic factors
quickly became one of the main causes for divisions among blocs of
deputies. On most important votes in the Estonian parliament, for
example, Russian-speaking deputies formed an opposition that was in
the minority on almost all issues. In the Russian parliament, representatives of non-Russian areas with autonomous republic status also
often *voted* as a bloc.

PARLIAMENTARY POLITICS

With the exception of the Baltic republics, political parties were only
beginning to be formed at the time the republic elections were held
in 1990. As is clear from Table 3.4, in all republics at the time of the
1990 elections a sizable portion of the body of deputies elected were
members of the Communist Party. There is a striking correlation
between Communist Party affiliation of deputies and relative conserva-
tivism/radicalism in the republics, shown in the ranking provided in
Table 3.4.

Everywhere at the time of the elections the Party remained the
ruling party, even if its authority was under constant assault – as in
Georgia and the Baltic republics. The status of ruling party gave
communists supported by the apparatus certain benefits in the election
campaign, such as access to the press, which was still mostly in the
hands of the Communist Party, as well as transport, publishing and
communications facilities. In areas where the Communist Party maintained a monopoly on political organization, it effectively prevented
a non-party opposition from emerging. In Tajikistan, for example
every candidate supported by the Party leadership was elected in the
1990 election.

Even where other parties and political movements existed, party

Table 3.4 Communist Party membership of deputies in republic parliaments at the time of the elections

Uzbekistan	95%
Tajikistan	95%
Kazakhstan	95%
Azerbaijan	92%
Kyrgyzstan	90%
Turkmenistan	89%
Ukraine	87%
Russia	86%
Belorussia	85%
Moldavia	81%
Armenia	70%
Estonia	58%
Latvia	54%
Lithuania	37%
Georgia	26%

Sources: In several cases (Belorussia, Armenia, Uzbekistan, Azerbaijan) the above figures reflect the results only of the first or first two rounds of voting. Belorussia: Michael Urban; Estonia: Cynthia Kaplan; Ukraine: Bohdan Harasymiw; Moldavia: William Crowther; Latvia: Juris Dreifelds; Lithuania (percentage includes both the Lithuanian CP and the loyalist CPSU faction): Laurie Salitan; Tajikistan: William Reisinger; Turkmenistan: Therese Zimmer; Armenia: *Komsomol'skaia pravda*, 21 August 1990; Russia: Regina Smyth; Uzbekistan: *Pravda vostoka*, 22 February 1990; Kazakhstan (of first 338 elected): *Kazakhstanskaia pravda*, 4 April and 18 April 1990; Azerbaijan: *Izvestia*, 11 October 1990.

affiliation was weak. Only in Estonia and Georgia was the candidate's party affiliation listed on the ballot, and elsewhere candidates were often put forward by several organizations at once. One should also bear in mind that many of the severest critics of past Party policies retained their membership in the Party at the time of the elections. It was not until the 28th Party Congress in July 1990 – after the elections in most republics – that a number of popular political leaders, including Boris Eltsin, Moscow mayor Gavril Popov, and Leningrad mayor Anatoly Sobchak resigned from the CPSU.

Only in Lithuania and Georgia was the share of Communist Party members in parliament less than half. In Georgia the election law prevented multiple affiliations, with the result that any candidate who wished to run under the label of another party had to resign from the Communist Party. Thus communist candidates were forced to run under the Party label, and the elections stimulated a mass exodus of prominent figures. In Lithuania the Communist party had already split by the time of the elections, and political life had begun to show signs of pluralist development.

The elections resulted in a new phenomenon in the politics of the republics: organized oppositions and parliamentary factions. This followed the experience at the national level where the Interregional Deputies' Group was formed as the first opposition deputy group within the Congress of People's Deputies. Many of the members of this faction were from the republics, and they later played a prominent role in governments and oppositions after the 1990 elections in their own republics.

Political developments in the republics were largely determined by the relative strength of deputy groups or factions. In many republics (all of Central Asia, Kazakhstan, Azerbaijan, Belorussia and Ukraine) Communist Party loyalists made up a majority of the deputies. In the Baltic republics, Georgia and Armenia nationalist, anti-communist movements had a clear majority in parliament. In the remaining two republics, Russia and Moldavia, popular reform movements had a slight edge over communist deputies but were dependent on alliances with independent legislators to obtain a working majority.

NEW LEADERS AND 'NEW' LEADERS

An important indicator of the balance of political forces within each republic after the elections was the selection of a Chairman of the Supreme Soviet. This was the most important leadership post in each republic, and all chairmen of the parliaments were chosen by a vote in parliament. Later, in most republics, the post was reduced in power as the top leader assumed the new post of President. The office of Chairman of the Supreme Soviet remained, but the role shifted from one of initiating policy to that of merely presiding over sessions of parliament.

The ease or difficulty with which a new leader was chosen at the first sessions of the parliaments reflected the political alignments of deputies at the time. In seven republics, nationalist and opposition movements in parliament were strong enough to elect their own leaders or sympathetic figures in the current hierarchy. In each case their choice underlined the extent of the change in elites brought about by the elections.

In the Russian republic, the most popular political figure in recent Russian history and Gorbachev's strongest rival, Boris Eltsin, was elected by the Russian Congress of People's Deputies with the support of the radical deputy group, Democratic Russia. In Lithuania,

Armenia and Georgia, leaders of anti-communist nationalist organizations were chosen to head the new republic governments. Vytautus Landsbergis was leader of Sajudis, the Lithuanian independence movement. Levon Ter-Petrosian, leader of the Armenian Pan-National Movement since 1989, had earlier been imprisoned at Butyrka prison in Moscow for six months for his role in leading protests over the Karabakh question.[7] Zviad Gamsakhurdia had been imprisoned three times for anti-Soviet activities and was the leading figure in the Georgian nationalist movement from the early 1970s. In the elections he headed the Round Table bloc of parties and was also leader of two of the component parties in the coalition.

There was a superficial continuity in Supreme Soviet leadership in Moldavia, Estonia and Latvia which masked profound political changes in these republics. In each case a communist official who had essentially gone over to the side of the nationalists and was willing to work closely with republic popular fronts was kept in power. In Moldavia, Mircea Snegur was a prominent official in the Communist Party who, in the course of 1989 and 1990, aligned himself closely with the Popular Front and was re-elected chairman of the new Supreme Soviet with its support. In Estonia, Arnold Ruutel had served in the same post since 1983, and he effectively adapted to rising nationalism in the republic. Similarly, in Latvia, Anatolijs Gorbunovs was re-elected to serve as Chairman of the Supreme Soviet, despite the victory by the Latvian Popular Front in the 1990 elections. All three men received the full support of the respective republic popular fronts and were viewed as moderates who could best chart the course toward future independence.

The politics of the election of parliamentary leaders varied greatly from republic to republic, as is shown in Table 3.5. In Georgia, opposition forces understood that they made up a tiny minority and did not try to offer an alternative. The disposition of political forces led to a free-for-all when it came time to select a parliamentary leader in the Russian republic. Despite his enormous popularity, Boris Eltsin was elected chairman of the Supreme Soviet by a narrow margin, in large part because of opposition from the large bloc of communist deputies in the Congress. Similarly, in Armenia, the selection process went four rounds before a majority supported Ter-Petrosian over the then leader of the Communist Party, V. Movsisian. A deadlock was avoided when a Party *raion* First Secretary broke ranks and argued that it was necessary to elect a candidate who had 'the trust of the people' – Ter-Petrosian.[8]

Table 3.5   Elections to top posts in the republics

Republic	Post	Date	Winner	Vote for/against
Armenia	chair SS	4 Aug 90	Ter-Petrosian	140/76
Armenia	prime min	13 Aug 90	Manukian	
Azerbaijan	president	13 May 90	Mutalibov	*316/3
Azerbaijan	chair SS	6 Feb 91	Kafarova	
Azerbaijan	prime min	7 Feb 91	Hasanov	
Belorussia	chair SS	15 May 90	Dementei	†
Belorussia	prime min	Jun 90	Kebich	*
Belorussia	chair SS	18 Sep 91	Shushkevich	214/98
Estonia	chair SS	2 Apr 90	Ruutel	
Estonia	prime min	3 Apr 90	Savisaar	54/32
Georgia	chair SS	Nov 90	Gamsakhurdia	*232/5
Georgia	prime min	Nov 90	Sigua	*
Georgia	president	14 Apr 91	Gamsakhurdia	*
Georgia	chair SS	18 Apr 91	Asatiani	*
Georgia	prime min	Aug 91	Gugushvili	*
Kazakhstan	chair SS	22 Feb 90	Nazarbaev	*
Kazakhstan	prime min	Feb 90	Karamanov	
Kazakhstan	president	24 Apr 90	Nazarbaev	*
Kazakhstan	chair SS	Apr 90	Asanbaev	
Kazakhstan	vice-pres	16 Oct 91	Ukin	
Kazakhstan	prime min	16 Oct 91	Tereschchenko	
Kyrgyzstan	chair SS	10 Apr 90	Masaliev	*293/46
Kyrgyzstan	prime min	13 Apr 90	Dzhumagulov	
Kyrgyzstan	president	Oct 90	Akaev	†
Kyrgyzstan	chair SS	Dec 90	Sherimkulov	
Latvia	chair SS	3 May 90	Gorbunovs	
Latvia	prime min	7 May 90	Godmanis	*131/46
Lithuania	chair SS	11 Mar 90	Landsbergis	91/38
Lithuania	prime min	17 Mar 90	Prunskiene	*107/6
Lithuania	prime min	Jan 91	Vagnorius	
Moldavia	chair SS	Mar 90	Snegur	
Moldavia	prime min	Mar 90	Paskar	
Moldavia	prime min	25 May 90	Druk	
Moldavia	president	3 Sep 90	Snegur	*
Moldavia	chair SS	Sep 90	Moshanu	
Moldavia	prime min	28 May 91	Muravschi	*185/na
Russia	chair SS	29 May 90	Eltsin	535/467
Russia	prime min	18 Jun 90	Silaev	
Russia	president	Apr 91	Eltsin	
Russia	chair SS	29 Oct 91	Khasbulatov	559/381
Russia	prime min	1 Nov 91	Eltsin	
Tajikistan	chair SS	12 Apr 90	Makhkamov	162/62
Tajikistan	chair CM	13 Apr 90	Khaeev	*
Tajikistan	president	30 Nov 90	Makhkamov	131/90

Table 3.5   continued

Republic	Post	Date	Winner	Vote for/against
Tajikistan	chair SS	1 Dec 90	Aslonov	121/89
Tajikistan	chair CM	Dec 90	Makhkamov	
Tajikistan	prime min	25 Jun 91	Khaeev	*178/6
Tajikistan	chair SS	Sep 91	Nabiyev	
Turkmenistan	chair SS	18 Jan 90	Niyazov	*na/1
Turkmenistan	prime min	18 Jan 90	Akhmedov	*
Ukraine	chair SS	4 Jun 90	Ivashko	278/61
Ukraine	prime min	28 Jun 90	Masol	229/134
Ukraine	chair SS	23 Jul 90	Kravchuk	239/76
Ukraine	prime min	Nov 90	Fokin	
Uzbekistan	president	24 Mar 90	Karimov	*
Uzbekistan	chair SS	Mar 90	Ibragimov	
Uzbekistan	prime min	26 Mar 90	Mirsaidov	
Uzbekistan	prime min	Nov 90	Karimov	
Uzbekistan	chair SS	12 Jun 91	Yuldashev	

* denotes that the candidate ran unopposed.
† denotes that the post was contested, but vote totals not available.

Sources: *FBIS Daily Report: Soviet Union*, press and wire service reports; Azerbaijan: *Bakinskii rabochii*, 7 and 8 February 1991; Kazakhstan: *Nezavisimaia gazeta*, 17 October 1991; Ukraine: *Izvestia*, 5 June and 24 July 1990; Russia: *The New York Times*; Tajikistan: *Kommunist Tadzhikistana*, 27 June 1991; Turkmenistan: Therese Zimmer.

The leaders of republic Communist Parties were chosen chairmen of the 'new' Supreme Soviets: in Ukraine – first Ivashko and later Leonid Kravchuk; Belorussia – Nikolai Dementei, though by the narrowest of margins; Kazakhstan – Nursultan Nazarbayev, who had been Communist Party First Secretary since 1989; Tajikistan – Kakhar Makhkamov, Party Chief since December 1985; Turkenistan – Saparmurad Niyazov, Party Leader since December 1985; Uzbekistan – Islam Karimov, Party leader since June 1989; and Kyrgyzstan – Absamat Masaliev, First Secretary since 1985. In Azerbaijan, Ayaz Mutalibov had been Chairman of the Supreme Soviet in 1989 and Party First Secretary since January 1990 (when Soviet troops entered the republic and imposed martial law). Mutalibov had already been elected president by the old Supreme Soviet and, when the newly elected soviet finally met in February 1991, it re-elected the previous Chairman and member or the Bureau of the Party Central Committee, Elmira Kafarova.[9]

Candidates for the top leadership post ran unopposed in Turkmenistan, Kazakhstan, Kyrgyzstan. In Central Asia and Kazakhstan, the reason was that there was no organized opposition within parliament at the time of the first sessions. In Tajikistan the competition was between the current and past leaders of the Communist Party.[10] In Kyrgyzstan efforts by a small group of deputies to run a candidate against the Party leader, Masaliev, were voted down by the communist majority.[11]

Communist Party leaders at first retained their top Party posts in Tajikistan, Kazakhstan, Uzbekistan, Turkmenistan and Azerbaijan. In Ukraine and Belorussia, Party leaders Vladimir Ivashko and Nikolai Dementei were pressured to resign the post of Party First Secretary in order to continue as head of state.

In an attempt to find common ground with minority blocs, the parliamentary majority in several republics elected a leader of the opposition to serve as a deputy chairman. A leading member of the Belorussian Popular Front, Stanislav Shushkevich, was chosen First Deputy Chairman of the Supreme Soviet. (He was later to be elected Chairman.) Similarly, in Azerbaijan, a leader of the Popular Front, Tamerlan Karaev, was chosen Deputy Chairman.[12] In October 1991, however, Karaev resigned his post, accusing his colleagues on the Supreme Soviet presidium of exceeding their authority and a lack of consultation.[13] In Armenia, where the Armenian Pan-National Movement was the largest deputy group, the compromise involved bringing a member of the Communist Party into the top parliamentary leadership. The head of the Armenian Communist Party's socioeconomic department was elected deputy chairman of the Supreme Soviet.[14]

In almost all republics, with the exception of the Baltic states and Belorussia, the new post of president was created in 1990–1.[15] This followed the precedent set by Gorbachev, when he convinced parliament to create the post of president with significant new powers in March 1990. Unlike Gorbachev, however, whose popularity was clearly waning, republic leaders sought the additional authority that would derive from being popularly elected. In 1991 direct popular elections for president were held in succession in Georgia, Russia, Azerbaijan, Kyrgyzstan, Tajikistan, Armenia, Ukraine, Uzbekistan, Kazakhstan and Moldavia. (In late 1990 Turkmenistan also held a popular vote to affirm the selection of Niyazov as president.) In all republics except Kyrgyzstan, the chairman of the Supreme Soviet was chosen to be president when the new office was created, and the popular elections merely confirmed this choice.

Political developments in Kyrgyzstan, Tajikistan and Belorussia shortened the tenure in office of several of these 'new' republic leaders. Masaliev's reputation in Kyrgyzstan was tarnished by violence in Osh province in June. When the new post of president was created in October 1990 – a post Masaliev expected to win – the no longer docile parliament chose instead the liberal head of the republic's Academy of Sciences, Askar Akayev. Masaliev resigned his Supreme Soviet post in December 1990, and in April 1991 he left Kyrgyzstan to take a post in the central party apparatus in Moscow.[16]

The failure of the August 1991 coup led the Communist Party majority in the Belorussian parliament to offer up a sacrifice in the form of their leader, Chairman of the Supreme Soviet, Nikolai Dementei. In May 1990 Dementei had been elected by a narrow majority (only 51.1 per cent of the deputies) in a contest with two opponents.[17] He was forced to resign in September 1991 after being accused of supporting the coup. Dementei was replaced, this time in the third round of voting, by S. Shushkevich, a nuclear physicist with popular front connections who had been a member of the radical deputies group in the USSR Congress of People's Deputies. The coup apparently resulted in a large number of deputies joining the side of radicals in the Belorussian parliament; these deputies rebuffed an attempt by the Prime Minister, long-time communist Vyachislav Kebich, to take over the post of Chairman of the Supreme Soviet.[18]

Demonstrations in Tajikistan in the aftermath of the coup led to the resignation of the republic's president, Kakhar Makhkamov, and the Chairman of Supreme Soviet, Kadreddin Aslonov, was named acting President. When Aslonov ordered the disbanding of the Communist Party and the confiscation of its property, the communist majority in parliament revolted. As was noted above, Tajikistan was unique in the large share (41 per cent) of Party and state officials represented in parliament. On 23 September 1991 the Tajik Supreme Soviet imposed a state of emergency and removed Aslonov as President, replacing him with the former leader of the Communist Party from 1982 to 1985, Rakhmon Nabiev, who had been Makhkamov's rival in the contest for President in 1990. The parliament declared Aslonov's moves against the Communist Party unconstitutional.[19] In a popular election in November, Nabiev won a majority of the vote for the post of Tajik president.

THE POST OF PRIME MINISTER

The other most significant post filled by the new parliaments was that of head of the government apparatus – the Prime Minister, or Chairman of the Cabinet (or Council) of Ministers. This division of responsibilities followed previous Soviet practice, which differentiated between the head of the legislature and the head of the government. As the post of President was introduced, however, the role of a separate and autonomous head of government became increasingly problematic. The Prime Minister had special responsibility in economic matters as the head of the republic bureaucracy. He was also responsible for putting together a new government – naming the heads of republic ministries and other top officials. The person chosen to be Prime Minister in almost all cases reflected the choice of the Chairman of the Supreme Soviet, though in several cases the decision was based on a compromise with other political forces within the parliament and outside it.

No compromise was viewed as necessary in republics where the Communist Party had a clear majority in the parliaments. In many republics Prime ministers were chosen who seemed particularly ill-equipped to lead their republics in the direction of a market economy. In Azerbaijan, Kyrgyzstan and Kazakhstan those then serving as Prime Minister (Hasanov, Dzhumagulov and Karamanov, respectively) were retained in their posts by the new parliaments. When Nazarbayev replaced Karamanov in 1991, he chose Tereshchenko who also had a background in the party-state apparatus.[20] The new Uzbek premier, Shukurilla Mirsiadov, won in a contest with the previous Prime Minister, Mirakhmat Mirkasymov. Mirsiadov had previously served as Deputy Prime Minister and Chairman of Gosplan.[21] In the Ukraine the first Prime Minister elected by the new parliament, Vitaly Masol, had been Prime Minister since 1987. The premier in Belorussia, Vyachislav Kebich, and the man chosen to replace Masol in November 1990 in the Ukraine, Vitold Fokin, were both communists who had previously served as head of the republic Gosplan.

In most cases, parliaments acceded to the wishes of the top leader on his choice for Prime Minister without much debate or opposition. In Turkmenistan, Kh. Akhmedov was elected by a show of hands after his candidacy had been put forward by Niyazov. In Belorussia, Kebich was chosen without any competition and was voted in almost unanimously, despite the divisions within parliament.[22] An exception to this rule was the Ukrainian premier, Vitaly Masol, who was elected only after three rounds of voting.[23]

In two Central Asian republics, Uzbekistan and Tajikistan, the top leaders – Islam Karimov and Kakhar Makhkamov, respectively – for a time held simultaneously the three most important posts in the republic: leader of the Communist Party, President and Prime Minister.

In the Russian republic, Eltsin chose Ivan Silaev for Prime Minister rather than other candidates who were more radical proponents of reform, such as Mikhail Bocharov.[24] A radical Prime Minister might have pursued a more divisive, confrontational strategy, directly challenging the role of the centre and the Communist Party. Silaev, on the other hand, had a career in the Party and state bureaucracy. While he was a supporter of reform, his style and experience made him more suited to the task at hand. After the August coup, Silaev was given the assignment of seeking to rebuild interrepublic economic relations in the form of an economic union, and he resigned his Russian government post in September. In November 1991 Boris Eltsin requested that the parliament allow him to combine the posts of President and Prime Minister in order to concentrate his political authority on implementing radical economic reforms.

In other republics the background of new government leaders broke sharply with the past. In three – Latvia, Armenia and Georgia (and later in Belorussia) – intellectuals with no previous government experience but who were active in new political movements were chosen as Prime Minister. Ivars Godmanis, leader of the Latvian Popular Front faction in parliament, was previously a lecturer at Latvian State University. In Armenia, a leading member of the Armenian Pan-National Movement, Vazgen Manukian, was nominated by Ter-Petrosian. He had been a lecturer at Yerevan State University. Both Godmanis and Manukian had been attached to the physics and mathematics departments. In Georgia, Tengiz Sigua, the head of a research institute and a political moderate who had distinguished himself as Deputy Chairman of the Central Electoral Commission, was named Prime Minister.

The Estonian Prime Minister, Edgar Savisaar, was one of the founders of The Estonian Popular Front and had previously been brought into the government as Deputy Prime Minister and Chief of Gosplan.[25] In October 1991, while continuing as Prime Minister, he became the leader of a new political party, the Popular Centrist Party, one of four that split off from the Popular Front.[26]

The post of Prime Minister and the policy line adopted by the new governments quickly became a focal point of controversy in many republics. The process of naming ministers for the new governments, one of the first steps taken by the newly appointed Prime Ministers, led to a number of extended parliamentary battles. Even in Belorussia, where the communists had a majority in parliament, the Prime Minister's choice for First Deputy Prime Minister and five candidates for ministerial posts were defeated.[27]

Prime Ministers resigned or were replaced within a relatively short time in Lithuania, Armenia, Moldavia and Georgia. Often this reflected the lack of generally accepted rules of the game in republic political life. Many Prime Ministers were genuinely offended by criticism voiced in parliament. When they felt support from the republic's leader and other members of parliament was inadequate, they resigned. Former Prime Ministers then often became a force rallying opposition to the political leadership of the republic. Paradoxically, then, the office of Prime Minister acted to facilitate the beginnings of political pluralism in several republics.

In Lithuania, an economist and leading reform member of the Lithuanian communists, Kazimiera Prunskiene, was named Prime Minister in March 1990. She clashed frequently behind the scenes with Landsbergis over economic policy and strategy towards Moscow. Prunskiene wanted more radical economic reforms and a more conciliatory approach to Moscow. After anti-governmental demonstrations and criticism of food price increases, an element of her programme for transition to a market economy, Prunskiene resigned in January 1991.[28] In the period after her resignation, Prunskiene remained a popular political figure and became one of the most vocal critics of the Lithuanian leadership.

Similar factors were behind the resignation of Vazgen Manukian, the Armenian Prime Minister. Manukian had introduced the most radical privatization of land of any republic. He resigned in September 1991 after criticism of his government went unanswered in the Armenian parliament.[29] There had also been a series of public disagreements between Manukian and Ter-Petrosian over relations with Moscow: Manukian was opposed to the decision to remain part of an economic union with Russia and other republics, arguing that it is best to get off a train before it crashes.[30] It was widely expected that Manukian would remain a factor in Armenian politics and that he would form a new political party.

In Moldavia, the first premier was Petr Paskar. He resigned after only two months in office when members of parliament criticized the government's inaction in the face of demonstrations and attacks on members of parliament in May 1990.[31] The parliament elected as Prime Minister a leader of the Popular Front, Mircha Druk. Druk was a Moldavian scholar who had been dismissed from the university in Kishinev because of his nationalist views and was forced to find work outside the republic.[32] Druk held the post for one year and was frequently attacked by conservative deputies from the 'Soviet Moldavia' faction in the parliament. He was replaced in May 1991 by the more moderate Deputy Prime Minister, Valery Muravschi, who was evidently the personal choice of Snegur, the President to fill the post.[33]

It was in Georgia that the conflict between President and Prime Minister had the most spectacular denouement. Tengiz Sigua resigned as Prime Minister in August 1991, after a number of disagreements over personnel and policy matters with President Zviad Gamsakhurdia. Sigua was replaced by another academic, a little-known social scientist, Vissarion Gugushvili, widely viewed as a Prime Minister who would be more easily manipulated by Gamsakhurdia. In the aftermath of the August coup, Sigua joined the extraparliamentary opposition and a breakaway faction of the National Guard and accused Gamsakhurdia of capitulating to the coup leaders. He also denounced the increasing authoritarianism of Gamsakhurdia, and claimed that he had obstructed genuine economic reforms. In December 1991 Georgian armed units loyal to the opposition, now led by Sigua and Tengiz Kitovani, the former head of the National Guard, fought a fierce battle with Gamsakhurdia's supporters in central Tbilisi. As a result, Gamsakhurdia fled the republic and Sigua became acting Prime Minister. New parliamentary elections were scheduled for the spring of 1992, while violence between Gamsakhurdia supporters and the opposition continued.

CONCLUSION

It was precisely those republics that elected non-communist majorities or pluralities to parliament in 1990 – the Baltic republics, Russia, Georgia, Moldavia and Armenia – that were the first to challenge the power of the centre to determine policy. Later even communist leaders, now ensconced as parliamentary leaders or heads of state in the remaining eight republics, sought to increase their effective sovereignty at the expense of the national government. The result of these pressures and the policy impasse that emerged in the course of 1991 was a draft union treaty that attempted to delimit the relative competence of central and republic organs.

The coup attempt of August 1991 was in part a last-minute, pre-emptive strike by proponents of a strong centre to prevent the signing of the new treaty. The failure of the coup in turn undermined what was left of the authority of the centre and led most republics to issue formal declarations of independence. Lithuania and Georgia had taken this step earlier, but organs of central power – All-Union enterprises, police, customs officials and the Soviet Army – continued to operate within their borders. Finally, in December 1991, efforts to preserve central authority in the form of a union collapsed in the face of strong opposition by the Ukrainian leadership. Eleven of the former republics agreed to form a loose 'Commonwealth of Independent States' (*sodruzhestvo nezavisimykh gosudarstv*). As a result, the USSR formally ceased to exist. The Baltic states, whose independence was already recognized internationally, chose not to join the new commonwealth, and at first neither did Georgia, which was on the brink of civil war at the time.

The increasing diversity of republic politics – reflected in their elites – was a key factor in these developments. To the extent that any new framework uniting the former Soviet republics depended on consensus, on achieving a 'least common denominator' in political terms, the diversity in republic leaderships ensured that only the most vague of formulations would be acceptable to all. Even on areas of common concern, such as control over the military and the structure of an economic framework for trade and currency regulation, republic differences quickly emerged to complicate joint decision making. Eltsin, who was simultaneously the most powerful and the most radical of the leaders in the new commonwealth, immediately launched an ambitious reform programme based on free market pricing, land reform and privatization. These measures were certain to be resisted by more conservative republic leaders, and the increasing economic splintering of the former union was inevitable.

NOTES AND REFERENCES

*   Editor's note. The title 'Moldova' was correctly used by the author of this Chapter. For consistency in the book, Moldavia has been adopted throughout.
1. *Pravda Ukrainy*, 21 January 1990; *Sovetskaia Rossiia*, 3 February 1990.
2. Based on a talk by Oleg Manaev, a Belorussian political activist and a sociologist at Belorussian State University, at Duke University, 3 May 1991.
3. See Chapter 6 by Vera Tolz.
4. On cooperatives, see Darrell Slider, 'Embattled Entrepreneurs: Soviet Cooperatives in an Unreformed Economy', *Soviet Studies*, September 1991, vol. 43, no. 5, pp. 797–821; and, on the new political role of cooperatives and their associations, Darrell Slider, 'The First Independent Soviet Interest Groups: Unions and Associations of Cooperatives', in Judith Sedaitis and James Butterfield (eds), *Perestroika from Below: New Social Movements in the Soviet Union*, (Westview Press, Boulder, co., 1991, pp. 145–64.
5. Valery Tishkov, director of the chief Soviet ethnographic institute, makes this claim in the article cited in Table 3.3.
6   Based on an analysis of the last names of the candidates and their place of residence.
7. An analysis of Ter-Petrosian's role in the national movement was given in *Soiuz* March 1991, no. 12 p. 11.
8. *Izvestia*, 5 August 1990; *Sovetskaia kul'tura*, 11 August 1990.
9. *Bakinskii rabochii*, 7 February 1991.

10. *Moscow News*, 30 December 1990 – 6 January 1991, no. 51 p. 6, and William Reisinger in D. Slider (ed) *Elections and Political Charge in the Soviet Republics*, Duke University Press, North Carolina, 1992.
11. Paper by Eugene Huskey in Slider (ed.), *Elections and Political Change*.
12. *Bakinskii rabochii*, 9 February 1991.
13. *Nezavisimaya gazeta*, 12 October 1991.
14. *Sovetskaia kul'tura*, 11 August 1990.
15. The Belorussian parliament voted in favour of introducing the post of a popularly elected president in June 1991, but had not passed a law on the presidency by October 1991. *Izvestia*, 21 June 1991.
16. Bess Brown, 'The Fall of Masaliev: Kyrgyzstan's "Silk Revolution" Advances', *Report on the USSR*, Radio Liberty, Munich, 19 April 1991, pp. 12–15.
17. *FBIS Daily Report: Soviet Union*, 21 May 1990, p. 113.
18. *FBIS Daily Report: Soviet Union*, 19 September 1991, no. 182, p. 65.
19. An interview with Makhkamov appeared in *Moscow News*, 30 December 1990 – 6 January 1991, no. 51, p. 6.
20. Tereshchenko had been chairman of the Chemkent province soviet: *Nezavisimaya gazeta*, 17 October 1991.
21. *FBIS Daily Report: Soviet Union*, 27 March 1990, no. 59, p. 121.
22. *Izvestia*, 23 July 1990. Kebich's biography appeared in *Izvestia*, 26 June 1990.
23. *FBIS Soviet Union: Daily Report*, 29 June 1990, no. 126, p. 113.
24. Bocharov was an experienced economic innovator whose programme foreshadowed the '500 days' programme that was later adopted by Eltsin and the Russian parliament.
25. Savisaar was the first to suggest organizing the popular front, on Estonian television in April 1988. See the article on the front in *Komsomolskaya pravda*, 13 October 1988. He became Deputy Prime Minister in July 1989.
26. *FBIS Daily Report: Soviet Union*, 18 October 1991, no. 202, p. 40. In January 1992 Savisaar resigned as Prime Minister after losing several parliamentary votes connected with his economic programme.
27. *Izvestia*, 23 July 1990.
28. *The New York Times*, 9 January 1991.
29. *FBIS Daily Report: Soviet Union*, 26 September 1991, no. 187, p. 71.
30. *Nezavisimaya gazeta*, 5 October 1991.
31. *Moscow News*, June 1990, no. 23, p. 6.
32. See Druk's interview in *Literaturnaya gazeta*, 13 June 1990, no. 24, p. 2.
33. Muravschi previously served as Minister of Finance, and had held a number of mid-level posts in that area from 1971 to 1990. *Sovetskaia Moldova*, 29 May 1991.

4. Social Groups, Party Elites and Russia's New Democrats

Sergei Mitrokhin and Michael E. Urban

The unexpectedly swift demise of the Communist Party of the Soviet Union (CPSU) has instantaneously created a vacuum of political organization in Russia. Who or what might be expected to fill it? One candidate for this role consists of those non-communist parties that had begun to form after constitutional restrictions banning party activity were lifted in March 1990. Although thus legally entitled to organize, the activity and recruitment efforts of Russia's new parties had nonetheless remained stymied by the CPSU's continued control of the organs of power. While it might fare poorly in competitive elections and even lose significant ones outright – as it did, for example, in city elections in Moscow and Leningrad (renamed St Petersburg in November 1991) in 1990 or in Russia's presidential election in 1991 – the CPSU had still held a firm grip on the central structures of government along with the lion's share of the means of communication. In consequence electoral victories won by the new 'democratic' parties seemed to count for little more than the right to populate various public offices, pass laws and decrees destined to remain unimplemented and put out newspapers in limited editions and with even more limited means of distribution. Moreover the CPSU had retained its elephantine size, even among that 10 or 12 per cent of members who had left it after its stormy 28th Congress in July 1990,[1] only a small handful have joined any of the new parties.

The sudden collapse of the CPSU would appear to have changed all this. Overnight some of these fledgling political organizations – previously referred to as minor or even micro parties – have become (for the moment, at least) the major parties in Russian politics. Beyond the level of formal accounts of their respective size, organizational structures, programmes and so forth[2] we have exceptionally scant knowledge about them. The present study, then, might be regarded as an initial step toward filling this gap in our understanding of party formation and development in Russia. It is based on the early results of a survey of activists, functionaries and officers in these new parties conducted under the auspices of Moscow's Institute for Humanist-Political Research.[3] We have selected two of the largest parties on the scene in 1991 – the Democratic Party of Russia (DPR) and the Social Democratic Party of Russia (SDPR) – in order to address three fundamental questions concerning the emergence of these new political organizations. First, which social groups have played the major role in creating democratically-oriented political parties in Russia? Second, do those in the sample exhibit distinctive status factors that might have had a bearing on their decisions to become active in these parties? And, finally, is it possible to draw meaningful distinctions between the DPR and the SDPR on the basis of the sociological composition of their respective elites?

A preliminary word might be said here about the two parties in our sample in order to clarify the significance of the last of these research questions. The offspring of various 'informal' political groups active principally in Moscow and Leningrad – primarily the Moscow Voters' Association and a wing of Leningrad Perestroika in the case of the DPR; Moscow's Democratic Perestroika and Leningrad's Social-Democratic Union in that of the SDPR – both parties were formally constituted at founding congresses that took place in May 1990.[4] The larger of the two parties, the DPR, has since maintained a membership of between 35 000 and 50 000, a figure that has varied from time to time as a result of successful recruitment and factional splits that have periodically depleted the party's ranks. At the moment it is the only party in Russia that has established organizations in every region of the country. The SDPR's membership, on the other hand, has been considerably smaller standing at the present time (1991) at about 5 000.

Judging by the formal orientations of these two parties, expressed in programmes and in the speeches of their leaders, there would appear to be very little that distinguishes them one from another. They both regard themselves as 'normal', 'parliamentary' parties oriented towards the creation of a market economy, a legal-rational state and a democratic political order.[5] What is more, they both seek to organize and to represent the same constituency, namely, what they regard as an emerging 'middle class' composed primarily of professionals, businessmen (managers in the state sector, entrepreneurs in the coop-erative and private sectors) and skilled workers.[6] The SDPR does place more emphasis on providing social security for those economi-cally dislocated during the transition to a market economy than does the DPR, but this may reflect no more than an attempt on the part of the SDPR's leadership to offer the concession of 'socialist' rhetoric to its Left Fraction[7] in return for the latter's support for its overall programme of marketization and privatization. Equally, inasmuch as the party's present size and standing in Russian politics make it highly unlikely that the responsibility of governing will be thrust upon it soon, the SDPR seems to face no major constraint against adding a 'socialist' plank to its largely free market platform. For the DPR, whose equivalent factional contentions have emanated from a Thatcherite right,[8] 'social security' is correspondingly rendered *sotto voce*. But, with allowances for programmatic manoeuvre, it would not seem mistaken to regard the orientations of the DPR and the SDPR as indistinguishable in the areas of social and economic policy.[9]

Differences between these parties are visible with respect to their views on federal relations and in the area of that always – slippery issue of political 'culture' or 'ethos.' As far as federal relations are concerned, the DPR has consistently favoured the maintenance of a union (albeit one composed of 'sovereign' members who have united voluntarily), whereas the SDPR envisages a looser, confederal arrangement based on the cooperation of sovereign, if not independent, states. In the case of the Russian Federation itself, the DPR has taken a position calling for the effective elimination of certain rights to self-government claimed by and for non-Russian peoples in their 'autonomous' regions and republics and the de facto reinstitution of the pre-revolutionary administrative system of guberniyas, with the Russian President appointing local prefects as the Tsar had done in a previous era. The SDPR, on the other hand, places more emphasis on the authority of legislative bodies and calls for the maintenance of national-territorial units within the Russian Federation that would enjoy a large measure of local autonomy.[10]

With respect to the other area of difference between these parties, that of political culture or ethos, one easily gains the impression in talking with their leaders and activists that these parties inhabit distinct cultural spaces or, to use Moshe Lewin's expression, different 'microworlds'.[11] Those in the SDPR seem more urbane, erudite, articulate and closer in manner to the social type, 'intelligent', in Russian society than do their counterparts in the DPR, whose straightforward and often curt comportment summons to mind certain traits associated with the culture of modern business. Observation of their respective party congresses would reinforce such impressions. Although SDPR congresses have been riddled with debates, these have proceeded in an orderly fashion, suggesting the presence of a subcultural code that emphasizes – as might befit a party self-consciously attempting to follow Western patterns – instrumental-rational action within the context of clearly defined and accepted rules.

Congresses of the DPR have been raucous, disorderly affairs, invariably ending in either shouting matches, walk-outs or both. The pattern, here, reflects a more emotive, expressive, one might say, more 'Russian' style, in which strong personalities and their loyal followers, rather than programmatic questions, form the axes of conflict. In this respect, speech seems to play quite different roles within these parties. Whereas it appears as persuasive argument in the subculture of the SDPR, it more often takes the form of declamation within that of the DPR. The same might be said of their respective newspapers; *Alternativa* and *Epokha* (SDPR) feature far more analytic articles than does *Demokraticheskaya gazeta* (DPR). SDPR discourse, then, belongs to a relatively discrete community, the intelligentsia, which values rational persuasion as its presumed leverage for affecting events; that of the DPR is geared towards action and bespeaks a world view in which physical things – equipment, party membership and the tightness of party organization – count for far more. DPR leaders regularly criticise their intellectual counterparts in politics as dilettantes and windbags who have no notion of real political action. Yet these same leaders continually endeavour to recruit leading intellectuals to the DPR – reflecting, perhaps, their own status deficiencies in the face of this more prestigious social group – only to chastise them when their efforts are rebuffed.[12]

With the results of our survey we intend to shed some light on the question of both the apparent similarities and the apparent differences that obtain between the DPR and the SDPR. That is, our aim is to treat both the similarities and differences that we have noted as problems, and to look for possible solutions to them in our sociological data on their respective elites. The data themselves have been collected by means of a survey questionnaire administered to delegates attending the Second Congress of the DPR and the Third Congress of the SDPR, both held in April 1991 in Moscow and Leningrad, respectively. The samples thereby drawn include just under half of the DPR's top leaders, activists and functionaries (190 out of some 400 delegates) and a little over half of the corresponding group in the SDPR (109 out of about 200 delegates). We begin our analysis by turning to the first of the questions set out above – which social groups have played the major role in creating democratically oriented political parties? We attempt to answer this question in the context of the representation of social groups within the elite composition of these parties.

SOCIAL GROUPS AND PARTY ELITES

For the purposes of this phase of our analysis, we use three variables that are standards in sociological research – education, income and occupation. Table 4.1 offers a comparison between the levels of education represented in the entire Soviet population in 1989 and that recorded in our sample of party elites (DPR/SDPR, combined). The differences between these two groups as displayed in the table should be qualified by noting that comparing Party elites against the entire population tends to skew the results in favour of the former, inasmuch as: (1) the figures for the entire USSR on higher education (10 per cent) are slightly lower than they are for Russia (11.3 per cent);[13] and (2) individuals 16 years of age or older are included in the All-Union data, lowering again – since some in this sample had not yet reached the age at which they might matriculate to a post-secondary institution – the scores in the upper row of the table. These relatively minor imprecisions notwithstanding, we might note the enormous differences here in terms of education that set apart these party elites from the general population. The first part of our answer, then, to the question of which social groups have taken the lead in organizing democratically-oriented parties in Russia would be: disproportionately, those with higher education.

Table 4.1   Education levels in the Soviet population* and among Party elites (percentages)

	Higher education	Some higher education	Secondary	Specialized secondary	Some secondary
Soviet population	10	1.7	30	18	20
Party elites	65	14	7	14	0

*Data for the full Soviet population were taken from *Sotsial'noe razvitie SSR 1989g: Statisticheskii sbornik*, Moscow, 1991, pp, 248–9. Those 16 years of age or older were included in the data for the whole of the USSR.

The rows in this table do not total 100 because those with education levels below 'some secondary' were not included.

We now repeat this exercise, using this time the variable 'income'. Owing to the considerable inflation that has occurred in Russia between 1988 (for which year published data on the general population are available) and 1991 (when our sample had been drawn) we have constructed five income categories for DPR and SDPR elites that we regard as proportionate to those applied to the general population in the earlier study. This inference is supported by the fact that responses to our survey question, 'What was your income five to seven years ago?' reveal a pattern consistent with the relative frequencies of their replies to the question of current income in 1991.[14] These sets of data seem to be reasonably comparable with each other, but we should note in passing that the comparison between per capita income for the population and individual income for the party elites would tend to inflate the figures for the latter, inasmuch as income earners are averaged together with their dependants in the first instance, while dependants are not included in the second. Table 4.2, then, by comparing the per capita income of the population against the individual levels of income reported by our respondents, would give the impression that our party elites enjoy higher incomes than they actually do. Bearing this in mind, a graphic representation of these data – as shown by Figure 4.1 wherein the five income groups that appear in Table 4.2 are represented as strata in an income hierarchy – nonetheless highlights the difference between the population at large and our party elites. This difference might be regarded as that obtaining between two rhombuses that find their respective 'centres of gravity' above (in the case of the population) and below (in that of the party elites) their geometric centres. Consequently we can add to our answer to the question of which social groups have become most active in democratically oriented parties with the observation that those from relatively disadvantaged income groups have played a disproportionately large role.

Table 4.2   Per capita monthly income levels in Russia and individual income of DPR and SDPR elites (percentages)

	Income (in rubles)				
	Below 75R	75–100R	100–150R	150–200R	Above 200R
Russian population*	6.3	13.1	34.0	24.6	22.0
	Below 210R	210–360R	361–600R	601–1000R	Above 1000R
DPR/SDPR combined	19	25	34	12	5
DPR	15	25	36	12	6
SDPR	26	24	31	12	3

*These data have been taken from *Statisticheskii ezhegodnik Estonii*, Tallinn, 1991, p. 270. Here and elsewhere in this chapter, rounding error accounts for row totals of percentages that do not equal 100.

*Figure 4.1   Income stratification of the Russian population and the
Party elites (DPR/SDPR combined)*

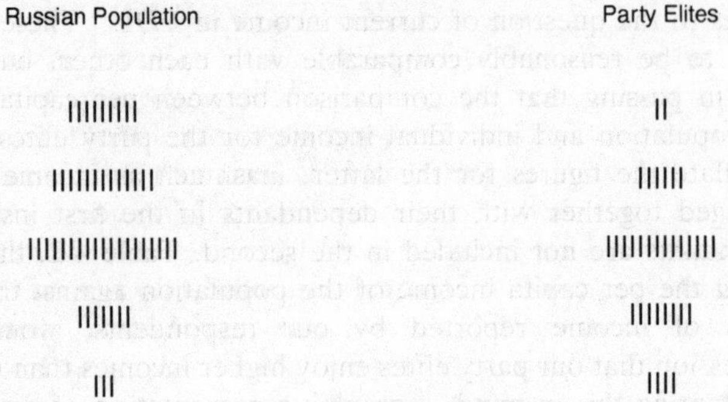

Russian Population   Party Elites

The third of our comparisons concerns the occupational structure
of the general population and that represented in our sample of party
elites. The relevant data, displayed in Table 4.3, indicate enormous
differences. Whereas the economically active segment of the Soviet
population is composed primarily of manual workers (61.8 per cent
in 1987), non-manual categories comprise the great bulk of those in
our sample of party elites (72 per cent). Even among those in this
category, however, those in our sample stand out as overwhelmingly
members of higher strata of the working class, with skilled workers
outnumbering the unskilled in a ratio 13:1. Similarly collective farm
peasants had accounted for 12 per cent of the Soviet workforce in
1987, while this group does not appear in our sample at all. This
indicator, then adds another dimension to our profile of party elites,
distinguishing them from the larger population as those most likely to
be found in urban areas working in non-manual occupations. Below
we return to the data presented in Table 4.3 – particularly to those
related to the occupational subcategories of *sluzhashchie*, ITR and so
forth – in order to draw comparisons between the elites of the DPR
and the SDPR.

PARTY ELITES AND THE CLUSTERING OF STATUS FACTORS

Having set out three standard sociological distinctions – education,
income and occupation – between our party elites, on the one hand,

Table 4.3   Occupational structures of the USSR (1987) and the DPR and SDPR* (percentages)

	USSR	DPR/SDPR	DPR	SDPR
Manual workers	61.8	15	15	15
Non-manual workers	16.2	72	74	70
Sluzhashchie		10	11	9
ITR		16	19	10
Intelligentsia		30	27	36
Businessmen		16	17	15
Collective farm				
peasantry	12	–	–	–
Students		6	3	10
Dependants		5	7	3
(unemployed, housewives and				
pensioners)				

*Data for the USSR are taken from *Narodnoe khoziaystvo SSR v 1987g: Statisticheskii ezhegodnik*, Moscow; Finansy i statistika, 1988, p. 351.
The subcategories used in our sample have been constructed as follows: *sluzhashchie* – state, CPSU and official trade union functionaries, petty military officers and other civil servants; ITR – from the Russian 'engineering technical workers', including managers and technical personnel in industry and agriculture; intelligentsia – those engaged in intellectual work outside the production sector (teachers, medical doctors, scientists and so forth); businessmen – those active non-manually in the non-state sectors of trade, finance and services.

and the general population, on the other, we turn now to a closer examination of the way these status factors cluster together for various groups in the party elites. Table 4.4, which cross-tabulates our sample by occupation and income, displays the first set of clusters. Reading this table by rows as the percentages of each of the occupational groups that have reached various levels of educational attainment, we notice, first, that, although the intelligentsia and ITR lead the other groups on this indicator, the scores posted by the *sluzhashchie* and businessmen do not lag far behind those of the leaders. The second cluster of note concerns skilled workers, whose presence in the educational structure of these party elites is most pronounced on the other end of the scale, namely, among those who have completed only secondary or specialized secondary education.

A fuller understanding of the significance of these status clusters emerges when we combine these findings with those presented in Table 4.5. Here we notice in the right-hand column of the table that those groups that rank lowest on the level of educational attainment – businessmen and skilled workers – are the same groups enjoying the

Table 4.4   Levels of educational attainment of Party elites (DPR/
SDPR combined) by occupational group (percentages)

Occupational group	Secondary	Specialized secondary	Some higher	Higher	Post-graduate
Sluzhashchie	7	18	2	68	2
ITR	1	5	7	79	8
Intelligentsia	0	6	9	68	17
Businessmen	7	12	21	58	2
Skilled workers	24	37	10	27	2

highest levels of income. Members of the intelligentsia, however, tend to cluster around the lower-middle level of the income ladder, earning appreciably less than their counterparts in the ITR and somewhat more than those classified as *sluzhashchie*.

Table 4.5   Levels of income of Party elites (DPR/SDPR combined)
by occupational group (percentages)

Occupational group	Income level (rubles per month)				
	Below 210R	210–359R	360–599R	600–1000R	Above 1000R
Sluzhashchie	16	35	32	10	3
ITR	6	23	58	6	2
Intelligentsia	11	30	44	10	1
Businessmen	20	18	20	20	18
Skilled workers	15	25	30	22	8

These results permit us to draw the following inference: taken as a group, the elites in our sample are distinguished by clusterings of status factors that mark our two rather distinct social poles. At one end, we find intellectuals, *sluzhashchie* and ITR, whose high scores on educational attainment are not matched by their incomes. At the other end, we notice that the reverse is true for businessmen and skilled workers. Especially in the case of skilled workers, their predominance in the representation in the higher income categories is sharply disproportionate to the levels of education that they have attained. Consequently it might not be amiss to speak of two forms of status incongruence that have contributed to the particular elite composition manifest in our data.[15] The first pertains to the intelligentsia, *sluzhashchie* and ITR for whom higher education and the status that accrues along with it have not been consistent with their levels of income. While it would be mistaken, in our judgement, to suggest that this incongruity 'caused' these individuals to become active in their respective parties, it would be equally mistaken, we think, to ignore its potential influence. For, as leading members of parties fundamentally opposed to the then-prevailing communist order, these individuals can be regarded as simultaneously opposing a system under which they had been educated and trained very well and yet remunerated rather poorly.

The second form of status incongruence would seem to have something of the reverse effect. At that pole occupied primarily by businessmen and skilled workers, we find that achievements in the world of work represented by income are not matched by the social prestige that would accompany the attainment of higher educational qualifications. For this group, then, becoming active in democratically oriented parties might in part be regarded as a method of offsetting their relatively low social standing by means of that emolument of prestige associated with holding office in organizations largely populated by more prestigious groups.

Finally we might remark on the fact that a rather sizable proportion of those occupational groups scoring highest on the variable 'income' are found at the lower end of the income scale. Since skilled workers have commanded relatively high wages in the Soviet economy, the fact that 40 per cent of those in our sample are found in the two lowest income categories would indicate the existence of an income gap between skilled workers in the party elites and their counterparts in the general population. Similarly, although a business class is a new phenomenon in Russia, it would be difficult to imagine that those entering it have done so with expectations of undergoing relative impoverishment, a characteristic of some 38 per cent of the businessmen in our sample.

Our examination of these party elites from the perspective of the status groups that compose them could be read as analytically grounded in the category of 'interest'. Certain groups have joined and have become active in these parties, one might say, because of some 'interest' that those in the groups are pursuing – obtaining more prestige, changing the distributive mechanisms of the social order to improve their position on the income ladder, and so forth. However we would reject this line of argument, for it amounts to no more than the imputation of 'interest', always a 'subjective' phenomenon, on the basis of social position – something that can be taken to be 'objective' or, at least, 'non-subjective'.[16] In defining what 'interest' might amount to in a given instance, the subject (whether an individual, a group or a social class) rather than the analyst is entitled to the first word.

The category of social interests is further complicated in contemporary Russia by the fact that the expression of such interests has been politically suppressed for many generations,[17] and because social structures and their attendant social relations are in the throes of fundamental change, so that group identities and interest are anything but stable and predictable at the moment. While avoiding, then, a robust usage of the 'interest' concept, we would nonetheless want to comment, however tentatively, on the question of those social clusters identified in our data, directing attention both to the sublimation of 'interests' during the period of party struggles against communism and to extant social cleavages in the elite composition of these parties that may engender conflict in future.

Understandably the agendas of all democratically oriented parties in Russia had been dominated by the desideratum of extirpating the communist order. As long as this order remained intact, their common projects for becoming 'normal', 'parliamentary' parties could not be realized. On the level of political organization, this unity of purpose among the parties has been embodied in Democratic Russia, an alliance of, effectively, all democratic parties, groups and forces that had been formed in October 1990 with the express aim of destroying the communist system and replacing it with a democratic one. On the level of political discourse, something similar seems to have been going on both within the democratic movement and, judging from our survey results, within at least some of the democratic parties a discourse of democracy that pointed outwards, towards things to come, either has occluded the expression of distinct social interests or has wrapped them all in the same indistinguishable packaging.[18] As a result, social differences within the movement and its member parties that might give rise to distinct political interest have remained latent. To illustrate this, we can take an 'extreme' case which was in fact emblematic of this period: striking coal miners and other militant workers have had no closer allies than business groups and pro-business political parties.[19]

What becomes of anti-communist alliances in the post-communist future is a question that remains, of course, open, but the cleavages in the social composition of DPR and SDPR elites indicated by our data suggest a potential for conflict among certain status groups that might grow now that one of the major factors encouraging their cooperation – the political dominance of the Communist Party – has disappeared. Equally the issue of the relationship between party elites and the particular constituencies that they seek to build appears to be susceptible to reinterpretation in communism's aftermath. One can scarcely expect such marriages of convenience as militant workers and business associations to survive long in the turbulent period accompanying Russia's transition to a market economy. It may well be that the particular 'middle class' to which these parties had addressed their appeals while struggling against the communist regime will be reconfigured now that that struggle has been won. In the context of such deep transformations in their environments, how can we expect these parties to cope with the (potentially) divisive effects of social cleavages within their respective elites? We can frame a response to this query by turning to the last of our three research questions, that of sociological distinctions between the DPR an the SDPR.

SOCIOLOGICAL DISTINCTIONS BETWEEN DPR AND SDPR ELITES

Our survey data on the levels of education among DPR and SDPR elites are reported in Table 4.6, while those for income have appeared above (Table 4.2). Apart from the 11 percentage points that separate these groups in the lowest income category (see the left-hand column of Table 4.2) the educational and income structures of DPR and SDPR elites seem quite comparable. Indeed even the income difference that we have noted would appear to be accountable in terms of other differences in our sample that concern the variables of occupation and age.

Table 4.6   Education of DPR and SDPR elites (percentages)

Party Elites	Incomplete secondary	Secondary	Specialized secondary	Some higher	Higher	Post-Graduate
DPR	1	5	13	14	57	9
SDPR	0	10	16	13	56	5

Returning to our data on the occupational structure of the party elites as set out in Table 4.3 (above), we might comment at this point on the differences that obtain here between the DPR and the SDPR. The salient ones seem to be these: ITR personnel are better represented in the DPR elite than in that of the SDPR (19 versus 10 per cent); and the SDPR's elite contains a larger percentage of both intellectuals and students (36 versus 27 per cent and 10 versus 3 per cent, respectively). The last of these distinctions, the percentage of student representation at the elite level in these parties, is correlated with the age differences between them (displayed Table 4.7) and probably accounts – since students usually subsist on small stipends – for the difference in income levels mentioned earlier. The data on the age structures of these party elites indicate that in both instances people between the ages of 30 and 50 constitute the bulk of our sample. Nonetheless it is also clear from these figures that the SDPR's elite is considerably younger, with a quarter of its members under the age of 30, where the comparable statistic for the DPR is only 9 per cent.

Table 4.7   Age structure of DPR and SDPR elites (percentages)

Years of age	DPR/SDPR combined	DPR	SDPR
under 23	6	3	11
23–9	9	6	14
30–9	34	32	37
40–9	32	36	25
50–9	14	17	8
60 and older	3	3	2

Before reviewing the findings on our final variable, time of entry into political activity, it would appear useful to sum up the differences so far encountered. First, while the SDPR's elite profile suggests that it is somewhat more a party of the intelligentsia than is the DPR, the latter is more a party of business and management.[20] Second, older age cohorts are better represented in the DPR's elite, younger ones in the SDPR's elite. Finally, the data show that our DPR sample is somewhat wealthier than that of the SDPR. While differences in this respect are not, in our judgement, large enough to indicate much in their own right, they suggest something of import when viewed in the context of social mobility. Although scores for the two groups in the area of education are nearly identical, with the DPR showing a slight advantage at the higher and postgraduate levels, the same is not true with respect to the level of education attained by the respondents' parents. Here we find that, whereas 38 per cent of the fathers and 30 per cent of the mothers of those in our SDPR sample hold degrees from institutions of higher education, the comparable figures for DPR respondents are 28 per cent and 20 per cent, respectively. On the side of the DPR, then, we can add 'more upwardly mobile' to our list of distinguishing social traits.

The data set out in Table 4.8 concern the time at which our respondents became active in politics (excluding Communist Party activity). The temporal intervals in this table are defined by the stages of development of *perestroika* and, accordingly, those of the democratically oriented opposition to communism. Consequently knowing when someone became active in the democratic movement is also, *ceteris paribus*, knowing something about that person's politics. The first row in the table (before 1986) is occupied by those who could be called 'dissidents'. They had entered into political activity while such activity remained the object of state repression. They had obviously displayed great courage in so doing. The second row (1986–8) concerns the period in which the so-called 'informals' came onto the scene. In these years, political activity had not yet been officially permitted but sanctions against it had been relaxed. In the eyes of the majority of the population, it might be fair to assume, such activity, if not regarded as criminal, would still be seen as unusual, improper and dangerous. Year 1989 (row three) represents a deep change in context as the first (relatively) free elections to the Soviet parliament simultaneously legalized political activity. Those appearing in row three, then probably became active through supporting candidates independent of the Communists Party.

Table 4.8   Date of entry into politics, DPR and SDPR elites
(percentages)

Date of entry	DPR/SDPR combined	DPR	SDPR
Before 1986	6	4	10
1986–8	17	12	27
1989	22	21	23
Jan.–May 1990	14	10	21
May–Dec. 1990	32	44	11
Jan.–April 1991	6	7	4

Since political mobilization accelerated in 1990, we have divided that year into two periods. The first (January-May) would be notable both because of the local and republic elections held in Russia, and because of the removal of constitutional restrictions against organizing independent parties. It will be remembered that both the DPR and the SDPR held their founding congresses in May 1990. Consequently it appears that those who entered into political activity during this period were attracted by the real opportunity to form parties. The second period in 1990 can be regarded as one in which parties, now established, began to expand their memberships and to attract those – from the standpoint of our sample of elites – who were interested in launching political careers. The final period in the table (row six) would capture those who began political activism rather late, but still found themselves elected to the party congresses from which our sample was drawn.

The differences between DPR and SDPR elites revealed in Table 4.8 are the largest that we have encountered in this study. They indicate that, whereas 60 per cent of the SDPR's elite had become active in the democratic movement prior to the unqualified legalization of political activity (see the top three rows of Table 4.8), a comparable portion of the DPR's elite (61 per cent) had deferred launching their political careers until *after* such official authorization had been extended (see the bottom three rows of Table 4.8). Moreover it would appear from the bottom two rows of the table that the DPR has recruited the majority of its elite (51 per cent) in the period following its constitution as a political party. Conversely SDPR's elite is over-whelmingly (85 per cent) composed of those who had been politically active prior to the formal inauguration of the party as such.

These sharp differences between the DPR and the SDPR in terms of the respective times at which their leading officers, activists and functionaries had begun to participate in one or another of the organiz-ations in the democratic movement enable us to draw some important distinctions regarding the sociopolitical character of these two elites and allow us to assemble some of the other differences between them that we have noted into a relatively coherent profile for each party.[21] With respect to the SDPR, we might observe that it has drawn its leadership largely from a politically active subculture, the 'informal' movement, which had functioned as something of a magnet for Rus-sia's non-conformist youth during the early years of *perestroika*. Non-conformism had, of course, been expressed via a number of different ideologies – Western liberalism, anarchism, democratic socialism and social democracy, to name but a few – but each had represented above all a vantage from which to criticize (and reject) the prevailing communist order. Those groups that comprised the core of the SDPR when it was founded in 1990 – Moscow's Democratic Perestroika and Leningrad's Social Democratic Union – had, represented a particular strand in the 'informal' movement, one that emphasized reason over radicalism and a *Western* orientation over a Russian one. A cadre of such activists then, had already formed around a particular political identity – Western social democracy – before the SDPR had been formally constituted. This cadre has remained rather stable, even as party membership, which seems to have reached its peak by late summer of 1990,[22] has declined somewhat thereafter. The Western orientation of those groups and individuals that created the SDPR seems to be congruent with the high percentage of intellectuals in the party's elite, its particular rational-discursive ethos that we remarked upon earlier and the universalist norms – emphasizing the self-determination and voluntary cooperation of peoples – that stand behind its programme in the field of federal relations.

With respect to the SPDR's top leadership, we might note that they achieved a certain prominence in Russian political life through activities associated with the rational-discursive ethos of their party. While only 30 years of age, Oleg Rumyantsev, for instance, has emerged as the leading figure on the Commission of the RSFSR's Supreme Soviet that has drafted Russia's new constitution. Following a long history of political activity in the circles of Moscow's dissident intellectuals, and later in those of the 'informal' groups spawned by the capital's intelligentsia, Pavel Kudyukin has earned a reputation for political-theoretical work that led to his appointment in November 1991 as Russia's Deputy Minister for Labour, the first such appointment awarded by Boris Eltsin to a member of any of the democratic parties. Similarly Aleksandr Obolenskii instantaneously achieved national notoriety by rising to challenge the one-candidate 'election' of Mikhail Gorbachev during the First Congress of People's Deputies of the USSR in 1989. In response to the uproar provoked by this disturbance of communist convention, Obolenskii patiently explained his self-nomination as an act designed not to secure his own election – there was simply no practical possibility of this – but one intended to establish a principle and a precedent. Democracy required elections, and elections would require competition. For each of the three leaders mentioned here, political activity would be more or less synonymous with persuasive argumentation, itself the forte of the SDPR. A commitment to this enterprise within the ideological framework of social democracy would seem to represent a powerful adhesive element for the party.

The DPR, for its part, has always lacked a solid ideological centre. Its inception was not antedated by the maturation of a cadre of like-

minded individuals with rather long histories in the informal movement. Its founders were relatively new to democratic politics; their
activities in many cases did not commence until the elections of 1989.
Having sat out the early years of *perestroika*, they responded to the
prospect of achieving tangible political results, namely, being elected
or working for the election of others to the national legislature. In
contrast to the SDPR's founders, then, their political histories suggest
a preference for action and results over programme and principles.
Accordingly ideology has been consciously soft-pedalled by the DPR's
leadership which has sought to cast its appeal as broadly as possible.
Since it is at the moment the largest party in Russia, we might con-
clude that this approach has been successful. On the other hand,
however, the relative absence of a coherent ideology has meant that
the DPR has lacked the adhesive medium of a common discourse
through which factions – speaking essentially 'the same language' –
might argue over and resolve their differences. Instead factional divisions within the DPR have surfaced at both of its congresses as
acrimonious contests for the leadership, followed by walk-outs on the
part of many or most of the defeated minorities.

The question of leadership has been pivotal in the history of the
DPR. Its Chairman, Nikolai Travkin, himself seems to personify many
of the collective characteristics of the party on which we have had
occasion to comment. His pre-political career was built in the construction industry where, beginning as a common labourer, he rose through
the ranks to become director of one of the largest – and perhaps the
most highly touted – construction trusts in the USSR. Accustomed to
giving directions and ever oriented to achieving results, Travkin has
not shunned taking what he considers correct and principled positions
on major political issues, regardless of their popularity at the moment.
In this respect, within the ambit of Russia's political lexicon, he cannot
be regarded as a 'populist'. His forceful persona has, no doubt,
attracted many supporters to the party and alienated a number of
previous supporters (usually members of the intelligentsia). Deservedly
or not, he has a broad reputation for an authoritarian style of leadership, a style quite consistent with the DPR's orientation toward federalism and its more 'Russian' ethos in the area of intra-party relations,
as discussed above. Our data help to ground this 'type' of leader or
this 'collective character' of the organization in the social traits evinced
by its elite. To all the ways thus far mentioned in which the elite
composition of the DPR would distinguish it from the SDPR – older,
more business-oriented, more upwardly mobile – we can add here the
fact that its elite seems to be more 'conformist' in the sense that the

great majority of its members had no experience in the non-conformist circles of the youth subculture in the late 1980s. Indeed its age profile indicates that it belongs mainly to an older generation that had come of age before this subculture developed. Accordingly, this 'conformism' has appeared in the form of taking up political activity only when it had become completely legal to do so and of joining an already established party.

These observations permit us to comment on the overriding similarities in the programmes of these parties in the field of social and economic policy on which we have remarked earlier. Judging by its roots in Russia's non-conformist youth subculture and its strong sense of identity as a Western-style social democratic party, the SDPR would probably experience serious difficulties in undertaking any significant departures from its present orientation towards class compromise, economic efficiency and social justice. Equally, we might assume, its current programme represents rather accurately not just what the party stands for – social democracy – but what the party, so to speak, 'is' – a party of social democrats. Such internal pressures against programmatic change do not appear to be as pronounced in the case of the DPR. Especially if our assessment regarding the results-oriented ethos of the DPR is correct, we can expect this party to adjust its programmatic postures as circumstances change and opportunities present themselves. Perhaps our data would suggest that promoting a large private sector in the economy would be the first order of business for this business-oriented elite. And well it might be. But the business of democratic politics is first and foremost a matter of winning elections and the efforts currently directed by the DPR toward that enterprise[23] would caution us against drawing facile conclusions on that score. We would expect it to be prepared to compromise on this issue, as with other of its goals, if such compromise has been judged important to its political success.

NOTES AND REFERENCES

1. This figure is taken from M. M. Malyutin, 'Perspektivy demokratii v Rossii', A report presented to the Higher Consultative-Coordinating Council of the Chairperson of the Supreme Soviet of Russia, August 1991, p. 15.
2. Vera Tolz, *The USSR's Emerging Multiparty System* Praeger, New York, 1990; M. A. Babkina (ed.), *New Political Parties and Movements in the Soviet Union*, Nova Science Publishers, Commack, NY, 1991; Vladimir Pribylovskii, 'Slovar' oppozitsii: novye politicheskie partii i organizatsii Rossii', *Sostoyanie strany*, April 1991, nos. 4/5.
3. These data were collected in April 1991. We wish to thank, in this respect, researchers at the Institute for Humanist-Political Research, Marina Razorenova,

Tatyana Shevshukova and Vera Pisareva for their work with data collection and processing, and Ilya Kudryavtsev for data analysis.

4. On the early histories of these parties, see Michael E. Urban, 'Party Formation and Deformation on Russia's Democratic Left', in R. T. Huber and D. R. Kelley (eds), *Perestroika-Era Politics*, M. E. Sharpe, Armonk, NY, 1991; Pribylovskii, 'Slovar' oppozitsii', pp. 6–7, 39–40.

5. For the SDPR, see 'Nashi printsipy' and 'Deklaratsiya', *Sotsial-Demokratiya; Informatsionnyi byulleten 1990 g.*, pp. 1–4. For the programme of the DPR, see 'Prilozhenie k vypusku No. 1', *Demokraticheskaya Rossiya*, July 1990, no. 1 pp. 2–6.

6. For the SDPR's position on this point, see 'Situatsiya v strane', *Alternativa*, (September 1990), no. 3 pp. 1–2. For that of the DPR, see section 7 of the programme adopted at the Party's Second Congress, 26–8 April 1991, p. 8.

7. According to the SDPR document, 'Levaya Fraktsiya v SDPR', 19 April 1991, prepared by G. Ya. Rakitskaya of the party's left wing, this group views itself as attempting to slow, if not halt, what it regards as the SDPR's slide toward liberalism by championing the causes of 'social justice', 'social security', 'human values' and the 'defence of the workers' against exploitation in a private economy that the SDPR is committed to bringing into existence.

8. This group in the DPR, the 'Liberal Fraction', has been led by Garii Kasparov and Arkadii Murashev. At the DPR's Second Congress, 26–8 April 1991, many in this group followed Kasparov's and Murashev's lead and left the Party, citing primarily their distaste for an insufficiently anti-communist orientation.

9. SDPR leaders have admitted this openly. See, for instance, the comments of Oleg Rumyantsev in ' "My" -partiya "oni"?', *Demokraticheskaya Rossiya*, 22 March 1991 no. 1, p. 9; and those of Pavel Kudyukin in 'Sotsial-Demokraty v Rossii: Byli. Kazhetsya est', *Demokraticheskaya Rossiya*, 12 April 1991, no. 4, p. 5.

10. Their differences on the issue of federalism surfaced clearly during the debate on the new union treaty whose signing was cancelled by the coup of August 1991. Whereas the SDPR aligned itself with those around Yurii Afanasev that opposed the treaty on the grounds that it promised an over-centralized federation, the DPR attacked the views of this opposition as extremist and proposed only marginal changes in the treaty's provisions. The positions of the DPR and those led by Afanasev can be found in 'Soyuznyi dogovor – polyarizatsiya mnenii i deistvii', *Soyuz*, 14–21 August 1991, no. 33, pp. 2–3; and in 'Chto bylo na nedele', *Kommersant*, 12–19 August 1991, no. 33, p. 2.

11. Moshe Lewin, *The Gorbachev Phenomenon*, University of California Press, Berkeley 1989, pp. 63–71.

12. Interviews conducted by M. E. Urban with Nikolai Alyabiev, Chairperson of the DPR's Moscow Regional Committee, 14 May 1991, and with Eduard Lorkh-Sheiko, Personal Assistant to the DPR's Chairperson, Nikolai Travkin, 24 August 1991. See also the interview given by Travkin to Andrei Karaulov, 'Radi odnogo naroda nelzya korezhit stranu', *Nezavisimaya gazeta* 8 August 1991, p. 6. Travkin, having at one time made a serious effort to recruit Yurii Afanasev and, later, Aleksandr Yakovlev to his party, spends considerable time in this interview arguing that these individuals represent effectively everything that is wrong with the Russian intelligentsia.

13. *Sotsial'noe razvitie SSR 1989 g.:Statisticheskii sbornik*, Moscow, 1991, pp. 248–9.

14. Since only a minority of the respondents had managed to answer the question on their incomes five to seven years earlier, we are not reporting those data here.

15. The concept of 'status incongruence' refers to a situation in which the status factors that an individual might present to others – say, his level of material well-being, his class standing as suggested by his dress or accent, his level of education and so on – do not match up with what these others have come to expect from experience as linked together. Status incongruence would then be negatively associated with status security and positively associated with action, including

political action whose object would be to alter the incongruence, the conditions producing it, or both. In the Polish context, some scholars have applied this concept with quite interesting results. See Andrzej Malewski, 'The Degree of Status Incongruence and Its Effects', *The Polish Sociological Bulletin*, 1963 no. 1, pp. 9–17; Alexander Matejko, 'Status Incongruence in the Polish Intelligentsia,' *Social Research*, Winter, 1966, vol. 33, pp. 136–58.

16. We are following here the thinking of Alvin W. Gouldner, *The Dialectic of Ideology and Technology*, Seabury, New York, pp. 210–28; and that of Charles E. Lindblom, *Politics and Markets*, Basic Books, New York, 1977, pp. 134–9.

17. We do not have in mind here petitions to the authorities, always permitted and even encouraged under the Soviet order, as an expression of social interests. On this question, see Michael E. Urban, 'Local Soviets and Popular Needs: Where the Official Ideology Meets Everyday Life', in S. White and A. Pravda (eds) *Ideology and Soviet Politics*, Macmillan, London, 1988, pp. 136–58.

18. Angelo Panebianco provides a useful discussion of this 'masking' of individual and group interest in his *Political Parties: Organization and Power*, Cambridge University Press, Cambridge, 1988, pp. 24–5, 31–2.

19. See, for instance, the joint statement on political goals issued by strike leaders and the representatives of business associations and the pro-business Interrepublican Party of Free Labour, 'Shakhtery poidut do kontsa', *Rossiiskaya gazeta* 23 April 1991, p. 1.

20. If we combine the scores for *sluzhashchie*, ITR and businessmen – the groups that represent the real or potential managerial-business class – that are reported in Table 4.3, we find that this group comprises 47 per cent of our DPR sample but only 34 per cent of that drawn from the SDPR.

21. Our analysis, here, draws on V. V. Igrunov, 'Public Movement: From Protest to Political Self-Consciousness', *Problema Vostochnoi Evropy*, 1990, nos 27/28, pp. 1–14; and Sergei Mitrokhin, "Molodezh' i politika v epokhu pereotsenki tsennostei (Rossiiskii opyt)', Institute of Humanist-Political Studies, Moscow, August 1991.

22. Denis Pankin, Executive Secretary of the SDPR, reported during an interview on 23 April 1991 that party membership had been 'more or less stable' since autumn of 1990 (interview given to M. E. Urban). Mikhail Malyutin, however, has stated that party membership has experienced some decline since the summer of that same year. See his 'A sushchestvuet li v SSSR mnogopartiinost'?', Moscow State University, Moscow, May 1991.

23. On the DPR's current efforts to organize a Union-wide 'disciplined' party to contest the upcoming elections to the union parliament, see 'Obrashchenie k sozdaniyu Ob"edinennoi Demokraticheskoi partii strany', *Demokraticheskaya gazeta*, July 1991, no. 8, p. 1; and V. E. Lyzov, 'Ob"edinennaya Demokraticheskaya partiya strany: kommentarii zainteresovannogo cheloveka', ibid., p. 3.

PART II

Civil Society

5 Professionalization

Anthony Jones

An important aspect of the policy of *perestroika* was the attempt to introduce 'professionalism' into Soviet Society.[1] In its simple formulation, this was nothing more than establishing the conditions in which decision making could be pursued on the basis of occupational standards and ethics, rather than on the basis of political considerations imposed from the outside. It was, therefore, an attempt to institutionalize rationality, to 'professionalize' the behaviour of job-holders so that the consequences of decades of politically shaped decisions could be avoided in the future.

On another level, reconstruction also created the conditions for a change in the status of those occupations that in the West are referred to as professions. This meant that they could move closer to what has been called 'guild status', the possibility of controlling the ways in which the occupation is pursued, making it more like a profession.[2] The historical experience of professions in the market-oriented societies of the West shows that the creation of a professional organization (or guild) takes a considerable amount of time, and so we should not expect the full flowering of professions in the USSR in just five or six years. It is suggested here, however, that several occupations have moved in this direction.

The greater emphasis on professional expertise in a system that was moving in the direction of democratization could also be expected to give the professions greater access to, and influence on, the exercise of power. Both as individuals and as organizational bodies, professional interests would stand a better chance of being represented and of affecting policy.

In what follows we shall indicate briefly how *perestroika* allowed the *process* of professionalization to develop, how it changed the organization of professional work and how it brought professionals into the political arena.

THE STATUS OF PROFESSIONS DURING THE SOVIET PERIOD

Discussing the status of professions in the USSR is difficult because the use of the term 'profession' is itself not wholly defensible. Even in the case of the non-socialist industrial societies there is a great deal of disagreement among scholars as to what exactly a profession is, and which occupations can truly be called professions. Most of those who study the professions, however, accept that it is an occupation which creates and maintains a boundary between itself and the outside world, in this way limiting the influence of extra-occupational forces. This boundary enables practitioners to exercise control over such matters as entry to the profession, the content of training, certification, the conditions of work, the development of standards of practice, policing performance and enforcing ethics, the claim to technical expertise beyond the jurisdiction of non-practitioners, and the sole right to make decisions on the basis of special knowledge.

In the Soviet Union it was extremely difficult for occupations to create boundaries and thereby to control their conditions of work. To an extent not found in other industrial societies, professional workers in the USSR were employees of the state and were not able to operate as free (independent or self-employed) professionals. More importantly, in the Soviet case the general environment in which all occupations operated was shaped by the state. Thus the state controlled the entire educational system and therefore access to all professional training. It set the conditions of employment, the number of jobs available in each speciality and the conditions of entry and exit. It set incomes, controlled occupational organizations and controlled the political and ideological environment within which practitioners operated. It was not just the bureaucratic setting in which professionals worked that set them apart from their counterparts in other societies, for there has been an increasing trend in industrial societies towards more and more professional work being done in such conditions. Rather it was the refusal of the party-state to allow the formation of independent organizations that could gain control of conditions of work and which could challenge and resist official policy.

All through the pre-*perestroika* period, the party-state sought to monopolize the right to organize, and to prevent any set of interests from influencing policy (and at times from even being expressed). In this respect, professionals faced the same constraints as other workers. But the professions present a special problem in that they are the bearers of the theoretical and practical knowledge without which the functional needs of the society cannot adequately be met. As a consequence, some professions (especially those involved in high-priority areas) were given a degree of autonomy not allowed to other groups.

PERESTROIKA AND PROFESSIONALIZATION

The changes introduced during the period of *perestroika* had both direct and indirect consequences for the professions. First, the decentralization of decision making and the reduction of the role of the CPSU meant that decisions could increasingly be made at the level of implementation, rather than at the centre. The purpose of this was to make it possible for decisions to be made on technical rather than on political grounds, with greater reliance on 'experts'.[3] This clearly expanded the opportunities for professionals, and for them to claim the right to make decisions on the grounds that their ideas are founded on a professional understanding of the matter at hand.

Second, *perestroika* changed the general environment in which professions operated. Democratization, the growth of a multi-party system, the decline of censorship and restrictions on the expression of opinion, and the establishment of the right to form unofficial groups to represent private interests – all provided opportunities for the creation of more autonomous professions. And last, the legalization of private enterprise meant that full-time employment for professionals outside the state sector was now possible, increasing the likelihood that professionals could gain control over their conditions of work and their incomes.

Given the need for brevity, we shall indicate in what follows only a few aspects of the progress made towards professionalization by physicians, lawyers, scientists and journalists.[4]

Physicians

The revelations during the *perestroika* period about the dismal state of Soviet health care focused attention on the medical profession and enabled doctors to stress the need for greater autonomy. During the three years that Evgenii Chazov was USSR Minister of Health, he spoke freely about the crisis facing health care, but was unable to bring about any improvements. His successor, Igor Denisov (who came not from the ranks of the ministry but directly from his post as a practising surgeon in the provinces) set about improving conditions by changing the financial foundations of the health system. Physicians' salaries, which by the late 1980s were on average about a third less than the average national wage, were set to be raised at the beginning

of 1991. This and other improvements were to be financed through
the introduction of a system of health insurance to be paid for by
employers out of company profits; non-working people would, however, continue to be provided for out of state funds. The draft law
for this appeared in August 1990. These changes followed the increasing activism of doctors in the late 1980s, in which they called not only
for better conditions for themselves, but also for a complete overhaul
of the health care system. These protests went as far as threatening
to strike, moves with which Denisov expressed some sympathy.[5] The
new minister's position on the private practices (cooperatives) that
were springing up was also positive, but only if they added to, and
did not compete with, the state providers.

The experience of these medical cooperatives is instructive in allowing us to see some of the forces at work that will help or hinder the
further professionalization of doctors. In 1986 and 1987 these new
cooperatives did quite well, establishing themselves as popular alternatives to many of the services provided by the state sector. The Ministry
of Public Health set out the qualifications people needed to work in
these private facilities, the procedures that were and were not allowed,
and the sanitary conditions that had to be met. There were considerable official misgivings on the issue of fees, however, for private
physicians could earn four to five times the official salary paid in the
state sector, and there was concern that large numbers of doctors and
nurses would move to the private sector, thereby making the conditions in state clinics and hospitals even worse. As a result there was
considerable official harassment of these cooperatives for the next few
years, with many being closed on some pretext or other. The campaign
waged against private medicine was often couched in terms of the
social injustice of having to pay for medical care and also of the
corruption that sometimes occurred in the use of state equipment and
in referring patients to the cooperative when services could have been
provided without charge in the state clinics. On the latter points there
were some grounds for legitimate concern, but, on the question of
fees, all of the evidence points to a willingness on the part of the
general public to pay for faster, and often better, treatment. As many
pointed out, the fees were usually considerably less than the bribes
that had to be paid routinely in the state sector in order to get even
remotely decent treatment.[6]

Reforming the medical system was not just a case of improving the
existing system, but also of increasing the diversity of ways in which
treatment could be obtained; that is, of providing patients with choices. Thus, in addition to the state and cooperative facilities, and the

introduction of an insurance scheme, there was a move towards the development of family practitioners, the cost of which is borne by the patient. Family doctors are envisioned as having smaller caseloads (400 – 500 patients) than the existing district physicians, while the introduction of fee-for-service will give doctors a financial stake in the results of their work (and undermine the corrupt practice of virtually extorting gifts from patients just to perform the routines to which patients are entitled). Surveys have shown that patients are more than willing to pay for treatment, as many as 87 per cent in one poll expressing approval of the new arrangements.[7]

This development should make the relationship between doctor and patient closer and more personal, and will probably enhance the professional responsibility of the physician. As one practitioner put it, family physicians have already begun to feel more like 'healers' and less like 'dispatchers' directing patients to one or another specialist.[8] Moreover increasing diversity is likely to increase the control that doctors have over their profession, since it not only gives them more choices in the ways they will approach patients, but it will make it more difficult for outside bodies to monitor and control the ways in which treatment is given and decisions are made. To the extent that this occurs, doctors will come closer to having guild control in addition to the considerable control that they had over treatment decisions during the Soviet period.

Lawyers

The profession that has benefited most from *perestroika* is probably the legal profession. The emphasis placed on the development of a state of laws, democratization and the practical steps taken to modernize the legal system, plus the legal issues that needed to be dealt with as the republics pulled away from the union, all increased the prestige of lawyers. As early as the 19th Party Conference in 1988, it was decided that there was to be a major reallocation of power within the profession away from those working in the procuracy toward those working as defence attorneys (that is, away from 'state employees' towards 'private practitioners'). The Conference also set out proposals that were clearly a step towards greater professionalization, such as enforcement of compliance with the constitution, longer terms for judges, making it a criminal offence to interfere with judges, introduction of a jury system and an increase in the power and autonomy of legal councils.[9] Further progress towards professionalization came in 1989 with the draft law that provided protection for judges from outside interference, including provisions for a professional standards collegium that would administer the examinations taken by candidates for judgeships, would control the certification process and would have the power to remove judges for unprofessional conduct.[10] That this step was seen as justifying greater resources can be seen from the comments of Justice Minister Yakovlev, who said that, if being a judge is 'an honoured profession, if this is a respected profession that is valued highly by the state, then it follows that appropriate financial and other conditions should be provided. When our foreign colleagues ask about the salaries paid to judges, we feel like sinking through the floor.' Moreover, he continued, high salaries are needed because then 'strong jurists who cannot be bossed around will come to serve in the courts. Judges who are professionally weak and who fear for their jobs can be bossed around.'[11]

Following this, in February 1989, defence lawyers created the USSR Lawyers Union, a self-governing body which had about 20 000 members within a year (approximately 80 per cent of all defence lawyers). By making membership open only to individuals and not to organizations, the Union avoided coming under the jurisdiction of the Ministry of Justice. The purpose of the Union (originally conceived of as early as 1985) was to protect the rights of lawyers and, by extension, of their clients as well. As the Chairman of the Board of the Union put it, defence lawyers needed to be removed from subordination to state agencies, and to be independent. Also, he noted, lawyers should not be held criminally liable, have criminal proceedings brought against them or be arrested, without the agreement of the Union's Board. If these goals were ever to be achieved, they would clearly move lawyers close to having professional autonomy.[12] Further the leaders of the Union were obviously concerned about controlling access to the profession, opposing lawyers' cooperatives on the ground that many people working in this sector did not have a legal education.

That there were opposing forces at work within the profession can be seen in the rivalry between the Lawyers Union and the Union of Jurists that was also set up in 1989. The membership of the latter organization consisted mainly of lawyers working in the state agencies and its leadership came from high officials in the Ministry of Justice, the Supreme Court and the procuracy. The Lawyers Union claimed that there was an anti-defence lawyer attitude in the Union of Jurists and, moreover, that the independence and legal protections sought by many lawyers could not be achieved if organizations retained close ties with the state agencies.[13] This division within the profession is a significant barrier to creating a unitary profession and, since even in the post-coup societies that will emerge the state will continue to be a major employer of lawyers, it is likely that the division will persist and remain an impediment to full professionalization.

Scientists

The importance of science for economic and military performance made it an obvious candidate for attention at the very beginning of *perestroika*. The past intrusion of politics, the lack of professional freedom to pursue research and develop new ideas, excessive centraliz-ation and a situation in which scientists 'came to be evaluated not on the basis of their scientific work, but rather on the basis of their personnel files and dossiers kept by . . . a KGB officer attached to every research institute'[14] all contributed to declining standards and increasing corruption in Soviet science. With *perestroika* it was finally recognized 'that better results would be achieved if scientists, not the Party, were allowed to decide how they should conduct their work'.[15]

Attempts at reform in the early years of *perestroika* resorted to old policies of tying salaries to contributions to the economy. Rather than liberating science, however, policies such as this resulted in increasing dependence on the whims of officials in the scientific establishment. By 1989, however, this had given way to efforts at decentralization of laboratories and projects, at improving higher education and giving it greater involvement in basic research, increasing links with foreign scientists and increasing freedom for scientists to set their own research and funding agendas.[16] That year also saw concerted attacks on the Soviet Academy of Sciences following its failed attempt to prevent highly visible and popular advocates of radical reform from becoming candidates for election to the Congress of People's Deputies. The Academy's lack of democracy was criticized and there was a call to set up a separate, independent association of scientists.

An important step towards greater professional status came in the form of a presidential decree in August 1990, in which the Academy of Sciences was granted independence from the state and was given ownership of all its assets and property. Salaries were to be decided by the Academy, contract research was to be encouraged and the state was supposed to increase its financial support of scientific research.[17] While necessary, this move did not solve the most practical problem of the Academy and its constituent institutes, namely the backward and poorly equipped facilities in which scientists had to work, and, without changing this, the brain drain of scientists that had developed in the freer conditions of the late 1980s could not be halted.[18] Nor does independence mean that the officials who had stifled Soviet science for decades can be easily swept away, unless the huge, bureaucratic structure of the research institutes is scaled down. Moreover the greater emphasis that was put on encouraging applied science posed a potential threat to basic research and to the pursuit by science of its own agenda.

As is the case with other professionals, many scientists have moved into the private sector, so acquiring greater independence and greater control over their activities, as well as higher incomes. A recent study of scientists in the cooperative (private) sector showed that their reasons for making this move were similar to those of other professionals, namely better opportunities to be able to act *qua* professionals.[19]

Support for improving the state of Soviet science comes from all parts of the political spectrum, however, and it is this which makes it likely that scientists will achieve more professional status in the near future. Evidence for this are the relatively uncontentious draft laws that were put forward in 1990 and 1991 and which dealt with such basic issues as the openness of scientific information, intellectual property, freedom of access to scientific information at home and abroad, freedom to publish and travel, and a legal basis for seeking redress for wrongful dismissal.[20] The role of the Higher Certification Commission (which certifies all scholars and scientists) has been reduced, but the effects of its long rule will take decades to overcome.[21] For scientists, all of these developments mean greater control over their conditions of work and hence a greater ability to resist outside interference in what should rightfully be scientific decisions. It is unlikely that scientists will create a corporate basis for their profession, though, given the variety of settings in which they work. Moreover many work as academics, and in every society this means that professional control is exercised more though peer review and control (as well as via departments and university administrators) than through guild-like organizations.

Journalists

A rather surprising development was the increasing professionalism of journalists, an occupation that before *perestroika* was one of the most politically controlled of any of the candidates for the title of 'profession'. The policy of *glasnost* depended for its success on a press that was more independent and free to raise issues and print information that were potentially embarrassing to officialdom. Policy on the press was rather ambiguous, however, for, although the Gorbachev leadership encouraged greater freedom for journalists, the latter were frequently chided for being 'sensationalistic' and for not being 'fair' in their news coverage and analysis. On the positive side, the Union of Journalists was designated a creative union in 1987, raising its prestige and increasing its control over its activities. At the same time, journalists were vocal in their criticism of the union for failing to protect them against interference from officials.[22]

Attempts to curb press freedom were frequent and vigorous all through the *perestroika* period, with one government ministry or another imposing restrictions on the physical movement of journalists, their access to information and situations, and (especially at the provincial level) continually attempting to censor news coverage. The long fight over the passage of a law on the press that guaranteed freedom and protection for journalists finally ended in victory for them, but the climate during this period was clearly not conducive to the development of professionalism. A significant element, however, was the emergence of an unofficial press which provided journalists with alternative sources of employment. The rapid growth of an alternative press, from 1987 on, for the first time provided opportunities in a private sector, though many of the new newspapers and magazines (and virtually all of the electronic media until the early 1990s) were owned by official or semi-private organizations. The degree of professionalism in this new sector, moreover, varied greatly.[23]

As long as employment was only available in the state- and Party-controlled press, there was no chance for journalists to develop a profession in the strict sense of the term. Even in those official publications which were taken over by editors who supported more independent reporting, there was always the possibility of threats and reprisals occurring. Even Gorbachev was not above publicly chastising an editor who strayed too far, or demanding his resignation. That this and other attempts to control journalists frequently failed is an indication that the desire for a more professional occupation was growing. At the same time, journalists resisted pressures not as a corporate body but as individuals. The lack of a concerted effort was due in large part to the fact that, for most people, employment in an official publication was the only path open, making it difficult to make a stand without risk of losing one's livelihood. In 1991, however, corporate and cooperative activities were becoming more noticeable: the Foundation for the Defence of Glasnost brought together journalists, filmmakers and television workers in a mutual protection organization, and the Committee for the Defence of Freedom of Speech and the

Rights of Journalists was created.[24] Divisions within the ranks of journalists continued to hamper unity, though, and led to the development of competing organizations (for example, the Independent Association of Democratic Journalists that was set up in June 1991, a splinter group from the Union of Journalists). Moreover, after the attempted coup of August 1991, conflict among journalists (and especially with editors) became intense.[25]

Organizational moves to greater independence did occur, though, beginning in the Baltic republics and spreading to other areas. Independent associations of journalists sprang up, often associating themselves with the newly developing press in the republics that was linked to (or owned by) separatist organizations. This provided not only cadres for the new press, but also protection for journalists from officials. There has even been a move to establish a code of ethics for journalists.[26]

PROFESSIONS AND POLITICS

Professionals were highly visible actors in the struggle to develop *perestroika*, as publicists and advocates, and as elected office holders and politicians. Economists and lawyers were especially prominent, including such people as Gorbachev, Sobchak and Popov. The elections to the newly-created Congress of People's Deputies in 1989 resulted in more than a doubling of the proportion of professionals in the state legislature (in comparison to their strength in the Supreme Soviet in 1984), up from 6 per cent to 14.3 per cent.[27] Especially noteworthy were the numbers of journalists (28), scientists (61), teachers (70) and physicians (67) who were elected to the 2044 seats that had been filled as of the end of April 1989.

These gains need to be put in perspective, however, for they are modest in comparison to the gains of lower-level administrators (such as farm chairmen) who increased their representation from about 48 per cent in 1984 to just over 60 per cent in 1989. The real losers in this reshuffle were ordinary workers and office employees, for they dropped from almost 50 per cent to about 23 per cent. Taken together, these numbers show a greater representation of people who are close to the practical implementation of decisions, rather than those closer to the policy-making end of the administrative spectrum, but not the domination of people who are expert in professional fields. It is true that many of the top and lower-level administrators have a specialist training, but this does not make them practising professionals, nor does it mean that their speciality makes them especially likely to fight for the professionalization of those who share this speciality. Frequently, the reverse seems to be the case, as is illustrated in the findings of a survey of Peoples' Deputies during their Second Congress: when asked whose interests they pursue in their work as deputies, 67 per cent said those of society as a whole, 52 per cent said their constituents, and only 19 per cent said the groups to which they belong.[28] Moreover many of those who rise to administrative positions do so precisely because they can be trusted to obey political dictates rather than insist on professional judgements being given priority. Also, as we saw in the case of lawyers, those professionals who work in the state sector often have a different agenda from those who work in the private or independent sector.

At the local level, professionals have risen to very influential political positions, but the evidence to date suggests that they did so not *qua* professionals but because of their ability to articulate the political views (and especially oppositional views) of the local electorates. This seems to have been true of such people as Sobchak, for example, while Popov represents success on the basis of his persona as an intellectual and as a man of integrity who stands for common sense. There does not seem to have been a mass willingness to elect people merely because they are practitioners of a profession.

While the new professional organizations have often been active in the support of candidates and parties, they have not themselves yet achieved places within the new political structure; also it is too early to know if this involvement will translate into support from politicians for the professions themselves. Some groups have, however, become very influential in helping to create the new order, as is the case, for example, of those lawyers who have been working with the central and republic authorities and with foreign advisers to create a new legal structure. As the new governmental elites establish themselves, they will come to rely more and more on the ability of professionals to supply those services without which the legitimacy of the governments will be in jeopardy. One of the most important failures of the old regime was its inability to provide for legal protection, good and reliable medical care, quality education and an efficient economy. Under newer (and often democratic) regimes, political survival will also depend on supplying the public's needs in these areas. This, of course, puts the professions in a strong position to bargain for greater autonomy in exchange for delivery of needed services. In this respect they will remain political players.

CONCLUDING REMARKS

The period of *perestroika* enabled many occupations to establish a more professional status and in this respect the desire of the reformers to introduce more professional behaviour into the society, and to base decisions more on technical expertise and less on purely political considerations, was partially achieved. But there were many forces at work that saw greater independence for professionals as undesirable. There were many constituencies whose interests would have been damaged if true independence for doctors, lawyers, journalists and others had developed. Those occupations which were most successful in professionalizing tended to be the ones that could claim that greater control over themselves was necessary for the achievement of socially desirable goals. Sometimes this meant a 'national' (USSR) need and sometimes this meant supporting 'local' (republic level or lower) agendas. For example, lawyers and journalists could easily play to local interests as well as national ones, and even play one off against the other. The growth of the environmental movement provided a useful opportunity for journalists and physicians to show how greater professionalism on their part could help overcome environmental problems; even scientists were able to attach themselves to this issue by forming a public interest group of professional scientists (the USSR Nuclear Society) to serve as a watchdog over the nuclear energy industry.

For some occupations, support by the central authorities was necessary for the development of more professionalism. The gains achieved by scientists were in no small way due to their having provided some of *perestroika*'s most public supporters and having provided advisers for the reform leadership. However the lack of central support for the technical professions, such as engineering, was probably linked to the fact that the technical intelligentsia was not highly visible in the reform process, certainly not to the extent that the creative and scientific intelligentsia were. Thus, while some professional gains were made by engineers, such as the formation of the Union of Scientific and Engineering Societies, attempts to create an academy of engineering that would have equal standing with other academies came to naught. Interestingly the aim of those who advocated such an academy was to set standards for the profession, to improve the quality of entrants to it and to raise the prestige and influence of engineers.[29] The development of the private economy, on the other hand, did much to increase the independence of engineers, many of whom opened their own consulting companies, engineering service centres and research centres.

It is tempting to predict that in the post-coup era the professions will move steadily in the direction of greater professionalization and that they will become more like their counterparts in other industrial societies. Fast change in this direction, however, is unlikely, for a number of reasons. First, even in the new states, most professionals will probably continue to be state employees rather than become independently employed. This will mean that the new political authorities will have a stake in overseeing these occupations closely and in setting their conditions of work and pay. This will be done, of course, in the name of the general good. It is probable that, until a real market economy is established, full professionalization will not be possible, not only because of the implied continuation of administrative controls, but also because the resources over which the professions will need control in order to increase their independence will not be available. Second, this division into state and privately employed specialists will probably continue to fragment the ranks within the professions, making it difficult to develop unitary, solidary organizations with a single set of goals and values. Third, for many professionals funding will continue to come from the state, since the sheer size of their needs cannot be met from private sources. In itself this should not be a barrier to professionalization, but it is likely to lower the ability of professionals to set the directions in which they would wish to move. The research-oriented professions are most likely to be affected in this way.

Fourth, and very important for professional status, is the issue of education, training and certification. Given the expense of this, the state will almost certainly continue to provide for most of these needs, and this will lessen the likelihood that the professions will gain much control over entry to the occupation, but it is also almost certain that they will be brought into the process as advisory bodies, and this will set the grounds for greater control in the future. The question of how new codes of ethics will be developed and enforced, and by whom, remains unclear. The absence of a tradition of strong professional ethics and the general corruption that reigns in all areas of what remains of Soviet society, pose some serious problems for the future.

Fifth, while allying themselves with local interests has certainly helped professionals in the short term, this may not guarantee support for greater independence later. There are already signs that local authorities are coopting professionals in the same way that the former central authorities did, with the result that professionals have no greater independence than they had before.[30] The development of civil society, and the gradual move towards guarantees of citizenship rights, on the other hand, should strengthen the position of professionals *vis à vis* officialdom, since the former can pursue greater independence as a right as well as for pragmatic, technical reasons.

For the future, then, we may expect a continued trend towards the development of independent, guild-like professional bodies and towards the creation of ethical and technical standards by which activities may be judged and policed. Given the interest which many constituencies have in the ways in which professional services are provided, and the costs that they will entail, it is not likely that professionals will soon (if ever) escape from external supervision and control. As what used to be the Soviet Union breaks up into new units, we should expect considerable variations in the extent to which greater professionalization will occur. This, however, will not make professionals different from their European and North American brethren, since for the latter the trend is away from self-governing professions. As more professionals work in bureaucratic settings, and as the general public becomes more concerned about the quality and cost of professional services, the professions are losing (not gaining) control over their activities. Moreover the European pattern has always involved greater state involvement in the professions than has been true in the case of the USA, and it is towards the European model that the societies of the post-Soviet period are likely to move. What democratization and modernization in the post-Soviet era are likely to produce, therefore, is not a growth in self-governing professions, but rather a better balance between the rights of professionals to act *qua* professionals and the rights and needs of those who are consumers of their services. The increasing material well-being of professionals that will undoubtedly accompany professionalization, and the greater complexity of stratification that the new societies will experience, will make it easier for the professions to recruit capable people to their ranks, and to enforce higher standards in return. To the degree that this occurs, the disastrous status of the professions in the USSR that has obtained since the 1950s will at last be reversed.

In conclusion, it needs to be stated that the degree of professionalization achieved will be in a large part dependent on the creation of a genuine law-based society. Without an institutionalized respect for the law, professionals cannot protect the practice of their skills from harmful outside interference and their clients can have no guarantee of redress for malpractice. In sum, the conditions for the emancipation of the professions are also the conditions for the emancipation of those who depend upon their services.

NOTES AND REFERENCES

1. This chapter draws freely from the accounts and analyses of professions in the USSR that were published in Anthony Jones (ed.), *Professions and the State: Expertise and Autonomy in the Soviet Union and Eastern Europe*,Temple University Press, Philadelphia, 1991, referred to hereafter as Jones, *Professions and the State*.

2. See Elliott Krause, 'Professions and the State in the Soviet Union and Eastern Europe: Theoretical Issues', in Jones, *Professions and the State* pp.3–42

3. It is interesting to note that in recent years many specialists in the USSR have taken to having the word 'expert' printed on their business cards, and to describing themselves to reporters as such. Often, what these people are experts in is not mentioned.

4. For a detailed account of this topic, see Jones, *Professions and the State*

5. See Margot Jacobs, 'Minister of Health Talks About Reform', *Report on the USSR*, Radio Liberty, vol. 2, no. 35.

6. For an account of medical cooperatives, see Anthony Jones and William Moskoff, *KO-OPS: The Rebirth of Entrepreneurship in the Soviet Union*, Indiana University Press, Bloomington, Indiana, 1991.

7. See *Izvestia*, 17 August 1990, p.2.

8. *Izvestia* 17 August 1990,. p.2: 21 February 1991, p.3.

9. See Julia Wishnevsky, 'The Party Conference Resolution on Legal Reform', 1988, Radio Liberty, p.302.

10. *Current Digest of the Soviet Press*, 1989, vol.41, no. 12, p. 26.

11. *Izvestia*, 30 November, 1988. p.4.

12. *Izvestia*, 4 January, 1990, p.3. For an account of the tactics used by officials to block the formation of this Union, see Julia Wishnevsky, 'Association of Legal Council to Be Established', *Report on the USSR*, 1989, Radio Liberty, vol. 1, no. 13.

13. *Izvestia*, 4 January 1990, p.3

14. Quoted in Michael Tsypkin, 'Turmoil in Soviet Science', *Report on the USSR*, 1989, Radio Liberty, vol. 1, no. 29, p.18.

15. Vera Tolz, 'The USSR Academy of Sciences in Crisis', *Report on the USSR*, Radio Liberty, vol. 2, no. 23, p.12.

16. See Aleksei Levin, 'Organizational Changes in Soviet Science and Learning', *Report on the USSR*, 7 December, 1990, Radio Liberty, vol. 2, no. 49, pp.3–5.

17. *Pravda*, 24 August, 1990, p.1.

18. *Izvestia*, 25 August, 1990, p.1.

19. S.N. Bykova, 'Spetsialist v kooperative sfery nauki' *Sotsiologicheskie issledovanie*, 1990, no. 11. pp. 89–96. These findings fit my own observations of, and discussions with, professionals in the private sector in the USSR.

20. Aleksei Levin, 'New Draft Legislation on Science Policy in the USSR', *Report on the USSR*, 1991, vol.3, no.22.

21. *Izvestia*, 13 January, 1991, p.3.

22. See Vera Tolz, 'The Sixth Congress of Soviet Journalists', Radio Liberty, 1987, p.110: Vera Tolz, 'Procurator General Rekunkov Attacks Journalists Who Critize Soviet Justice Apparatus', 1986 Radio Liberty, p.265.

23. Vera Tolz. 'Alternative Press in the USSR', *Report on the USSR*, 24 May, 1991, vol. 3, no.21, pp. 6–11.

24. *Izvestia*, 8 June, 1991, p.1.

25. *Izvestia*, 24 August, 1991, p.2.

26. *Izvestia*, 12 April, 1991, p.3.

27. The actual percentage varies, depending upon whether or not professionals acting as administrators are counted. The number I am quoting does include them. See *Izvestia*, 6 May, 1989, p.3. Due to multiple answers these percentages sum to more than one hundred.

28. These findings do not mean that narrow interests are never served, of course. See V.A. Zots and A.S. Kapto, 'Trud – glavnaia tochka otscheta', *Sotsiologicheskie issledovania*, 1990, no.4, pp.. 34–42.
29. See Viktor Yasmann, 'The Technical Intelligentsia, a Potential Ally for Gorbachev', 1988, Radio Liberty, p.82.
30. For an example of this, see the report on the cooptation of journalists in Georgia, in *Izvestia*, 13 March, 1991.

6. The Role of Journalists and the Media in Changing Soviet Society

Vera Tolz

It is clear that in the course of his reforms Mikhail Gorbachev has gone much further than Nikita Krushchev in assigning to intellectuals, and especially journalists and writers, a new, more constructive role in politics. Why did the Soviet leader decide, when he embarked on his new course in 1985, to begin his reforms by drastically changing the role in society of intellectuals, and above all of journalists? Why were journalists relatively well prepared to assume a new role? And, finally, what has been the effect of the media on society in the past few years? These are the issues that are analysed below.

HOW THE POLICY OF *GLASNOST* WAS BORN

Although Mikhail Gorbachev was the first Soviet leader to give meaning to the concept of *glasnost* in the press, neither he nor his leadership invented the term as such. *Glasnost* – in the sense of public information about the activities of the country's authorities – first entered Russian political thinking as early as the mid-nineteenth century. In a series of political essays written at the end of the 1840s, the Russian poet Fedor Tyutchev attempted to convince the Russian tsars that, by providing the population with more information about their policy making, the rulers of the country would contribute to narrowing the gap between the authorities and society.[1] In the Soviet period, all Gorbachev's predecessors from Lenin to Andropov, including both Stalin and Brezhnev, used *glasnost* as one of the concepts in their propaganda arsenal.

Glasnost appeared in the Soviet Union in a new context in the mid–1960s, when openness with respect to the functioning (and malfunctioning) of the Soviet system became one of the main demands of the newly born human rights movement in the USSR. Calls for broadening openness in the media did not, however, assume the form of a coordinated campaign until Mikhail Gorbachev came to power.

Summing up the events of 1986, the poet Evgenii Evtushenko proudly stated that writers and artists had not been granted 'restructuring and openness' as a gift from above but had fought for years for a liberalization of Soviet intellectual life 'in the face of incomprehension and, on occasion, offensive attacks'.[2] There is, indeed, an element of truth in this statement, since a limited number of intellectuals did press the authorities for the relaxation of ideological control, but the statement does not adequately reflect the whole truth. It is more than likely that those Soviet intellectuals who were critical of the Soviet regime would have had to spend quite a few decades more battling for restructuring and openness, had not the top Party leadership met them halfway. In sum, Gorbachev and his reform-minded associates deserve great credit for launching a campaign aimed at making the Soviet media more open and intellectual life in the country more free.

On 11 March 1985, in his speech to the plenary meeting of the Central Committee of the CPSU that had elected him Party leader, Gorbachev promised to provide Soviet citizens with more information about the work of the Party.[3] Soon afterwards, numerous articles appeared in the Soviet press stressing the need for more 'openness' in reporting on Soviet domestic affairs. The Gorbachev leadership apparently began to think of changing the situation in the Soviet media when it realized that the leadership itself needed trustworthy information about the situation in both the Soviet Union and the outside world. It seems that already, in the initial stage of revising traditional Soviet ideological dogmas, Gorbachev and his colleagues had come to the following conclusions: first, the old way of governing the country had made Brezhnev and his associates the victims of their own monopoly on information. Even assuming that they had wanted to, they were unable to put together an adequate picture of the Soviet Union. Second, the broadening of the information revolution in the world meant that any effort to maintain the old secretive way of ruling became damaging for the economy as well as for the political situation in the country.

These concerns find support in the first political actions of the Gorbachev leadership. Indeed Gorbachev launched *glasnost* by starting to make changes in the functioning of his own information networks. In a memorandum to the CPSU CC Politburo in November 1985, Gorbachev wrote that distortion of the information received by the CPSU Central Committee from all over the Soviet Union and abroad was inadmissable. Gorbachev said: 'We are particularly in need of objective information that depicts not what we would like to hear, but what really is . . . , more concrete analysis of current developments, more fresh proposals'.[4] Gorbachev's memorandum and statements by other Soviet leaders show clearly the initial aim of the policy of *glasnost*. First, the leadership, believing that Communist Party rule would come under threat if it did not embark on some sort of reforms, started to look around for viable ideas about how to reform the social and political system, especially the economy. Second, it sought to mobilize as many sections of the population as possible in support of reform. The intelligentsia was the first target.

Third, the leadership wanted to increase the credibility of the Soviet media. They envisioned the increase in openness of the domestic press as a pre-emptive strike against the Western information revolution, the achievements of which were well understood by the new leaders. For instance, one of the main architects of reforms in the Soviet ideological sector, Aleksandr Yakovlev, told a meeting of ideologists in October, 1986:

> Today's world is becoming ever smaller in the communications sense, ever more interconnected. To think that it is possible in this world to create some sort of niche or cloister cut off from external influences and to sit it out there in timid resignation is not only to indulge in illusions but also to doom ourselves to defeat. We need to be active ourselves, to adopt an offensive stance, one that guarantees not only absolute priority in our own house but also a steady strengthening of our . . . influence on the outside world.[5]

Fourth, the leadership wanted to rout out corruption, flourishing in the Soviet economy as well as in its political and social institutions, by using openness in the press against particular individuals, groups or even whole institutions within the Soviet political system. And last but not least, *glasnost* was a useful tool for Gorbachev to get rid of his rivals and enemies.

JOURNALISTS AND PUBLICISTS READY TO RESPOND

The reform drive of the Gorbachev leadership posed new challenges to a number of different groups of the Soviet population. The response of these groups demonstrated that in many ways society was far readier for reform than outside observers and even domestic intellectuals had dared to believe. One can argue, though, that those groups that were called upon to respond to new ideological demands (journalists among others) showed greater readiness to accept the new challenges than many Party officials or even the general population who were invited by Gorbachev's reforms to seize new opportunities in the sphere of political activities. Why was this so?

Any period of drastic social and political reconstruction will be accompanied by a renewal of the ruling elite. Naturally, before replacing the old one, the new elite must start to emerge and mature within a society. Under the conditions of civil society this process is natural. It is different in systems where a single party has a monopoly of power and controls almost all spheres of political and social life. Under the latter conditions a new political elite has virtually no room for emerging and maturing. This was precisely the situation in the USSR, where the formation of political elites independent of the CPSU was impossible until Gorbachev's reform drive started and the existence of organizations free of CPSU domination was finally permitted. No wonder, then, that at first the new political organizations in the country (which became active from about 1988) were feeble and able to put forward programmes that amounted to little more than the rejection of the existing system, and failed to offer concrete creative ideas. For this reason the CPSU continued to play an important role in the country until the attempted coup in August 1991.

In addition to a political elite, an intellectual (or ideological) elite is also essential. This is especially true for a country like pre-revolutionary Russia and the USSR, where traditional restrictions on political activities resulted in a situation where the intelligentsia, especially writers and journalists, have played a unique sociopolitical role, turning literature and journalism into the main battlefield of various social and political ideas. It seems to have been the understanding of these historical realities that made Gorbachev put such a strong emphasis on gaining support from intellectuals for his reforms.

During the Soviet period relations between the political leadership and the intellectuals were based on a deep mutual distrust. After Stalin's death and the subsequent 20th Party Congress, the ideological and political pressure exercised earlier by the regime was relaxed and ties with the outside world intensified. The result was the flow of Western and émigré literature (often through underground channels) and ideas into the country; domestic intellectual life became livelier. Consequently the number of intellectuals rejecting the existing regime (not necessarily rejecting socialism) grew considerably, and the number of those in the intellectual sphere who were sincerely loyal to the ruling powers became very limited.

Indeed the post-Stalin years witnessed a tremendous resurgence of independent culture, the appearance of political *samizdat*, and the establishment of vocal human rights movements. By the 1970s voices

in the non-Russian republics were already clamouring for the preservation of their national languages and cultural heritage. It was as early
as the 1960s and 1970s that the so-called *shestidesyatniki*, or children
of the 20th Party Congress (who were to play a major role as the
ideologists of *perestroika*) had formed their ideas as well as a theoretical and factual base for their rejection of the Soviet system. (Some of
them remained Leninists until the late 1980s, but Stalinism was
rejected by them as early as the 1960s.) *Shestidesyatniki*, who became
activists of *perestroika* in the late 1980s, for example, Yurii Burtin,
Yurii Karyakin, Fedor Burlatsky, Len Karpinsky and others, came
into conflict with the authorities (they lost their jobs or were expelled
from the CPSU) during Brezhnev's rule. Therefore, as soon as they
were given a chance by Gorbachev, those intellectuals who by 1987
would form a new ideological elite demonstrated their readiness to
operate under the new conditions.

NEW OPPORTUNITIES

The greatest opportunity obtained by journalists as a result of Gorbachev's reforms was the broadening of the range of topics that could
be discussed in the press. There were so many pressing problems, the
discussion of which had been suppressed earlier, that journalists alone
could not have performed the immense task of rethinking the country's
past and present condition. Therefore journalists were promptly joined
in press debates by other intellectuals – economists, philosophers,
historians and, above all, writers. The latter have even been criticized
for abandoning literature for journalism.

With the passage of time the situation changed and it was not so
much the authorities as journalists and other intellectuals who started
to determine how far *glasnost* should go. In 1990, when the press law
was adopted, journalists received the legal right to set up their own,
independent periodicals – something which they had not had since the
early 1920s.[6] As *perestroika* and *glasnost* continued journalists and
other intellectuals gradually ceased to take into account the point of
view of the top leadership and started to run the media the way they
thought appropriate. The ultimate result of this change was that the
new information policy, originally introduced in the USSR in order
to strengthen the Soviet system, came increasingly to contribute to
the actual destruction of the regime. This result seems to confirm
Alexis de Tocqueville's idea that revolutions start not in stagnant
societies, but in periods when the leaderships in such societies initiate

reforms. The collapse of repressive regimes comes largely as a result of changes initiated by their own governments.

These new freedoms have applied throughout the years of *perestroika* to journalists of all political views – from radical reformers to Stalinists. While reformists and anti-Stalinist periodicals such as *Ogonek* and *Moscow News* obtained the freedom to criticize Stalinism and push for the speeding up of Gorbachev's reforms, periodicals at the other pole of the political spectrum – *Nash sovremennik, Molodaya gvardiya, Sovetskaya Rossiya* – also became able to carry material, the publication of which would have been unthinkable before. These periodicals became a mouthpiece of opposition to Gorbachev's reforms, which they condemned as pro-Western and anti-Russian.[7] Moreover the anti-Semitic articles that have appeared in the last three years in periodicals such as *Molodaya gvardiya* could not have been published before press control was relaxed. In other words, all Soviet periodicals, regardless of their political stance, benefited from the policy of *glasnost*. Conservative publications enjoyed the possibility of publishing what would previously have been censored just as much as liberal ones did, even though the 'right' was initially slow to take advantage of the new situation.

However it was hardly to be expected that Gorbachev himself and his colleagues would support all shades of intellectual opinion equally. It was only in the first years of *perestroika* (in 1985 and early 1986) that Gorbachev appealed to all intellectuals, ranging from the liberal Evgenii Evtushenko to the Russian nationalist Valentin Rasputin, regardless of their views. From mid–1986, the top politicians, first of all the country's main ideologist Aleksandr Yakovlev and Gorbachev himself, started to side openly with Western-oriented reformers. This was only natural since it was this group of people that strongly supported the new reform course and gave it an intellectual impetus. In the first three years of *perestroika* the political leadership and liberal intellectuals demonstrated an unprecedented unity. Later (from about 1989) the reformist media started to push reforms further than was initially planned by the top leadership and as a result relations between Gorbachev and liberal intellectuals, including journalists, became more complicated.

Journalists promoting anti-reform views also had their advocates in the top political echelons, with Egor Ligachev being the main figure until his ousting at the 28th Party Congress in 1990. On the whole anti-reformists in the media have lost to a considerable extent the position as well as the privileges that they enjoyed in the pre-*perestroika* era.

MEDIA FIGURES IN KEY POSTS

The promotion of new people to important positions in the media started in 1986 with the appointment of 'liberals' to the post of chief editor of the main central Soviet periodicals: Vitalii Korotich to *Ogonek*, Georgii Baklanov to *Znamya* and Egor Yakovlev to *Moscow News*. (Prior to these appointments these periodicals were run by loyal communists or even Stalinists.[8]) And it was initially through these restructured periodicals that various categories of intellectual (not only journalists and writers, but also political scientists and economists) became known throughout the country for the new ideas they promoted.

The second important stage, when many media people, already known for publications critical of the existing system, received further opportunities to influence the situation in the country, were the 1989 elections to the USSR Congress of People's Deputies and the 1990 elections to the local soviets and republican parliaments. According to *Zhurnalist*, 92 media people were elected USSR people's deputies in the 1989 elections.[9] Most of them were representatives of the liberal media. Among them were such well known activists of *glasnost* as Vitalii Korotich, Fedor Burlatsky, Yurii Chernichenko, Mikhail Poltoranin (now RSFSR Minister of the Press and Mass Media) and Egor Yakovlev. Also elected were chief editors of major literary journals – Sergei Zalygin of *Novyi mir*, Chingiz Aitmatov of *Inostrannaya Literatura*, Anatolii Ananev of *Oktyabr* and Boris Nikolsky of *Neva*. At the time the popularity of these journals, which had started to publish previously banned émigré, *samizdat* and Western works, was extremely high among the reading public.

Not only Moscow and Leningrad journalists, but also those from the Union republics, known for the promotion of their republics' national interests, won seats in the USSR Congress. Among them were an Armenian correspondent of *Literaturnaya gazeta*, Zorii Balayan, an active campaigner for the transfer of Nagorno-Karabakh to Armenia, Dainis Ivans, a member of the board of the Latvian Journalists' Union and head of the Latvian Popular Front, and Marju Lauristin, chief of the department of journalism at the University of Tartu, and at the time a leading member of the Estonian Popular Front and now speaker of the Estonian parliament.

It should be noted that of these 92 only ten were nominated as candidates by the USSR Union of Journalists. The others had to compete in territorial (or national-territorial) electoral districts and won because of the wide popularity of their journalistic as well as political activities.

In March 1990, 55 media people were elected to the RSFSR Congress of People's Deputies.[10] It was not surprising that the most widely read periodical, *Argumenty i fakty*, was able to get as many as five of its representatives elected to the Congress. The five included chief editor Vladislav Starkov and his first deputy Aleksandr Meshchersky. Representatives of the most popular television shows also won seats. Among them were Bella Kurkova from Leningrad TV; Aleksandr Lyubimov, Aleksandr Politkovsky, and Vladimir Mukusev of the outspoken TV programme, 'Vzglyad', and Leonid Gurevich of Gosteleradio in Murmansk.

The 1990 elections in the RSFSR marked the first instance when representatives of truly independent (formerly *samizdat*) periodicals and press agencies took part and won in the election to the state organs, although the CPSU launched an intensive campaign against them. They were Aleksei Manannikov of the Independent Siberian Press Agency, Valentina Linkova, an editor of the Tartu-based independent periodical, *Doverie* (she was nominated candidate and elected in the RSFSR city of Noginsk) and Viktor Mironov, chief editor of the Moscow independent periodical, *Khronika*.

ACHIEVEMENTS AND RESULTS

The main achievement of the Soviet media in the period of *perestroika* is very easy to define – the Soviet press has become exceptionally interesting reading and television has become interesting to watch. Of course Soviet journalists have not been able in such a short space of time to attain the standards of the best Western journalism. Many provincial and especially recently-created independent newspapers are not professional as regards either content or appearance. Some press articles are marked by intolerance – a general problem of Soviet society; some material is unbalanced, and many journalists fail to distinguish between fact and opinion (a failing of many news programmes on RSFSR television and radio).[11] And yet what the 'liberals' have achieved in the country has been amazing – thanks to the support of the mass media; in a short period they have managed to change radically the intellectual atmosphere in the country. Vladimir Shlyapentokh has rightly pointed out that 'in fact, it took less than one hundred liberal intellectuals to effect a change in viewpoint of the mass intelligentsia and of the politically active part of the rest of the population'. In sum, since 1986 the media have been shaping public opinion more effectively than ever before in Russian and Soviet history.[12]

The best illustration of the impact the media have had on the population in the past few years can be found in the events related to the attempted coup in August 1991. These events showed that neither the population nor the media were any longer ready to tolerate in silence sudden turns in the country's politics – a development the organizers of the coup had completely failed to take into account. The reaction of the changed population to the attempted coup also dispelled some fears that, as had been the case so often in Russian and at least once in Soviet history (the ousting of Khrushchev), a reform drive would be succeeded by conservative counter-reforms.

A crackdown on the Soviet mass media was, not surprisingly, high on the agenda of the group of eight hard-liners who seized power in Moscow in the early morning of 19 August. Announcing the group's media policy – the closing down of all but nine central newspapers and the imposition of a ban on the operation of the RSFSR TV and radio network – acting President Gennadii Yanaev said that the media bore much of the responsibility for the 'current chaos' in the Soviet Union.[13] Journalists, however, immediately started resisting the new line. Even at the height of the crisis, on 19 and 20 August, many managed to perform their duties.

Despite the declared imposition of strict censorship and control over the media, the organizers of the coup seemed from the outset to experience great difficulty in implementing their policies. On the evening of 19 August even the news programme 'Vremya', noted for its generally conservative attitude, managed to give the impression that it supported Russian President Boris Eltsin and the democratic forces and opposed the coup. 'Vremya' screened film of protest demonstrations in Moscow and Leningrad and interviews with citizens who had come to defend their democratically elected leaders. Sergei Medvedev, the commentator, also managed to indicate his sympathy for the protesters.[14]

When martial law was declared in Poland a total news blackout was imposed that lasted for three days. The situation in Moscow could hardly have been more different. Western correspondents were allowed to operate relatively freely. CNN, for example, was able to show Western viewers up-to-the-minute film of the situation in the Moscow streets. Particularly striking was footage shown on 19 August 1991 of Eltsin standing on top of a tank and delivering a speech to the crowd gathered outside the headquarters of the RSFSR Supreme Soviet. In addition leading political figures and independent journalists in Moscow and other Soviet cities were freely interviewed by Radio Free Europe/Radio Liberty (RFE/RL) and other Western radios. (This echoed the situation in January of 1991, when Western correspondents were not expelled from Lithuania in the wake of the military crackdown in Vilnius.)

The decision not to expel foreign journalists seemed to have been taken deliberately by the Emergency Committee in an effort to avoid open confrontation with Western countries. The committee's failure to enforce its ban on domestic publications, however, was another matter and was one of the main signs of weakness on the part of the self-proclaimed authorities. On 20 August, *Moscow News, Megapolis-ekspress, Kuranty* and *Rossiya* managed to publish emergency issues despite the ban. In an interview with RFE/RL on 21 August, deputy chief editor of *Moscow News*, Stepan Kiselev, described how the issues of his paper were prepared. He said that four copies were produced using a typewriter and then xeroxed. The xeroxed copies were distributed to people in Moscow and also posted in places such as subway stations. In another violation of the ban, 11 suppressed newspapers in Moscow prepared a joint issue entitled *Obshchaya gazeta*. Kiselev told RFE/RL on 21 August that the issue was printed outside Moscow and then smuggled back to the capital. (On 23 August it became known that the publishing houses of two newspapers in Moldavia had helped with the publication of *Moscow News* and *Nezavisimaya gazeta* during the coup. Some issues of *Moscow News* were also printed in Tallinn.[15])

In Leningrad, on the morning of 19 August, the then commander of the Leningrad military district, Colonel General Viktor Samsonov, went on local radio to announce that military censorship was being imposed. Yet almost all Leningrad newspapers, including the outspoken Leningrad Komsomol newspaper, *Smena*, and the organ of the Leningrad Soviet, *Nevskoe vremya*, were published.[16] The independent radio station 'Svobodnyi gorod' was also able to resume broadcasting on 20 August and devoted its programmes to documents issued by the leadership of the RSFSR. Leningrad television, too, remained under the control of the opposition. There were reports on 19 August that OMON troops had occupied the city's television centre, but, late that evening, Leningrad mayor Anatolii Sobchak and several other liberal local deputies were given airtime. They called on the military to hand over to the city authorities all officers who had helped to organize the illegal seizure of power.

Russian Television managed to broadcast briefly on 20 August and the independent 'Ekho Moskvy' was broadcasting most of the time during the coup.[17] The RSFSR Supreme Soviet managed to set up its own radio station in the headquarters of the RSFSR government. In

short the functioning of the media during the coup was a good illustration of the strong union of democratic forces that existed within
the country. The aid given by Moldavian and Estonian publishing
houses to the banned Moscow newspapers is a good example of such
unity.

JOURNALISTS DEMONSTRATE THEIR MATURITY

Journalists demonstrated their maturity also after the coup. They
immediately decided to use the opportunity that had arisen to turn
glasnost – which still depended to some extent on the good will of the
top leadership – into freedom of information. The attempt by the
organizers of the coup to suppress the activities of the media,
especially on television and radio, encouraged journalists to seek independence from CPSU and state organs. Many newspapers, with *Izvestia* in the lead, announced that they would in future be run and
published by their work collectives.[18] The desire to become joint-stock
companies was expressed by employees of the main government
agency *TASS* and the semi-official *Novosti*.[19] A group of journalists
from Central Television demanded the creation of an independent
news service within the All-Union State Television and Radio Broadcasting Company. A similar proposal was put forward the same day
by journalists of the RSFSR Television news service, 'Vesti'.[20] In their
turn, already existing independent radio stations, like 'Ekho Moskvy',
started to campaign for abandonment of the state monopoly over the
means of communication (transmitters first of all) and for the adoption
of legislation on radio frequencies, which would assign two-thirds of all
frequencies to non-governmental radio stations.[21] Finally many media
representatives showed their political wisdom by criticizing as illegal
Boris Eltsin's decree of 22 August in which he ordered, among other
things, the suspension of the activities of the CPSU newspapers,
*Pravda, Sovetskaya Rossiya, Rabochaya tribuna, Glasnost', Moskov-
skaya pravda* and *Leninskoe znamya*.[22]

In the new situation created after the coup in Moscow, political
censorship seems to have practically become a thing of the past, and
the main problem now facing many publications, and particularly those
that previously belonged to the CPSU, is that of finding the necessary
financial resources. Many newly emerging as well as traditional publications will also have to establish a new identity and clearly define
their audience.[23]

CONCLUSION

By the time Gorbachev started to unveil and implement his reforms, a large group of Soviet intellectuals, including journalists, had already formed a theoretical base for supporting drastic changes in the Soviet political system and therefore was ready to respond to the new challenges posed by Gorbachev's policies and to take advantage of the new opportunities they offered. In the early years of *perestroika*, in particular, the Soviet leadership considered liberal journalists its allies and encouraged their active participation in political life. A large section of the media responded with almost unrestrained support for the leadership and performed many important tasks, including the denunciation of the country's Stalinist past and of present-day bureaucracy, as well as the elaboration of various reform projects.

In the period of Gorbachev's reforms, the Soviet media had an unprecedented impact on the Soviet population. It should be noted that, in the period of *perestroika*, works of journalism elaborating new social, political and economic ideas have become the main reading of the Soviet population and far surpassed the popularity of the belles lettres, notwithstanding the publication of previously banned works of prose and poetry.

NOTES AND REFERENCES

1. Fedor Tyutchev, *Politicheskie stat'i*, YMCA Press, Paris, 1976, pp. 82–3.
2. *Sovetskaya kul'tura*, 3 January 1987.
3. *Pravda*, 23 March 1985.
4. *Izvestia TsK KPSS*, no. 2, 1989, pp. 39–41. See also Radio Liberty (RL) 313/89, Victor Yasmann, '*Glasnost* Versus Freedom of Information: Political and Ideological Aspects', 6 July 1989.
5. *Pravda*, 22 October 1986.
6. For the text of the USSR press law, see *Izvestia*, 20 June 1990. (Article 7 of the law regulates the establishment of new mass media.)
7. See RL 23/89, Julia Wishnevsky, '*Nash sovremennik* Provides Focus for "Opposition Party" ', 12 January 1989; and RL 113/89, Julia Wishnevsky, 'Ligachev, "Pamyat", and Conservative Writers', 28 February 1989.
8. Vitalii Korotich took over *Ogonek* in 1986, replacing a Stalinist, Anatolii Sofronov; Georgii Baklanov took over *Znamya* in July 1986. He replaced Yurii Voronov who became head of the CPSU CC Cultural Department. Egor Yakovlev became chief editor of *Moscow News* in August 1986, replacing Gennadii Gerasimov who was transferred to the post of the USSR Foreign Ministry's spokesman.
9. *Zhurnalist*, nos. 5–7, 1989. 2250 deputies altogether were elected to the USSR Congress of People's Deputies in 1989.
10. *Zhurnalist*,nos. 6–8, 1990. Altogether 1068 deputies were elected to the RSFSR Congress of People's Deputies in 1990.
11. At a conference on the USSR after the attempted coup held on 19 and 20 September 1991 at RFE/RL Research Institute (Munich) deputy chief editor of *Nezavisimaya gazeta*, Igor Zakharov, said that these shortcomings are especially

true in cases of young journalists working for the new press. For the summary of the proceedings of the conference, see *Report on the USSR*, 1991, no. 43.

12. Vladimir Shlapentokh, 'Soviet Intellectuals and Political Power. The Post-Stalin Era', I. B. Tauris and Co Ltd Publishers, London/New York, 1990, p. 265.

13. This comment was made at the press conference given by members of the Emergency Committee on 19 August 1991 (Central Television, 19 August 1991; *Pravda*, 20 August 1991).

14. Political commentator Vladimir Tsvetov revealed on 22 August 1991 that Leonid Kravchenko, the then head of the All-Union State Television and Radio Broadcasting Company, had demoted Medvedev because of his stance. Kravchenko was reportedly acting on a request from three members of the Politburo – Aleksandr Dzasokhov, Oleg Shenin and Moscow Party leader Yurii Prokof'ev.

15. The issue of *Moscow News* for 21 August states that it was printed in Tallinn. In addition, the same day, a separate, combined issue of *Moscow News* and *Nezavisimaya gazeta* appeared in Kishinev.

16. On the evening of 19 August 1991, Leningrad Mayor Anatolii Sobchak proclaimed all restrictions on the media imposed by Samsonov illegal. On 20 August the only major Leningrad newspaper that did not appear in its usual format was *Vechernii Leningrad*, an organ of the Leningrad City Soviet, which contained gaps where censors loyal to the Emergency Committee had removed Boris Eltsin's declarations; all other Leningrad newspapers appeared without the censor's interference.

17. In a report delivered at the RFE/RL Research Institute Conference on 20 September 1991, chief editor of 'Ekho Moskvy' Sergei Korzun said that his radio was switched off three times in the course of the coup. Every time, however, its workers managed to resume broadcasting.

18. *Izvestia*, 23 August 1991.

19. *TASS*, 25 August 1991; *Novosti*, 26 August 1991. On 27 August an independent news service, 'Info-Nova', was set up within *Novosti*. *TASS*, however, still remains the main All-Union government agency.

20. *TASS*, 26 August 1991.

21. These ideas were elaborated in the above-mentioned report (see note 17) by Sergei Korzun.

22. For a critical assessment of Eltsin's decree, see *Komsomol'skaya pravda*, 24 August 1991.

23. In some former Union republics (Georgia, Moldavia) political censorship of the media has been reintroduced by nationalistic governments which replaced communists.

7. Manual Workers and the Workforce

Elizabeth Teague[*]

This chapter looks at the impact of Mikhail Gorbachev's *perestroika* policies on Soviet workers. Reform of the Soviet economic and political system promises ultimately to leave every member of society freer and better off. But, as Boris Eltsin warned the Russian Federation parliament when he announced his economic reform programme on 28 October 1991, the short- to medium-term costs of reform will be high and will be borne by the general population.

Since radical reform will by definition require drastic changes in the pattern of national economic activity, Soviet workers will play, willy-nilly, a key role in the reform process. At present, there is not much evidence either of a worker 'push' for change or, conversely, of a 'pull' by the leadership to bring the workers in as active constituents. Blue-collar workers – a social stratum not deprived of the ability to defend itself, but one that is nonetheless at present poorly organized and ill-prepared for the major readjustments economic reform will demand – seem to have been very much on the sidelines of the reform constituency so far. They are, however, likely to be among those most affected; only pensioners and others on fixed incomes are likely to be harder hit in the initial phases.

According to the orthodox Soviet definition, blue-collar workers (*rabochie*) make up by far the largest group in the Soviet labour force. In 1989 they were estimated to number 78.7 million people, or 62 per cent of the entire working population in the state and kolkhoz sectors. White-collar workers (*sluzhashchie*) were estimated to form 28.9 per cent of the working population in the state and kolkhoz sectors, with collective farm peasants making up 9.1 per cent.[1]

In any assessment of the social impact of the changes initiated under Gorbachev's leadership, the analyst must decide on which groups of people to focus. It will be argued here that the traditional social categories of Soviet doctrine – workers, peasants and employees – have little value for analysis today. An alternative approach might be

114

to distinguish, within the economically active population, between the *nomenklatura* and the rest. This would conform to the perception widely held in Soviet society of a divide between 'them' (the nachal'-stvo or 'bosses', that is the holders of *nomenklatura* state and Party posts) and 'us' (all the rest)[2] as illustrated in Alexander Zinoviev's aphorism that a Soviet general has more in common with a Soviet academician than with a Soviet soldier.[3] But while the *nachal'stvo* may in the past have been a class in the traditional sense, conscious of its interests as a class, it is now split, within what used to be the USSR, both on lines of nationality and also between traditionalists who feel threatened by radical change and those former *nomenklaturshchiki* who are trying to transform themselves into a new business class.[4]

The analysis developed here is based in part on this simple 'them/us' divide, with a particular focus on blue-collar workers. In other words, the workforce is taken initially to be those people who are neither part of the old *nomenklatura* nor amongst the emerging non-*nomenklatura* business class: in short, the unprivileged. This is a group that includes white-collar as well as blue-collar workers. It does not follow, however, that the workforce in this sense, even within specific republics, shares similar interests, let alone that its members are conscious of common interests and feel themselves united by a sense of class solidarity. There are divisions amongst the unprivileged (in addition to nationality divisions) as well as amongst the privileged. This is true within the category of blue-collar workers as well as more widely.

In a landmark study published a decade ago, Alex Pravda asserted that the existence of a homogeneous Soviet 'working class' was a myth cultivated by Soviet ideologists as a means of legitimizing the rule of the Communist Party and the Soviet state. Drawing on the research of Soviet social scientists, Pravda argued that the Soviet 'working class' was in reality composed of widely differing strata, each with its own interests, and that it was, moreover, growing increasingly hetero-geneous. Rather than marking blue-collar workers off from other social groups, Pravda went on, the major divisions in Soviet society cut so deeply through the manual workforce as to cast doubt on the usefulness of the concept of the 'working class' as a tool for analysis. For example, differences between blue-collar workers' educational and skill levels showed as much a generational as a class dimension. Pravda suggested that Soviet workers might be more appropriately divided into 'old' and 'new' segments, with younger, more highly-skilled workers in relatively high-technology production tending to display a

different set of interests from older, less highly-skilled ones in traditional 'smokestack' industries.[5]

Attention to the importance of economic and social change has also
been drawn by other Western scholars.[6] Walt Connor, for example,
has stressed that Soviet society was still relatively homogeneous in
1953, when Stalin died and Nikita Khrushchev became Party leader.
It was a poor society ('one that judged itself in terms of how many
motorcycles and radios there were per hundred members of the population').[7] Moreover it was still a predominantly rural society. Even
many of those who in the 1950s were considered for statistical purposes
to be urban dwellers were first-generation city dwellers; that is, they
had been born in the countryside; many of them, Connor has pointed
out, lived not in real towns or cities but in so-called urban settlements.
It was a society that was uneducated and underskilled but highly
mobile. Society was not differentiated enough for classes or social
groups to coalesce and to articulate demands and force them on
the state. It was, in many ways, a pre-modern or even semi-feudal
society.

A SOCIETY IN TRANSITION[8]

By the time Mikhail Gorbachev was elected Communist Party leader
in 1985, Soviet society had changed dramatically from what it had
been a generation before. Gorbachev's USSR was predominantly an
urban society. The shift from the country to the towns occurred in
the USSR both later and more rapidly than in most other major
industrialized countries. In 1940 only 33 per cent of the Soviet population were urban dwellers and it was not until 1960–1 that the USSR
reached the point where more than 50 per cent of the population lived
in towns. Thereafter urbanization proceeded apace. Migration from
the country to the towns can be seen from the following data from
the All-Union censuses carried out in the USSR in the post-Stalin
period.[9]

	Size of population (millions)	*Percentage living in towns*	*Percentage living in rural areas*
1959	208.8	48	52
1970	241.7	56	44
1979	262.4	62	38
1989	286.7	66	34

The 1989 census revealed that rural to urban migration was occurring in the 1980s in all Soviet republics except the four Central Asian ones (Turkmenistan, Uzbekistan, Kyrgyzstan and Tajikistan).[10] In the Russian Federation, the figure was considerably higher than the All-Union average: by 1989, 74 per cent of the population of the RSFSR were urban dwellers, up from 69 per cent in the 1979 census.[11]

In the USSR as a whole the urban population in the 1980s became increasingly concentrated in large towns. Thus, in the period between the 1979 and 1989 censuses, the number of Soviet citizens living in towns of between 100 000 and 500 000 inhabitants increased by 9 per cent; the number living in cities of up to one million inhabitants went up by 18 per cent; and the number living in cities with over a million inhabitants grew by 23 per cent.[12] At the time of the 1989 census, the overwhelming majority (87.5 per cent) of the RSFSR's urban dwellers lived in towns or cities; only 12.5 per cent were still living in 'urban settlements'.[13]

The citizens of Gorbachev's Soviet Union tended to be appreciably better educated than their forebears. In the USSR, as in other industrialized countries, the standard of education was generally higher in large towns and cities than in rural areas and, as the USSR became more urbanized, there tended to be an improvement in the level of education of the population.[14] In 1939 those with secondary education accounted for only 10 per cent of the Soviet population over the age of 15 years. By 1989, 81 per cent of the population over that age had secondary education.[15] At the time of the 1989 census, 72.7 per cent of those aged between 45 and 59 inclusive had higher or secondary education, whereas the figure for those aged between 25 and 44 inclusive was 98 per cent. Of those in the older age-bracket, 12.2 per cent had higher education, whereas the figure for the younger age group was 16.7 per cent.[16]

Following the shift of population to the towns, the 1970s and 1980s saw a slow but steady tendency for blue-collar workers to move into white-collar employment and from less skilled to more highly-skilled jobs. By Western standards, to be sure, the proportion of manual workers remained high. Leonid Gordon and Alla Nazimova of Moscow's Institute of the International Working Class Movement have estimated that, in the early 1980s, about 65 per cent of those employed in agriculture and 45 per cent of those in construction were engaged in manual work.[17] Nonetheless the trend was clear: older workers were tending to become concentrated in lower- and semi-skilled professions, while younger workers were tending to enter more skilled ones.

STRATIFIED SOCIETY, MONOLITHIC POLITY

The result of all these factors was that Gorbachev's USSR was a far more complex society than that over which either Stalin or Khrushchev had ruled. Education and skill differentials had stratified the society that had been, only a generation before, relatively homogeneous. National elites had emerged within the more than one hundred ethnic groups inhabiting the Soviet Union. As Soviet society became more differentiated, so the interests of its various strata began to diverge and the potential for social conflict became more acute. And, as the demands placed on the state by society grew more insistent, so too did the need for institutions that could represent those demands.

However the Soviet economic and political systems remained as if fossilized. Soviet society was changing, yet the institutions by which it was governed hardly changed at all from those created by Stalin. Claiming that capitalist society was riven by conflicting class interests, Marxist-Leninist (that is Stalinist) ideology closed its eyes to Soviet society's increasing diversity and continued to insist that socialism was characterized by a single 'social interest' and would, moreover, become increasingly homogeneous the more 'mature' it grew. Supposedly the interests of blue-collar workers did not differ in any fundamental way from those of any other social stratum. The Communist Party based its monopoly of state power on its claim to be uniquely qualified to determine and administer the 'general interest'.[18]

WORKERS IN THE PRE-*PERESTROIKA* PERIOD

In the pre-Gorbachev period, blue-collar workers had little influence on state policy. Lip-service was paid throughout the Soviet period to the advantages allegedly bestowed on the working class in what Stalin's *Short Course* called 'the first Socialist State of Workers and Peasants in the world',[19] but, in reality, Soviet workers were without political or economic clout.

First, blue-collar workers had no effective role as voters in the pre-Gorbachev political system. In this they differed little from most other members of Soviet society. Since Stalin's day, voters going to the polls to elect both local government officers (deputies to the local soviets) and members of the All-Union parliament (deputies to the USSR Supreme Soviet) were presented with a ballot paper on which there was a single name for each post. Moreover the single candidate had been pre-selected by the officials of the Communist Party organization at the appropriate level. Deputies to the USSR Supreme Soviet were carefully chosen in accordance with quotas to ensure representation of women, national minorities, workers and so on.

Since deputies were nominated from above, not chosen in competitive elections by the voters, they responded not to the electorate but to the Party apparatus to whom they owed their posts. The fact that in 1984 (the last time the USSR Supreme Soviet was elected by the old quota method) 32.5 per cent of the deputies to the Soviet parliament were classified as blue-collar workers did not, therefore, mean that these deputies saw it as their duty to defend the interests of ordinary members of the working population. They knew they owed their allegiance to the apparatus. It was to be 1988 before any Supreme Soviet deputy dared to vote against a proposal put forward by the Party leadership in the Soviet parliament.[20]

Second, manual workers had no autonomous organizations to defend their interests *vis-à-vis* the state and the rest of society. The CPSU presented itself as a party representing the interests of the whole of society and embracing within its ranks a wide cross-section of the Soviet population. In reality, the CPSU was never a normal political party in the generally accepted sense of the word, that is, it never competed for power in elections on an equal footing with other parties, and it represented the interests of no-one other than the bureaucracy. According to Ivan Laptev, former chief editor of *Izvestiya*, there were always 'at least three parties' within the CPSU. The first was made up of the rank-and-file members who, 'although they constituted the majority of the Party, never determined its real identity or its policies'. The second consisted of a small group of Party leaders who 'personified the Party in the eyes of the population and of the world'. The third and most important group, according to Laptev, was the Party apparatus, which 'represented the Party members to the leaders, the leaders to the Communists, and the Party to the masses'.[21]

Evidence that blue-collar workers did not perceive the CPSU as representing their interests is furnished by the amount of energy the Party traditionally had to put into what was clearly the difficult job of recruiting workers as members. At the beginning of 1990 manual workers made up only 27.6 per cent of the membership, while employees made up 40.5 per cent.[22] When, later that year, Party membership began to drop, the evidence indicated that blue-collar workers were the first to quit.[23]

'The workers have rejected the CPSU,' ran an article in the newspaper *Rabochaya tribuna* on 9 October 1991; 'will they [now] turn to the trade unions?' The author, Igor Zaramensky, a former official of the CPSU Central Committee, was not hopeful. The Communist

Party, he wrote, had turned its back on the workers by permitting their 'alienation from power'. Since the Party was aided and abetted in this by the official trade unions, many workers had turned against the unions too, Zaramensky concluded. As Zaramensky acknowledged, the very trade unions to which Soviet blue-collar workers belonged were firmly controlled by the Party-state apparatus. Indeed the official unions – the only labour unions permitted to exist in the USSR until the Gorbachev era – were (and remain) so tightly tied to the state that they are perhaps best described as part of it. Charged with the quasi-governmental function of administering social security payments, the unions received (and still receive) financial allocations directly from the USSR state budget. Just like Supreme Soviet deputies, union officials were appointed on the say-so of the Communist Party. Therefore they looked up to the apparatus for their instructions, not down to their worker-members. Organizers of strikes and unofficial trade unions, on the other hand, were harshly repressed by the authorities.[24]

While they were estranged from political and economic power, Soviet workers did have a high level of job security, though at a low level of real income. In addition the Soviet economy for many years provided its workers with full, even over-full, employment; moreover low levels of workplace discipline were routinely tolerated. Whether this came about by accident or design has for some time been the subject of dispute among Western scholars. Philip Hanson has suggested that full employment and job security were unplanned and ultimately dysfunctional side-effects of centrally-planned economies in which enterprises operate with soft budget constraints.[25] Others, including Peter Hauslohner and the late David Granick, have postulated the existence of an implicit 'social contract', under the terms of which blue-collar workers were fostered by the Soviet authorities as a source of political support for the regime.[26]

If there was such a thing as a Soviet 'social contract', the workers' side of the bargain would require them to remain politically passive. The state in return would guarantee them job security, full employment, and lax labour discipline; it would implement an active incomes policy aimed at minimizing wage disparities between blue-collar workers; and it would ensure, in contrast to the situation in the developed capitalist countries, that blue-collar workers were relatively better paid than white-collar ones.

At first sight this explanation is persuasive – pay for certain skilled and professional personnel, such as teachers and doctors, was notoriously low for example – but it soon runs up against the problem that plagues all attempts to evaluate real wage levels in the USSR. The difficulty is that, while income disparities were generally smaller in the USSR than in the West, Soviet citizens had widely varying degrees of access to consumer goods. Such goods were in short supply through-out the country, and this encouraged the creation of all sorts of distribution networks that ensured that state officials and workers in prestigious plants had privileged access to special outlets. A member of the *nomenklatura* would have the right to order luxuries from a closed store; a worker in a factory producing high-priority goods could eat in a specially stocked canteen. Moreover, it was a major source of real-income advantage to possess a Moscow residence permit, or merely to have time to spend standing in line, which of course had nothing to do with performance at work. This element of access played a real but unquantifiable role in creating significant differentials between different groups of Soviet citizens.

Others again have argued that relations between leaders and led, even in the post-Stalin USSR, were characterized less by the kind of interdependence suggested by the term 'social contract' than by mutual fear. Soviet leaders, according to this interpretation, were poorly informed about the state of public opinion and their ignorance made them deeply mistrustful of the population and, in particular, of the workforce.[27] Further elaboration of the relationship between blue-collar workers and their bosses has been proposed by Donald Filtzer, who argues that Soviet shopfloor workers came over generations to exercise a significant amount of negative, 'veto' power over the speed, organization and quality of their work, but this could hardly be described as much more than 'the freedom to work badly'.[28] In other words, Soviet workers had 'exit' but not 'voice'.[29] From 1985, with the launching of Gorbachev's reform policies, this situation has begun to change.

WORKERS UNDER *PERESTROIKA*: PHASE ONE

The working population was assigned a central role in Gorbachev's early reform efforts, the initial aim of which was to revitalize the flagging Soviet economy. The first period of *perestroika* (1985–6) was characterized by initiative from above; during this first period Gorba-chev used a combination of carrot and stick to try to prod the popu-lation into working harder and more conscientiously. There was much talk at this time about widening wage differentials, increasing worker participation and even, perhaps, using the threat of unemployment as a way of spurring the workforce to greater effort. One of Gorbachev's main ideas in this first phase of *perestroika* was that increased responsibility and participation in decision making on the part of rank-and-file workers would release a surge of productivity. 'Activating the human factor' was therefore an integral feature of Gorbachev's early policies of 'intensification' and 'acceleration'; that is, achieving enhanced economic growth by more efficient use of inputs (manpower in particular) and the application of modern technology in the workplace.

The early years of Gorbachev's leadership also saw growing acknowledgement of the existence of conflicting group interests, both of workers as a whole and of different groups of workers, and more scope was allowed for articulation of these interests (though not at that stage for their organized expression). Gorbachev envisaged a modernized Soviet Union as a society in which the public could and should be given more information and responsibility and in general be trusted by the rulers more than before. In a major speech delivered in Krasnodar, in September 1986, Gorbachev for the first time described the 'democratization' of Soviet society as his main priority. He said that, when he was talking to crowds on the city streets earlier in the day,

> I thought of how much our people have grown up, of what intellectual potential they possess, creative potential, and of how, in resolving issues in the country, we still do not make use of this potential, relying on administrative injunction, giving orders and issuing commands.

'We must,' Gorbachev went on, 'include the people in the process of restructuring via the democratization of society.'[30] 'Our people,' he stated the following day, 'have matured to the extent that they must be trusted to administer themselves.'[31]

WORKERS UNDER *PERESTROIKA*: PHASE TWO

The other side of the coin was that Gorbachev expected the population to work harder and with less economic security than before. This aspect of his programme did not meet with widespread public approval. Indeed Gorbachev's initial efforts to revive the economy by exhortation and tinkering changes failed to arouse popular support. The reason for the population's failure to respond was that, for all Gorbachev's efforts to increase participation and openness, what he was engaged upon was a within-system reform. The overarching dominance of the CPSU and the central planning apparatus remained undiminished and powerful institutional interest groups retained the ability to block reforms. As a result, ordinary people were mistrustful since they feared that, as had happened in the past, change could be easily reversed. In 1987, therefore, the Soviet leader turned to deeper political reforms. During the next phase of *perestroika* (1987–9), much greater political openness was permitted and the formation of unofficial trade unions and ad hoc strike committees was tolerated.

In particular the USSR Law on the State Enterprise of 1987 sought to involve workers in the management of their factories and plants by offering them the power to elect their managers and, through the institutionalization of councils of the work collective, to enforce the rights of codetermination that workers had been promised – but had been unable to exercise – under the 1977 USSR constitution.[32] In the vast majority of cases, however, the 1987 law ran up against fierce resistance from the branch ministries and the official trade unions, neither of which was eager to share its powers with the elected representatives of the workforce, and the law failed to operate in the way it had been intended. It was eventually superseded by the 1990 USSR Law on Enterprises which stripped the work collective of the right to participate in enterprise decision making in anything other than a purely advisory capacity.[33]

Also characteristic of the second phase of *perestroika* was Gorbachev's attempt to revamp the Soviet parliament by making it more responsive to the desires and needs of ordinary people. High hopes were placed in the new USSR Congress of People's Deputies and Supreme Soviet when they were elected in the spring of 1989. The Congress was the first Soviet parliament since 1917 to be elected on a multi-candidate basis. Ultimately, however, this experiment also turned out to be a failure. The reason was simple. It was that, while two-thirds of the 2250 members of the USSR Congress of People's Deputies were directly elected, one-third were not elected by the general public but were instead nominated by establishment institutions, including the CPSU and bodies dominated by it, such as the official trade unions. The golden rule – 'one man, one vote' – was violated. Ordinary people had one vote, but members of the elite had two or three.

Voters' choice was further restricted by the fact that candidates were screened by local electoral commissions before their names could appear on the ballot: in numerous cases these commissions excluded candidates considered 'undesirable' by the local authorities. Large numbers of candidates ran uncontested, and there were numerous reports of attempts to manipulate the outcome of the voting. The net

result was that the Supreme Soviet was not a representative body and
could not be called a truly democratic parliament. Probably, therefore,
it was not a matter of great importance that, in the general elections
of the spring of 1989, only 18.6 per cent of those elected to the USSR
Congress of People's Deputies were classified as workers (as opposed,
as mentioned above, to 32.5 per cent in the 1984 elections).[34]

If the first phase of Gorbachev's *perestroika* was greeted with apathy
on the part of the workforce, the second phase saw the population
begin to respond to the increased opportunities his reforms offered,
though not always in the way Gorbachev had hoped. As a result, his
leadership found itself increasingly obliged to react to events, rather
than directing them. For example, the formation of the first unofficial
trade unions and strike committees took place against an escalation
of industrial action, much of it sparked by ethnic and national grievances. In general, strike activity by Soviet workers proved in this
period far more likely to be sparked by ethnic conflicts than by the
kind of bread-and-butter demands normally viewed as typical workers'
issues.[35] In response the official Soviet trade unions began to agitate
for the legalization of the right to strike: since workers' protests were
becoming commonplace, the unions sought (unsuccessfully) to secure
the exclusive right to organize them.

The miners' strike of July 1989, which made nearly half a million
workers idle, was a major turning-point in the relationship between
workers and the state. Strikers ignored their official union representatives and spontaneously organized their own strike committees. Even
more significant, the miners resolved to keep these strike committees
in existence after the strike was over in order to monitor the government's compliance with the agreements on the basis of which the
miners returned to work. The experience spurred the Gorbachev
leadership into introducing a bill legalizing strikes – though the new
law contained so many restrictions that it was clear that its aim was
to make it harder rather than easier for workers to organize their
protests.[36]

THE OFFICIAL UNIONS REORGANIZE

The miners' strike of July 1989 prompted the official trade unions –
long a bastion of conservatism – to undertake a fundamental policy
review. At the Sixth Plenum of the All-Union Central Council of
Trade Unions (AUCCTU) in September 1989 the unions announced
that they were formally abandoning the role, which they had played
since the days of Lenin, of 'transmission belts' of Communist Party

policy to the masses. From now on, the unions declared, they would operate in complete independence from the CPSU.[37] The unions, which had rarely been known to defend any interests other than those of the Party-state apparatus, retained their anomalous, quasi-governmental function of distributing state social welfare benefits, but asserted that, henceforth, the protection of working people would be their prime task.

There were several reasons for this change. The communist-dominated official unions had been badly frightened by the hostility to them shown by the miners during the 1989 strike, and resolved in future to court the workers with promises to defend them against the hardships (which the unions stressed at every available opportunity) of the switch to a market economy. In addition the official unions saw the writing on the wall a good deal sooner than the Communist Party did. Evidently aware of how unpopular the CPSU and its doctrines were among working people, the unions anticipated the move to a multi-party system. They sought to distance themselves from the Party in the public eye and proclaimed their readiness to work with any political party approved by the population.

PERESTROIKA: PHASE THREE

Perestroika moved into its third phase (1990–1) as Gorbachev and the central government lost the initiative to newly self-assertive governments in the republics which, in a number of cases, were responding to and being driven by popular pressure. Economic chaos, not economic reform, was the result of the collapse of central authority and the 'war of laws' that ensued. Working people were alarmed by the fall in their living standards and by threats of unemployment and dislocation. The urge for national self-determination grew stronger in an ever-increasing number of regions. Again the trade unions seemed to grasp earlier than the Communist Party the fact that, once the CPSU lost its monopoly on power, the Marxist–Leninist ideology that glued the USSR together would also dissolve. In October 1990, in anticipation of such an event, a congress of the official unions decentralized the union structure and turned the AUCCTU into a loose confederation, renamed the General Confederation of Trade Unions of the USSR (VKP).[38] From then on, as power flowed to republican bodies, the All-Union trade union centre began to look more and more like a dying organization.

Particularly significant was the establishment, early in 1990, of the Russian Federation of Independent Trade Unions (FNPR).[39] Despite the word 'independent' in its title, this organization sprang from the official trade union structure and continued to maintain close links with the state. Even more conservative than its All-Union parent, indeed, the FNPR lost no time in expressing its opposition even to the timid proposals for 'a regulated market economy' advanced by the then Soviet prime minister Nikolai Ryzhkov in autumn 1990. After the election of Boris Eltsin as head of state of the Russian Republic in the spring of that year, the FNPR sought to present itself as the Russian government's natural negotiating partner on economic and social issues.

Trade union federations in other republics acted in a similar way as did, on the All-Union level, the VKP which, under its then leader Gennadii Yanaev, offered to sign an annual 'collective agreement' with the government on behalf of the workforce.[40] The VKP proposed that, as long as the government kept its side of the bargain, it would dissuade its members from embarking on strike action. But, the union hinted darkly, should the government fail to keep its side of the bargain, then it would call its members out on strike.

Even as they courted the workers with promises of support, therefore, the unions projected themselves in a corporatist role as guarantors of industrial peace; in return they demanded an assured place in whatever configuration of political forces took shape in the USSR. Observers expressed doubts, however, as to whether the USSR's VKP or the official trade union federations in the various Soviet republics really enjoyed enough influence among Soviet workers to be able to control the behaviour of the workforce in such a way.

Similarly, in abandoning the role of 'transmission belt' and moving into an explicitly adversarial role *vis-à-vis* the government, the official unions seemed to be taking a leaf out of the book of Poland's OPZZ (National Alliance of Trade Unions). From its inception, the OPZZ disavowed the role of 'transmission belt'; instead, it deliberately adopted an attitude of confrontation, first towards Poland's communist government – in order to attract workers into its ranks and to defuse their anger through the protests it organized – and later towards the Solidarity-led government.[41] Overall the official Soviet unions have shown every sign of learning from the experience of Eastern Europe, where the unions have displayed an ability almost unique among formerly communist-dominated organizations to retain their property and much of their membership in the post-communist world.[42]

For the time being at least, it seems, the official Soviet unions have assured themselves a role in the post-communist era. One of the leaders of the (genuinely independent) Independent Miners' Union,

Aleksandr Sergeev, even believes that Eltsin may, sooner rather than later, find it more to his advantage to arrange a deal with the official Russian trade unions (if the latter prove able to keep worker unrest to a minimum) than he would with a militant free union such as the Independent Miners' Union or the other genuinely independent unions of airline pilots and air traffic controllers – all three of which spoke out immediately in defence of Eltsin during the August coup.[43]

THE WORKERS' ECONOMIC POSITION AT THE END OF *PERESTROIKA*

The failed coup of August 1991 marked, for many observers, the end of Soviet socialism. Though that judgement may yet prove premature, the putsch and its aftermath certainly changed the borders of the Soviet state, entailing its break-up; the Communist Party and its Union-wide system of *nomenklatura* appointments were destroyed; and an end was put to *perestroika* which, conceived as a radical reform from above and as something closer to a New Deal than to a revolution, had brought the country to the verge of economic collapse.

By August 1991 the average levels of material welfare of the Soviet population had declined sharply. At the same time, income differentiation had probably increased: certainly traditional patterns of differentiation had been drastically changed. These changes could not be reliably measured, however. Neither inflation rates nor real levels of supply could be tracked through 1991, though it seemed probable that, in the first three quarters of 1991, per capita real consumption in the USSR fell by a little less than 12 per cent.[44] Real wages were falling. Those who worked in cooperatives and joint ventures (around three million people) were receiving very high incomes by Soviet standards – typically, some two to four times the state-sector average. But every member of the population was subject to the impact of rapid inflation, possibly approaching 400 per cent a year in August 1991.[45] The State Statistics Committee, (Goskomstat) no longer provided an average state wage figure, but the closely equivalent 'enterprise consumption fund per worker' was 400 rubles a month in January-September 1991, and the average income per household member of worker (*rabochie*) families was reported as 274 rubles per month.[46]

Estimates of the 'poverty level' proliferated and varied widely - between 166 rubles a month and 500 rubles a month in autumn 1991. Certainly, on many of the definitions that were circulating in the USSR, the *average* member of a worker household, on 274 rubles a month, would have been below the 'minimum income level' (*prozhito-*

chnyi minumum), while the average pensioner, on 182 rubles a month, would have been well below most definitions.[47] On 28 October 1991, indeed, Boris Eltsin told the RSFSR parliament that 55 per cent of families in the Russian Federation were living below the poverty line.[48]

Meanwhile workers began to brace themselves for the widespread cyclical and structural unemployment that threatened to accompany the Soviet Union's long-awaited move to a market economy. In January 1991 the USSR adopted a framework law on employment that called for the creation of a Union-wide State Employment Service that would, for the first time since the 1920s, register the jobless, maintain a bank of job vacancies, administer training programmes and coordinate the payment of unemployment benefits. The service was to be financed through mandatory contributions (equivalent to one per cent of payroll) by state-run and private enterprises, factories, cooperatives and joint ventures.[49]

The USSR Employment Law envisaged the adoption of further legislation by each of the republics. Laws on employment have so far been enacted in the Baltic states, the Russian Republic, Ukraine, Kazakhstan, Belorussia, Azerbaijan and Kyrgyzstan. Other republics in Central Asia and the Transcaucasus claim they cannot afford to pay for the training and unemployment benefits required by the USSR law.[50] Even the RSFSR while it can afford unemployment benefits, does not have enough money to provide retraining.[51]

The Russian Republic is proud that the unemployment benefits it pays are higher than those in other parts of the USSR. However they are not lavish: they decline in size as time progresses and cease altogether after one year, or if the unemployed person rejects two suitable job vacancies proposed to him or her by the Employment Centre. Thereafter a person who is unable to find work will be eligible only for minimum social welfare support.

The Moscow Employment Centre, which opened in February 1991, has launched a particularly ambitious programme to cope with unemployment. However Moscow's experience is in many ways unique: the city has high white-collar unemployment (90 per cent) and 90 per cent of its jobless are female. (High female unemployment is also reported from other parts of the USSR and is characteristic of blue-collar as well as white-collar personnel.)[52] Moscow's main problem is that the majority of job vacancies in the city (85 per cent) are for blue-collar workers. Many white-collar workers refuse even to consider blue-collar jobs because they see them as representing a sharp drop in social status.[53]

As 1991 drew to a close, unemployment was still low in the USSR.

Goskomstat, which had in 1989 admitted to the existence of unemployment in the USSR for the first time since the 1920s, continued to
claim that total Soviet unemployment on ILO definitions was only
about two million people. With employment in all sectors (state and
non-state) averaging 137.5 million during January-September 1991,
this meant the estimated unemployment rate was 1.5 per cent – a
figure dismissed by most knowledgeable observers as far too low. In
nine former Soviet republics for which data were given (excluding the
newly independent Baltic states and the strife-torn Transcaucasus)
269 200 jobless people were recorded as having sought employment
through the State Employment Service in September 1991, but only
a tiny minority of these met the conditions for receiving unemployment
benefit at that time.[54]

Meanwhile a plethora of independent unions and worker-oriented
organizations began to compete for the worker constituency. As 1991
neared its end, the Independent Miners' Union (created in 1990) was
debating whether it was strong enough to set up a confederation of
independent trade unions to rival the VKP. On the Stalinist 'right',
the arch-conservative United Workers' Front (founded in 1989) was
trying to organize worker opposition to the market. In October 1991
members of the Socialist Party, the Anarcho-Syndicalist group and the
CPSU's former Marxist Platform joined forces to form a Party of
Labour. Modelled on the British Labour Party of the 1920s, the new
party would be aimed specifically at workers, who would mobilize in
support of the (official) trade union movement. Also in October, the
Interrepublican Union of Work Collectives met in Moscow to hammer
out policy on worker ownership and self-management; with strong
support in defence industry enterprises, the union made it its aim to
save the jobs of skilled workers in the military-industrial complex. On
the liberal 'left', the independent union 'Sotsprof' was trying to build
a grassroots base by helping workers to defend their rights through
the courts. New organizations aimed at workers were also springing
up in other parts of the former USSR.

However officials in the new independent organizations complained
about the difficulty of mobilizing the workers, the majority of whom,
the activisits alleged, were 'lumpenized' and as yet uninterested in
collective action. Their complaints underscored the conclusions
reached in this chapter; that is, that the traditional Soviet view, according to which blue-collar workers formed a self-conscious, homogeneous
'working class', is of little value as a tool for analysis in today's
conditions. As Peter Rutland exclaimed in November 1991, 'There's

no organized workers' movement in the Soviet Union today because there's no working class.'[55]

It has been argued above that, despite the changes wrought during the Gorbachev era, the interests of workers are still rather poorly represented in the Soviet political system. A case might be made that the existence of strong workers' organizations, prepared to fight in defence of workers' interests, could derail efforts to institute a market reform and that the absence of such bodies in the USSR today therefore bodes well for the reform's success. An equally good case might also be made that the absence of strong defence mechanisms threatens to leave Soviet workers with so little protection that they may have little choice but to resort to strikes and even violent protests to express their grievances. The leaders of the former Soviet Union will tread a knife-edge in the coming months as they try to balance the interests of the working population against the imperatives of the reform process.

NOTES AND REFERENCES

*   The author is grateful to Professors David Lane and Philip Hanson for their valuable comments and advice on the early drafts of this article.

1.   *Narodnoe khoziaystvo SSSR v 1989 g.*, 'Finansy i statistika', Moscow, 1990.

2.   Michael Voslensky, *Nomenklatura. Die herrschende Klasse der Sowjetunion*, Molden, Vienna 1980; Mervyn Matthews, *Privilege in the Soviet Union*, Allen and Unwin, London, 1978.

3.   Alexander Zinoviev, *Kommunizm kak real'nost'*, Lausanne, L'Age d'homme, 1981.

4.   See Chapter 11 by Olga Kryshtanovskaya.

5.   Alex Pravda, 'Is There a Soviet Working Class?', *Problems of Communism*, November-December 1982, pp. 1–24. See also Alfred Evans, Jr., 'The Working Class and Reform', paper presented at the Annual Convention of the American Association for the Advancement of Slavic Studies in Chicago in November 1989; Evans provided a perceptive overview of leading Soviet and Western analyses of the composition of the Soviet working class.

6.   See, for example, David Lane, *Soviet Society under Perestroika*, Unwin Hyman, Boston, Mass. 1990; Walter D. Connor, *The Accidental Proletariat*, Princeton University Press, Princeton, NJ, 1991; Blair A. Ruble, 'The Social Dynamics of Perestroyka', *Soviet Economy*, April-June 1987, pp. 171–83; 'The Soviet Union's Quiet Revolution', in George W. Breslauer (ed.), *Can Gorbachev's Reforms Succeed?* Berkeley-Stanford Program in Soviet Studies, Berkeley, CA, 1990, pp. 77–94; and 'Stepping off the Treadmill of Failed Reforms?', in Harley D. Balzer (ed.), *Five Years That Shook the World: Gorbachev's Unfinished Revolution*, Westview Press, Boulder, CO, 1991, pp. 13–21. A similar focus is found in the works of Geoffrey Hosking, Jerry F. Hough, Moshe Lewin and S. Frederick Starr.

7.   This paragraph is based on the contribution of Walter D. Connor to the round-table 'Khrushchev and Gorbachev as Reformers', at the Annual Convention of the American Association for the Advancement of Slavic Studies in Washington, DC, in October 1990.

8.   This section was first presented at the 1991 International Summer Course on National Security at Christian-Albrechts University, Kiel.

9.   All-Union censuses have been carried out in the USSR in the post-Stalin period

roughly every ten years. Data from the 1989 All-Union census are being published piecemeal in the Soviet media. Rural/urban figures are taken from *Pravda*, 29 April 1989.

10. *Pravda*, 29 April 1989. See also CIA Directorate of Intelligence, *USSR: Demographic Trends and Ethnic Balance in the Non-Russian Republics*, Washington, DC, April 1990, pp. 4–5.

11. *Izvestia*, 29 April 1989. In the USA at that time 74 per cent of the population were urbanized; in Britain, 76 per cent; in Japan, 77 per cent.

12. Ibid.

13. *Sovetskaya Rossiya*, 11 May 1989.

14. See Lane (1990), Connor (1991) and Ruble (1867), op. cit. in note 6 above.

15. Data from the 1989 census relating to education appeared in Goskomstat, *Uroven' obrazovaniya naseleniya SSSR po dannym Vsesoyuznoi perepisi naseleniya 1989 g.*, 'Finansy i statistika', Moscow, 1990. The author is grateful to Ann Sheehy for this material.

16. Ibid.

17. L. A. Gordon and A. K. Nazimova, *Rabochii klass SSSR: tendentsii i perspektivy sotsial'no-ekonomicheskogo razvitiya*, 'Nauka', Moscow, 1985, p. 202, as cited by Alfred Evans, Jr., 'Social Structure, Social Change, and the Soviet Working Class: Changes in Theoretical Perspective from Brezhnev to Gorbachev', paper delivered at the Fourth World Congress for Soviet and East European Studies in Harrogate in July 1990, and forthcoming in a volume of congress papers being edited by Michael Urban.

18. See Elizabeth Teague, *Solidarity and the Soviet Worker*, Croom Helm, London, 1988, Ch. 14; 'Redefining Socialism in the USSR', in John Tedstrom (ed.), *Socialism, Economics, and the Challenge of Perestroika*, Westview Press, Boulder, CO, 1990.

19. *History of the Communist Party of the Soviet Union (Bolsheviks). Short Course*, Foreign Languages Publishing House, Moscow, 1939, p. 1.

20. *Moscow News*, 1988, no. 45, as cited in Julia Wishnevsky, 'First Shoots of a Civil Society', Radio Liberty, *Report on the USSR*, 4 October 1991, no. 40.

21. *Argumenty i fakty*, 1991, no. 40.

22. *Izvestia TsK KPSS*, 1990, no. 4, p. 113.

23. *The Guardian*, 27 April 1991.

24. See Kevin Klose, *Russia and the Russians: Inside the Closed Society*, Norton, New York, 1984, chs 1–3.

25. See Philip Hanson, 'The Serendipitous Soviet Achievement of Full Employment: Labour Shortage and Labour Hoarding in the Soviet Economy', in David Lane (ed.), *Labour and Employment in the USSR*, Brighton, Wheatsheaf Books, 1986.

26. See David Granick, *Job Rights in the Soviet Union: Their Consequences*, Cambridge University Press, New York, 1987; Peter Hauslohner, 'Gorbachev's Social Contract', *Soviet Economy*, January-March 1987, pp. 54–89. Granick, Hanson and Hauslohner presented their views at the round-table, 'A New Social Contract? The Implications of Economic Reform for Job Security in Eastern Europe and the Soviet Union', at the Fourth World Congress for Soviet and East European Studies in Harrogate in July, 1990.

27. Teague, *Solidarity and the Soviet Worker*, p. 322.

28. Donald Filtzer, *Soviet Workers and De-Stalinization*, Cambridge University Press, Cambridge, forthcoming; 'The Contradictions of the Marketless Market: Self-Financing in the Soviet Industrial Enterprise, 1986–1990', mimeo nd.

29. Albert O. Hirschman, *Exit, Voice, and Loyalty*, Harvard University Press, Cambridge, MAs., 1970.

30. Central Television, 18 September 1986.

31. Radio Moscow, 19 September 1986.

32. *Izvestia*, 1 July 1987.

33. *Izvestia*, 12 June 1990.

34. For details, see Dawn Mann, Robert Monyak and Elizabeth Teague, *The Supreme Soviet: A Biographical Directory*, RFE/RL, Munich and Center for Strategic and International Studies, Washington, DC, 1989. Workers fared even worse in the spring 1990 elections to the RSFSR parliament, when no more than 5.6 per cent of those elected were classified as workers.

35. Elizabeth Teague and Philip Hanson, 'Most Strikes Politically Motivated', *Report on the USSR*, 24 August 1990, no. 34; Elizabeth Teague, 'Ethnic Tensions Remain Main Cause of Work Stoppages', *Report on the USSR*, 12 October 1990, no. 41.

36. *Pravda*, 14 October 1989.

37. *Trud*, 6–9 September 1989.

38. *Trud*, 24 and 25 October 1990.

39. *Trud*, 19 and 20 September 1990.

40. *TASS*, 18 April 1990.

41. See the contribution by Louisa Vinton to the round-table 'Trade Unions in Post-Communist Society', *Report on the USSR*, 11 October 1991, no. 41.

42. Contribution by Judith Pataki, ibid.

43. Author's interview, Moscow, October 1991.

44. For an assessment of inflation rates and changes in real consumption, see UN Economic Commission for Europe, *Economic Bulletin for Europe*, United Nations, New York, 1991, no. 43.

45. Ibid.

46. Data from the Goskomstat report in *Ekonomika i zhizn'*, 1991, no. 43, possibly referring to only nine republics.

47. L. Pronina, 'Pensioner i rynok', *Ekonomika i zhizn'*, 1991, no. 41.

48. *Russian Television*, 28 October 1991.

49. Elizabeth Teague, 'Tackling the Problem of Unemployment', *Report on the USSR*, 8 November 1991, no. 45.

50. *Izvestia*, 1 July 1991.

51. *AP*, 9 July 1991.

52. A Zverev, 'U bezrabotitsy – zhenskoe litso', *Izvestia*, 30 October 1991.

53. Author's interviews, Moscow, October 1991.

54. *Ekonomika i zhizn'*.

55. Taking part in a round-table discussion on 'Soviet Workers and the Politics of *Perestroika*' at the National Convention of the American Association for the Advancement of Slavic Studies, Miami, FL, November 1991.

8. The Emergence of New Family Farmers: The Countryside of Estonia in Transition[1]

Ray Abrahams

This chapter focuses on the current re-emergence of family farming and accompanying transformations in state and collective agriculture in Estonia. Broadly similar processes are also taking place throughout much of Eastern Europe and the Soviet Union. In the wake of recent affairs, it is scarcely necessary to note here that Estonia was a small independent country of Finno-Ugric speakers in the 1920s and 1930s, and that it is now beginning a second period of independence after its enforced incorporation in the Soviet Union in the 1940s. Pre-Soviet Estonian agriculture was comparable to that in many other parts of northern Europe, and it has been among the most productive and efficient in the Soviet Union. This should be borne in mind, along with the relatively late imposition of collective farming in Estonia, when comparing the contemporary situation there with that in older Soviet republics such as Russia.[2]

My research was conducted in 1991 at a time of rapid change and much uncertainty about the viability of new farms and the adaptability of state and collective enterprises and their workers to new demands. New legislation is awaited on land ownership, and the scale and impact of different kinds of foreign aid are still unclear, as is the future of the Russian market for Estonian farm produce. Party politics are only just emerging.

THE COLLECTIVE AND ADMINISTRATIVE SCENE

As in other erstwhile Soviet republics, two main sets of formal institutions have been operating in contemporary Estonia at the local level. These are the village soviets (*külanõukogu*) and the collective and state farms. Both at present face the prospect of reform and even, in the case of farms, of dissolution, though resistance to this has begun

133

to crystallize in some sections of society. The village soviets have recently been renamed *vald*, a term harking back to pre-war independence.

Two major trends can be identified in the development of large-scale agriculture in Estonia. There has been some tendency for farms to expand through the amalgamation of smaller units into larger ones, and there has also been some movement from collective (*kolhoos*) to state farm (*sovhoos*) production.[3] This has only been a partial shift, however. In most regions of the country the number of collective farms and their combined areas are substantially greater than those of state farms, and there is no longer an official preference for state farms. It appears, moreover, that the formal differences between these two types of organization (in the first the workers are in some sense the collective owners and in the second they are state employees) have not always been as great in practice as one might expect, and the word *kolhoos* is sometimes used loosely to refer to either form. Direction from above by the farm's leadership and by the Party have been a common feature of both kinds of institution for much of their history, and ordinary people's preferences appear often to have focused more on the character of leaders and on economic factors than on constitutional principles and differences. Thus the issue of being an employee or a shareholder seems to have been less interesting to many workers than the security and size of income which one institution or another has been able to offer at different times; and in any case both forms have been seen by most people as alien institutions imposed by an occupying power. Recently, however, some differences have been emerging a little more clearly. It appears that the new democratic tendencies, which have become visible in most areas of Estonian society, are more easily realized in a *kolhoos* setting with its internally elected leadership committee. At the same time it has also been suggested to me that, as *kolhoos* and *sovhoos* try to become competitive enterprises in a modern economic setting, the appointed and more authoritative leadership of a *sovhoos* director and his staff may have advantages for efficient management.[4]

The areas in which the research was carried out fell mostly within the territory of Edasi *kolhoos*, in Võru region, and Kalevi *sovhoos* in Saaremaa.[5] Both were fairly large establishments by Estonian standards, though considerably bigger ones exist in some areas. Edasi *kolhoos* covered an area of 11 549 hectares in 1989, and had four main divisions including one devoted largely to producing apple juice. There are at present about 1300 adult members of the *kolhoos*, and about 500 of these are *kolhoos* workers, while many of the rest are pensioners. There were about 7500 hectares of fields in 1989. There were about 1200 milk cows (now about 900 while a cowshed is being renovated) and over 4000 pigs. There is a wide range of agricultural and other machinery, and there are large machine repair shops equipped with lathes, drills and iron-forging and welding equipment. The farm was built up to its present size by the gradual incorporation of several different farms, and the creation of four subdivisions followed a realization that it had become too large to run from a single centre on a day-to-day basis.

Kalevi *sovhoos* was formed in 1965 from two collective farms to which a third was added in 1971. There are now about 10 000 hectares of land but not all of it is in good condition. There are about 220 *sovhoos* workers, more or less equally divided between the sexes. The farm mainly produces milk and meat. There are about 750 milk cows and a little over 2000 heifers, calves and young bulls bred for meat. Last year there were 2000 pigs, but the number has been drastically reduced since then, to around 600, owing to fodder supply problems. As in Edasi, there is a wide range of machinery and there are many large buildings for livestock housing, grain processing and storage, and machine repairs. Both farms also have some centrally situated housing, mainly in the form of flats, but it is important to note that many past and present workers live on house sites which belonged to former family farms in different parts of the farm territory.[6]

In both areas the territories of the collective or state farm and of the village soviets are more or less the same, and they share the same administrative buildings. In Saaremaa both units had the same name, Kalevi, but in Võru the soviet and farm had different names. This territorial linkage was a fairly new development in Kalevi and it seems that it is common elsewhere. Despite the overlap between them, the *vald* (as it will be called from now on), with its own staff and committees, is nonetheless a formally separate organizational unit from the state or collective farm. It acts as a registry office for records of births, marriages, deaths and population movement, collects local taxes, and its council has now been vested with the power to process land applications from new family farmers. It also provides some local services such as a library and a kindergarten in some areas, and it is expected to have an increased role in the school system. It is also possible that it will in time take over some of the welfare functions of the local *sovhoos* or *kolhoos*, for example with regard to housing provision and pensions, and possibly leisure facilities. The maintenance of such welfare services in years to come is an important issue which is often raised by those who are opposed to the collapse or abolition of state and collective farms. On the other hand, even some of their supporters seem to feel these days that they will best survive as hard-headed economic enterprises with considerably smaller workforces, even if this means unemployment and hardship for many of their present workers.

There is considerable consultation between *vald* and state or collective farm, and this is not surprising when the latter are the main employers and producers in their areas, and when the *vald* council processes requests for land. The degree and direction of influence from one institution to another is another matter, and difficulties can arise. I was told that the proposal to create a new smaller soviet in Kalevi originated from the local *sovhoos* director, who is rumoured by some to have had ambitions to increase his power through the move. However this may be, some conflicts over policy have arisen between *vald* and farm. One source of these is the creation of new farms and the threat to the *sovhoos* which they are seen to constitute. This threat arises most practically from the loss of land and labour which the new development entails, but there is also the broader ideological challenge which the small-scale private sector now presents to such large-scale enterprises.

NEW DEMOCRATIC PROCESSES

The present Kalevi *vald* was created as a new village soviet in February 1990 by dividing the previous much larger unit in two. This followed a referendum on the issue, in which a large majority voted for the change. The referendum was held only after someone had argued that there ought to be a clear demonstration of popular support for the *sovhoos* director's proposal, and the director is said to have seen this, not unreasonably, as a challenge to his ability to speak for local people in such matters. In addition elections were held to choose a 'chairman', who would oversee the creation and establishment of the new council, and three candidates stood for the post. When the new council was established there were further elections, and 11 places apparently being contested by 14 candidates. Such contests seem to be a new departure from the earlier pattern in which officials apparently sifted out various candidates who would be nominated and elected without competition. In addition, the new council's decisions are not quite so strongly dominated by the small group of individuals – not all on the council – who constitute the *vald*'s executive committee (*täitevkomitee*). These are typically local bureaucrats and/or technical experts, and one does not need to go to Estonia to see such influence exerted.

A further important aspect of the situation is of course the collapse in the last year or two of Communist Party dominance and even membership, which has fallen drastically in this and other localities.

INSTITUTIONAL RESPONSES TO CHANGE

The response of state and collective farms and other state enterprises to new challenges and problems have been varied. There have already been a number of privatizations, but these have been almost wholly confined to non-agricultural establishments. Thus Saare Kalur, the big fishing collective on Saaremaa, has become a limited company, as have one or two state building and state transport enterprises there. Similarly the large Kirov fishery *kolhoos* outside Tallinn and also some factories have gone private. But the transformation of the many large-scale grain and livestock farms – which constitute the bulk of state and collective productive institutions – seems to be more problematic. There appear to be a number of related reasons for this. Firstly, it is not at all clear that such farms constituted truly effective production units even in Estonia, which has probably had the most efficient agriculture in the Soviet Union; and their situation these days is especially difficult. As has been noted, large-scale state and collective agriculture is seen, reasonably enough, as an alien imposition by an occupying power, and many of the foundations on which the successful running of such farms was based have been increasingly eroded in recent years. Absenteeism and poor work discipline are said to be on the increase, and pilfering and misuse of farm property are common. Those who try to impose discipline are, it seems, likely to be branded as diehards or 'red barons' – a term which nicely merges Soviet and feudal idioms. Also their future is uncertain as they have lost land to the new individual farmers and may lose yet more under new legislation.

Only one case was found where clear plans for privatizing a large farm have been formulated and a serious attempt at implementation has been made. Väimela *sovhoos*, in Võru region, at first did relatively little beyond allocating land to some workers who wished to farm for themselves, but last year its directorate began to develop a more coordinated plan in the light of the organizational problems mentioned above. They claim, not implausibly, that many of the holdings which individuals will acquire will be too small to be viable, and they say that they are also interested in safeguarding the future of workers who do not wish to farm for themselves. The plan involves the creation of a number of large farms, each of about 900 hectares, and these are being run as cooperatives which it is hoped will eventually become companies in single or corporate ownership. The directorate do not seem to have reacted negatively to demands for land for family farms, but claim now to know how much land is required and how much will be left for these larger-scale plans. How well the plan will work has still to be seen, but it is interesting as constituting much more than the common pattern of ad hoc reactions to individual requests for land and the growing problems of trying to manage an enterprise which is gradually running down.

Edasi *kolhoos* provides an example of this. The farm seems so far to have reacted to the new situation in a positive but piecemeal way. In 1987 it allocated 20 hectares of land to Mart S. on a contractual basis, and he became Estonia's first new private farmer. The main terms of the agreement were that he should provide for the *kolhoos* as much produce as they would expect to have got from the land under collectivized production, and the rest he could keep for himself. He easily met this demand, and he was later able to increase his land holding and become a relatively free agent. Since then Edasi land has been allocated to many other members who have requested it, and the amount of land which members can have at their own disposal while continuing to work on the farm has also been increased from 0.6 to 3 hectares. This seems to have been intended as a sort of palliative, but it has had negative effects according to some officials there. Workers have been tempted to spend more time on their plots and less at work, and absenteeism has become a problem.

Kalevi *sovhoos* has so far reacted in a similar way but there are signs of serious change. After a period in which substantial numbers of new private farms were started, the director has tried to put a brake on new developments, and possibilities for privatization of a sort comparable to those in Väimela are being considered. Meanwhile the director has issued a verbal warning to his drivers not to use *sovhoos* machines to help new farmers, and he has delayed access to further land for new farms until at least the autumn. He has also sharply cut back the farm's labour force in a drive to increase farm efficiency. Although he has something of a reputation as a 'red baron', he seems much more a businessman than a committed communist. In interview he came across as a man keen to maintain his own economic interests and those of the *sovhoos*, and as one who is taking as tough a line as he can with the competition in the form of the new family farmers.

THE NEW PRIVATE FARMERS

The contemporary emergence of family farming in Estonia harks back directly to pre-soviet days. The pattern in the countryside in the 1930s and early 1940s was rather similar to that in Finland at that time. Post-independence land reform resulted in a wide distribution of land ownership, though many farms were fairly small. In Kalevi area in the 1930s, around 30 per cent of farms were under 10 hectares and 45 per cent were between 10 and 30 hectares. The situation seems to have been broadly similar in the Edasi area, though it should be said that bigger farms seem to have been more common in some other parts of the country. These farms were then collectivized in the late 1940s, with some of the bigger farmers sent off to Siberia as *kulaks*, and it is, broadly speaking, the same farms which are being re-established under current legislation.

The contemporary legal position is in fact extremely complex, since the legislation necessary for the full establishment of land-owning farming families is not yet complete. An early period of individual collective and state farm decisions, made apparently with Moscow's blessing, allowed a few farmers like Mart S. to get started, and this was followed in 1989 by an Estonian farm law. This allowed the owners of farm houses and house sites to apply to farm the land previously attached to these farmsteads. Ownership of such houses and house sites has been obtained in a variety of ways. Often the owners are members of the original farming family, but sometimes distantly related kin, or even unrelated friends, have been left the property by will. In other cases the property has been bought, most commonly from previous owners or their heirs, but occasionally also from the collective or state farm itself whose ownership seems mainly to have arisen through the dying out or disappearance – sometimes in Siberia – of the original farming family. The legal status of some of these transactions may be open to question and it is not yet altogether certain whether the allocation of land to those in possession of a former farm house or house site will be liable to some form of contestation or redefinition in the future when property rights are clarified by new legislation. A commonly expressed viewpoint is that some compensation may have to be paid to those former owners or their heirs who are not in actual possession of the land and have not formally surrendered their rights to it. Whether this is actually the case, and who will have to pay such compensation – the new farmers or the state at one or other level – remains to be seen.

There are now several thousand new farmers in the country and the numbers of those applying for land to farm are rising every day.

Many of them only obtained their land this year and have yet to get properly started. The educational and career backgrounds of such people vary quite a lot. Several of those encountered are graduates of the Estonian Agricultural Academy in Tartu, and many more have special training and skills in such fields as engineering or livestock management. A number have held managerial positions in collective or state farms, and some have been school teachers. Others are less educated and have worked at lower-level jobs on the large farms, perhaps as tractor drivers or milkers, while others have worked as lorry drivers or builders. For most of them, however, the move to private farming has not been a totally new step. Older ones were children in the 1940s when private farming was still going on, and the large majority of them have kept up their own small plots and livestock holdings at home in addition to their formal employment on a large farm or elsewhere.

ACCESS TO MACHINERY

A major difficulty facing almost all new farmers is access to machines which are in good condition and appropriate to the scale of their activities.[7] Those who got started by the late 1980s have been better placed in this regard than later starters. They were able to buy machinery relatively cheaply before inflation in both official and 'free market' prices became too much of a problem, and there was also less competition than at present for machines and other goods in short supply. Some of them, like Mart S. and Uuno S., who was the first Saaremaa new farmer, attracted attention in Finland and Sweden, and they were able to get special help from there. Such help is still available – local communities in Gotland and in southern Finland, for example, have been sending over old machines to Saaremaa – but it has to be spread more and more thinly. Some people clearly foresaw this problem: one woman farmer told how her brother, who was a distinguished *kolhoos* chairman and himself opposed to private farming, had advised her that, if she wanted to farm, she should do so as quickly as possible.

New farmers have been able to mitigate these problems of machine supply in various ways. Some of them have jointly bought new or second-hand machines and some machinery donated from abroad has also gone into joint ownership by small groups of farmers. There is also a considerable amount of exchange of help between farmers and this seems on the whole to be preferred to paying and receiving cash and vodka for such work, though this is sometimes necessary. One factor here is the ever-diminishing value of the ruble, but there is another, broader, issue of the value of persistent relationships as against short-term monetary transactions. This is not of course restricted either to Estonia or to farmers, and it is a well-known feature of Soviet society and economy more generally. People are constantly dependent on their connections to others for all sorts of basic supplies. According to one joke, it is announced that capital punishment is to be abolished in the Soviet Union. Its replacement is to be a harsher penalty of '15 years without acquaintances'.

In many areas new farmers have received help with machinery from the local collective or state farm, since few farm leaders seem as yet to have taken as hard a line as the Kalevi director. Normally the charges for such help are double those paid by farm members, and there can also be problems of timing since it may be hard to get the use of a machine just when it is needed.

PRIVATE PLOTS ON STATE AND COLLECTIVE STATE FARMS

It is well known that work on private plots has contributed substantially to the production figures of state and collective farms, since most of the milk and some of the meat produced at home was sold to and through the farms. This was even acknowledged by those in favour of the Soviet system and, in a publication on the state and collective farms of Võru region, one such supporter quotes figures for 1984 of 30.8 per cent of total milk and 22.7 per cent of total meat production in the area coming from what he calls the 'individual sector'.[8] Until recently such individual holdings were supposed to be only 0.6 hectares, sometimes with access to hay land and pasture, but they have increased in many places in the last two or three years, as was mentioned for Edasi *kolhoos*. Even on smaller plots, families have tended to keep themselves in potatoes and other vegetables, and often grow strawberries and other fruit. They also commonly keep one or two milk cows, a couple of pigs and perhaps some sheep and chickens. In some cases it is difficult to distinguish between such farm workers' smallholding activities and those of the new independent farmers. Indeed it was pointed out that some farm workers' families can produce substantially more than many a new farm on their private plots, especially if one or more family members are machine operators.

A particular example, albeit rather an extreme one, may be useful here. Sirje K. is 39 years old and drives a tractor for the local *sovhoos*. She lives at her father's old place, and the farm used to have about 36 hectares of land. She is married, but her husband, who is a hard-working but rather quiet man from a village a few kilometres away, prefers her to represent the farm to the outside world as *peremees* (farmer, master, literally 'man of the family'). They live there with her mother, who is a former *sovhoos* worker, and three sons aged 20, 19 and 9. Her husband is a *sovhoos* lorry driver, and the two older boys are tractor drivers for the *sovhoos*, like their mother. By last year they had managed to get the use of almost seven hectares of hay land and a similar amount of arable, but this year the *sovhoos* director has been cutting back such allocations. Even so, they still manage to get six hectares, since the allocations are for separate individuals and their families, and the two older boys have managed to have themselves defined as separate units even though they live at home and are unmarried. Nonetheless they fear that things might get worse, and they have decided to put in a claim for land from the old farm. They will only ask for half the land in question and they would not have bothered if the *sovhoos* director had not started to be difficult about land allocations for the workers. They have more livestock than many of the better-stocked new farms. They have six milk cows, 12 heifers, four young bulls, nine pigs including a breeding pair, nine sheep, and about 50 chickens. They produced a little over 20 metric tons of milk last year and they have been getting about 2500 kilos per month this year. This means an income from milk alone of about 2000 rubles per month on top of their salaries as *sovhoos* workers, which are probably around 300–400 rubles each before extras.

When they formally set up the new farm it will be registered only in Sirje and her husband's name, and the boys will continue to work on the *sovhoos*. The great advantage of such work for them is their access to machinery, rather than the wages it brings in. They can use the machines they drive for themselves, and they can make deals with other drivers to exchange help with them. The *sovhoos* should be paid for such use, but it is not clear that this always happens. In addition they have acquired some machinery from the *sovhoos* for themselves. Such machinery is sometimes written off after a period of years, even if it is still in quite good condition, and it can then often be bought by its driver. Sirje's husband bought a lorry from the *sovhoos* in this way; they paid only 3000 rubles for it earlier this year, as against a probable free market price of 30 000 rubles. They have also acquired other machines in similar fashion, and they have bought yet others for themselves through other channels. Consequently their own stock of machinery rivals that of many of the better-equipped new farmers and far outstrips that of very many others. In addition they are building a new house for the boys with *sovhoos* help.

This is an extreme case of a family which does a great deal of profitable farming for itself without having been tempted, until recently, to apply for the return of land and formally register as private farmers. It is sometimes said that the 'individual sector' can help to put a brake on radical change to the collective system, and this and several other less extreme cases seem to offer some support for this view.[9] Yet, as experience in Edasi shows, and indeed as the hardening attitudes of the Kalevi director also suggest, it has been hard to keep this sector under tight control and to maintain an equilibrium between it and the state and collective farms under whose umbrella it operates. At the same time the private plots have also helped to keep the people's hand in, as it were, in readiness for the re-emergence of private farming. It is clear that Sirje K. and her family hope that the *sovhoos* and their connections with it will not collapse completely, but they are also relatively well set up to survive and even prosper as family farmers in their own right if this happens.

ALTERNATIVES TO FARMING

There are still many people in the rural areas who do not wish to farm. Secretarial and book-keeping staff on a state farm, for example, often lack the necessary interest, skill and access to a labour force, and many older people are in a similar position, especially if their children live in towns and have become used to urban life. Some individuals with technical expertise also prefer to take their chance as consultants of one sort or another, if the state and collective farms collapse. Some such people also have no claim to land, but it is worth noting that not everyone who now intends to claim land wants to farm, though whether they will succeed in getting it under new property reform legislation passed in the summer of 1991 is unclear. I have met several people who want to make a claim before the current January 1992 deadline simply because it seems sensible to obtain a title to land rather than to let it lapse. Some of them hope that younger members of the family may wish to farm, or that there may be something to be gained from later sale or rental of the land to others. One man, who has already been allocated land under the Farm Law, grows almost nothing on it. He allows a neighbour to farm some of it for the sake of appearances. He has a flat in the nearby town and uses the farm house site as a base for a small building materials factory where he employs a couple of young men to make cement blocks and also local-pattern roof tiles on old machines which he has renovated. He also has some valuable pre-war car and lorry bodies and spends some time renovating these. There is apparently much money to be made from such rare treasures: in Võru it was said that some Swedes had offered to cover the substantial costs of transporting used farm machinery there if local farmers could find them an old BMW motor-cycle.

THE VIABILITY OF NEW FARMS

It is very probable that many of those who do begin to farm will fail to make a go of things. Shortages of machinery and materials, and produce prices which fail to keep pace with inflation, are likely to create serious problems for many, and relatively few farmers have the capital to withstand a long period of difficulties. The absence of large privately owned timber holdings, which have been a vital form of capital for Finnish farmers in recent decades, is especially noticeable. Of course all this has to be considered in the light of the relatively poor incomes and the ever-rising prices which are now the lot of many collective and state farm workers. And there is also the desire to turn one's back on the whole Soviet system. One new farmer I met had claimed his land and begun farming with his son. They had a fourth share in an old tractor which had come from Sweden and they had shown great ingenuity in adapting old horse-drawn machines and even cobbling together a small three-wheeled 'tractor' out of a suitably modified old motor-scooter. They had a few sheep and three pigs, and they had so far got very little income from the venture, but they said proudly that they at least produce food for themselves, and that they did not earn much anyway when they had jobs. And the man proudly proclaimed, 'Olen vaba mees!' ('I am a free man').

Many of the more successful farmers also show considerable adaptability and ingenuity. Some have been able to put their mechanical skills to good use both for themselves and as a valuable service for their neighbours. Some are also experimenting with new forms of income generation. One former state farm vet has specialized in breeding nutria which he sells for their skins and also for their meat, which is processed for human consumption. Another family has a more conventional farm but also breeds polecats. Some too have strong entrepreneurial talents and are involved in a wide variety of business activities. Thus one farmer concentrates successfully on milk production on his own farm, but he sometimes also trades as an agent for other produce in the Leningrad area, where factories are willing to exchange building and other materials for food. He also earned hard currency last year by looking after Finnish tourist groups and small groups of hunters who come down to hunt wild boar, and he expects to entertain some hunting groups again this autumn. He is rather exceptional in the scale and the wide scope of his activities, and he is the only farmer so far met who employs a full-time labourer – his sister's husband – on the farm. This farmer also works on many of his business ventures in partnership with his wife's brother, who relies solely on such activities for his own income.

CONFLICTS AND NEW POWER BASES IN THE RURAL SECTOR

Local conflict arising from the creation of new farms was mainly visible in Kalevi where it largely took the form of strain between the farmers and the *sovhoos* directorate, as outlined above. This was to some extent a special case, which was partly dependent on the past history of relations between those involved, but it clearly reflects new structural tensions in both the political and the economic sphere. The leadership and influence of the old guard has been eroded by the new developments, and new claims to economic and political power and status are emerging. Some of the more successful new farmers are already earning far more than they did as administrators, specialists or labourers in the public sector and some of them have begun to make their voices heard politically in *vald* and wider contexts, including even the occasional parliamentary candidature. In some cases encountered, former Communist Party officials had changed sides radically and applied their old political expertise to new roles as representatives of private farmers' interests. There was, predictably, considerable suspicion of the motivation and reliability of some such individuals, and it was felt that they might easily turn back again if it proved expedient to do so. Such suspicions were not, however, typically voiced openly, and most people seemed content to wait and see. This may partly have reflected a more general caution and uncertainty about the future, but it was also clearly recognized that a large proportion of Communist Party members had been under pressure to join the Party and that most of them were 'radishes' – red on the outside and white underneath.

As yet there is relatively little sign of other conflicts. At the level of relations between neighbours, a striking feature was the way in which some older people who have claims to land, but do not wish to farm themselves, have willed their houses over to others who might wish to do so. Similarly some of the new farmers provide generous help to neighbours, and especially the old and infirm. It is easy to see hard-headed strategy in all this, but there is also some sense of moral community at work in such cases. Nonetheless it is clearly possible that further conflicts will develop, especially if new farmers emerge as a relatively well-off class, while others suffer as collective and state farms become less viable. Some farm workers and other villagers are already said to be annoyed that the new farmers obtain special privileges, for example with taxation, to help them get started, and that they have also received aid from overseas, not only with machinery but also with supplies of scarce consumer goods such as sugar.

It is also possible that such issues will gain more attention as party politics develop. The Agrarian Centre Party (*Maa-keskerakond*) is strongly in support of the development of private family farming, while the Agrarian League (*Maa-Liit*) is more strongly in favour of gradual change and the maintenance, if locally desired, of state and collective farm structures. There are sharp differences of opinion between them about the significance and ownership of land and the rights (and also the character) of collective and state farm workers who might not wish or be able to farm for themselves. With a few notable exceptions, there was relatively little interest among farmers in these parties in mid–1991. Partly this stemmed from a suspicion of the motives of the national and other Party leaders, who were often said simply to want power, but some people were also worried, with some justification, that the new direction of changes could easily be reversed and that it was better to keep one's political head down. The coming of independence may now change such attitudes.

More important than political parties for most farmers was the National Farmers' Union (*Eesti Talupidajate Liit*) and its local branches, in which membership does not imply allegiance to a party. All new farmers and some intending ones seemed to be members, and they received a great deal of help through the union, which organized many of the vital overseas contacts as well as the distribution of machinery and other help which came through these. Local leaders of the union work very hard, and few of them seem to want to keep their posts for long, since they are subject to constant demands for information and help as farmers try to cope with the many problems and uncertainties which face them. A few of these leaders are among the former Communist Party personnel mentioned earlier, and a reluctance on the part of others to do such work may also partly account for their current acceptability. Many collective and state farm managers and directors belong to regional 'Producers' Associations' which are nationally confederated. Like the Farmers' Union, these associations distance themselves formally from party politics, though overlaps in membership in both cases suggest some affinity between them and the Agrarian Centre Party and Agrarian League, respectively. Unlike the associations, however, both parties seek a broader support base than either new farmers or old farm management can provide, and this is especially true of the League which vigorously claims to represent the interests of all sections of the rural population, rather than those of the 'red barons', as its opponents like to argue. In their turn, and taking the opposite tack, League politicians rarely fail to tell one that the chief spokesman of the Agrarian Centre Party – albeit unlike many of his colleagues – is a city academic and professional politician rather than a countryman and farmer. Meanwhile many farmers so far see little benefit accruing to themselves from the party political arena, and their main interest in the Farmers' Union is in the special services they can receive through membership.

BACK TO THE FUTURE?

The uncertainties of the contemporary situation make it very difficult to foresee how family farms will fare during the next few years. A common opinion expressed locally by those in favour of such farms, as well as those against them, is that probably at least a third of them will fall by the wayside. Some see such a failure rate as a potential source of further land and increased prosperity for more successful farmers, while others see it as a justification for maintaining large-scale institutions, which may themselves be able to benefit from the opportunity to reacquire land from those who fail. Some of those who see a more efficient, trimmed-down family farming sector in the future also expect that some failed farmers and some of the people currently employed on state and collective farms will need to be absorbed as labourers on more successful private farms. Others foresee increased migration to the towns, perhaps accompanied by the movement of new landowners from town to country. However this may be, it is clear to many farmers and non-farmers alike that the kind of freedom in which the 'vaba mees' quoted earlier so bravely rejoiced, is unlikely to do much for his or for Estonia's prosperity. The present system is in some danger of recreating both the farms and many of the farming conditions of the 1940s. In this situation it must be remembered that, while this farming pattern was destroyed by the Soviet collective system in Estonia, it was also radically transformed during the same period in nearby capitalist Finland and Sweden. Consequently its resurrection seems likely to be only a first and possibly a short-lived step to further substantial change.

NOTES AND REFERENCES

1. The research on which this chapter was based was carried out in summer 1991 on the island of Saaremaa and in Võru region. The research was supported by a grant from the ESRC as part of its East-West comparative research initiative. I am very grateful for help from the Estonian Academy and especially Professors J. Kahk and A. Park. I am also much indebted to G. Grünberg, M. Haab, E. Kuusman, M. Ligi, T. Pehk, M. Saldre and many others in Tallinn and in the two areas in which I worked.

2. For a history of Estonia see T. V. Raun, *Estonia and the Estonians*, Hoover Institution, Stanford University, 1987. For a valuable general discussion of decollectivization, see F. Pryor, 'When is Collectivisation Reversible?', *Studies in Comparative Communism*, March 1991, XXIV, 1, pp. 3–24.

3. Cf. Raun, *Estonia*, pp. 176f. and 200f.

4. The significance of these two forms of institution for local populations has varied both historically and locally in the Soviet Union. D. Anderson, in 'Property rights and civil society in Siberia' (forthcoming in *Praxis International*) notes how Evenki hunter/herders see *sovhoos* organization as a strong threat to their land rights which early forms of *kolhoos* protected.

5. These are not the real names of the two farms in question.

6. Patterns of settlement differ strongly between the two areas in which I worked. Võru region, like most of rural Estonia, has scattered settlement, whereas there are compact villages in Saaremaa. A number of such villages are to be found in an area the size of Kalevi *sovhoos*.

7. Shortages of building materials and the failure of produce prices to keep pace with inflation were other problems regularly reported.

8. Cf. A. Männiste, *Haanjamaa Leib*, Eesti Raamat, Tallinn, 1987, p. 25.

9. Cf. S. Hedlund, *Private Agriculture in the Soviet Union*, Routledge, London, 1989, p. 2 and *passim*.

9. Soviet Youth

Jim Riordan

There are moments in history when young people take the national stage and make a decisive impact on events. Such was the case in the West in 1968, when many youthful rebels made the qualitative leap from particular grievances to universal transformation, challenging hierarchy, institutional totems of bourgeois culture, gender, discrimination, racial oppression and the colonization of everyday life by the state and militarism. Such was the case in Eastern Europe in 1989, when young people were instrumental in revolutionizing their societies: in Romania, Poland, East Germany, Hungary, Bulgaria and Czechoslovakia, even Lithuania, Latvia and Estonia. Their collective pressure brought down governments, introduced tentative democracy and gained the right to free speech, travel and elections. This chapter examines the part played by youth in the unfolding drama in the erstwhile Soviet Union since *perestroika* was launched in 1985.

DEFINITION

It is important to establish from the outset what 'youth' means. For the concept is uncommon to Britons (unlike *molodyozh, jeunesse, Jugend*) who confine youth to the teenage years. The Soviet Union, like continental Europe and UNESCO, sets broader parameters: roughly from age 15 to 30. This makes Soviet youth a sizable body of people – slightly less than a quarter of the entire population of 291 million. In 1977 there were some 70 million persons in the 15–30 age group, but with the falling birth-rate the number declined to 64 million in 1987.[1]

The variations in social and economic development between regions of the USSR are so vast that young people may well be born and grow up in utterly different historical epochs. Such variations range from barely literate juveniles in remote areas of the Soviet Far North and Central Asia to the well-educated (a full 6–17 schooling) in most of Central Russia, the Ukraine and Belorussia, as well as the three

Baltic states. In one and the same republic young people may engage in primitive farm work (such as milking cows by hand three times a day) and space research. In the country as a whole they comprise 43 per cent of the 158 million able-bodied workforce and over 50 per cent of people employed in advanced technology (electronics, computers).[2] In social terms the differences are also great. In the Central Asia republics it is customary for native girls to marry early (15–16), have large families (six or more children) and live by Islamic *shariat* (arranged marriage, payment of bride price, secondary female status). At the other end of the country, in the Baltic states, however, marriages are relatively late (24 for men, 22 for women) and most couples have one-child families.

So Soviet youth is a fairly abstract notion. Any discussion of youth 'in general' can lead to crude conclusions and gross errors. All the same, to gain an overview of young people, we will consider survey material which, for the first time since the 1920s, provides a more or less realistic portrayal of Soviet youth.

HISTORICAL ROLE OF YOUTH

Young people have sometimes played a prominent role in Soviet history and, at least initially, were entrusted with leading positions. For example, the average age of Red Army commanders in the Civil War was 27. Of the first seven Komsomol leaders (up to 1938) three were under 20 (one was 17) and four were under 27 on taking office.[3] Lenin himself, 47 when the Revolution took place, was known in the Party as *starik* (the 'old man') – a mere stripling, of course, in comparison with Brezhnev's Politburo 'geriatrics'.

Young people made up the bulk of the fledgling Red Army, they were the battering ram used against religious citadels in the 1920s, the shock force of industrialization and the collectivization of agriculture; they were the cheap, reliable and dynamic labour force employed in building the railways, blast furnaces, power stations, canals, dams and the vast iron and steel mills in steppe, taiga and tundra; later they cultivated the virgin lands in southern Siberia and Kazakhstan. Until recently, students helped bring in the harvest each September and worked on construction brigades in the summer vacation.

The noteworthy feature of the youth role, however, is that young people were steadily pushed so far into the background of power that they found themselves, by the mid–1930s, virtually outside the historical process. The number of under–30s in administration declined, thereby producing decrepitude in the rulers and indifference in the ruled. After 1938 no Komsomol leader took charge aged under 35 (seven years over the Komsomol age limit). While lauding young people for their labour enthusiasm, the Soviet leadership in all spheres grew to *fear* youth for its political activity. Even when the Party had wiped out all other youth organizations and brought to heel its own youth wing, it still found it necessary to execute six of the first seven Komsomol leaders in the late 1930s.[4]

Outside politics, Party paternalism everywhere implanted wary, distrustful attitudes. The spiritual basis of this paternalism was dogmatism and authoritarianism; the acme of good manners was 'communist consciousness' – the ability of the disciple to memorize and repeat a 'catechism' after the teacher, without deviating from society's political and ideological norms. In culture, paternalism meant intolerance and repression. Any aspect of independent youth culture, or subculture, in art, music, dance, fashion (short or long hair or skirts, wide or narrow trousers, plaits or beards), science, literature or general demeanour was not tolerated. Youth creativity was stifled at birth. The natural youthful desire to create a subculture as protest against the cultural traditions of the older generation was regarded as an assault upon society's political edifice; it could therefore only exist clandestinely. This led to the emergence of an underground culture and market, an orientation towards, even obsession with, Western youth culture, frequently in its extreme variant, and a distorted emulation of that culture's attributes.

Another consequence of paternalism and 'stagnation', particularly for young people born and brought up in the Brezhnev era, has been apathy and indifference to political processes and ideas. By contrast with the radical youth of the early Soviet years and of Eastern Europe in the late 1980s. Soviet youth have been noteworthy for their absence from the political stage. The processes of *perestroika* and *glasnost* received their impetus from the middle-aged, the 'men and women of the 1960s', who received their political education and stimulus – and hope – during the Khrushchev 'thaw'. The Gorbachev leadership tended to cultivate this group, especially those who retained a belief in idealism, in humanitarian and socialist values, and ignored young people as a support and motive force for *perestroika*. What is remarkable about young people during the 1985-August 1991 period of *perestroika, glasnost* and democratization is that they did not participate actively in the new political parties, local councils and parliaments – or in the top political process in general. The reasons for this must be sought in the pervasive disillusionment felt by young people with the values and institutions of their own society, and the extent of their alienation from politics.

YOUTH AND THE KOMSOMOL

Anything originating outside the Komsomol, even constructive youth initiatives, ran into bans and persecution. This applied to the song and poetry clubs, the jazz groups, youth housing cooperatives and various socialist political societies of the 1960s. Such activity was often punished by individuals being expelled from school or college, or from the Komsomol (so putting a black mark on future character references) and sometimes by criminal prosecution. For example, Valery Andreyev, leader of the popular rock group Arax, spent two years in gaol, the youth activist Boris Kagarlitsky was imprisoned for 13 months for publishing a Eurocommunist journal, and Boris Grebenshchikov, leader of Aquarium, was expelled from the Komsomol, sacked from his job and banned from singing in public.[5] Youth deviance from adult-prescribed behaviour was therefore punished severely. In 1980 as many as 78 per cent of all 14–29-year-olds found criminally guilty were sent to prison or labour camp; significantly the figure had fallen to 55 per cent by 1989.[6] Young people were therefore reduced to being a transmission belt for adult experience and values. Any deviation from the norm was seen as a betrayal and a failure in youth training.

The extent of youth revolt against the Komsomol has been strikingly apparent in several surveys, which reveal that the Komsomol was *the most unpopular institution in the USSR* (more so than the Party, the KGB or the Trade Ministry!).[7] The lack of trust came partly from the fact that the Komsomol was perceived as ignoring the interests of young people, with its leaders more concerned with feathering their own nests than attending to youth issues. Partly, too, the lack of popularity was due to the fact that *perestroika* and its consequences undermined the prestige of all official organizations, the Komsomol included. As the revelations mounted of the Komsomol's implication in the crimes of the past (the personality cult, purges, extermination of all opposition, distortion of history, stagnation, links with the security forces, corruption and debauchery) so the revulsion grew. The Komsomol was generally seen as a stick with which to beat young people. It did not escape attention that two previous Komsomol leaders (Semichastny and Shelepin) went on to become security police chiefs or, as the 21st Komsomol Congress (April 1990) materials revealed, that 42 000 Komsomol members were still employed by the KGB.[8]

The unpopularity was reflected in the rapid decline in membership. As recently as 1987 the Komsomol aspired 'to encompass the entire younger generation', since 'constant growth in the Komsomol's ranks is a sign of successful activity and authority among young people'.[9] Its junior wing, the Young Pioneers, set its sights on embracing *all* 9–14-year-olds. Yet within a few years not only was the monopoly of the Party-controlled youth organization broken, but it began to disintegrate swiftly. In September 1990 the Pioneers formally broke with the Komsomol and Party, becoming the Federation of Children's Organizations, which firmly rejected politics and ideology, swapped its red neckerchief for a blue one, and its old Scout motto 'Be Prepared' for the new 'For Country, Goodness and Justice'. By 27–28 September 1991, the Komsomol had no more than 19 million members, a loss of 25 million members since *perestroika* began. It therefore decided to dismantle itself.[10]

THE KOMSOMOL AND ELITES

In the last few years the accusation has grown that the Komsomol was a 'state within a state'. Maria Pastukhova, herself a member of the Komsomol Central Committee Bureau, has written that 'The Komsomol Central Committee is a state within a state. Many people see the Komsomol not as their organization, but as a nest of gentry functionaries.'[11] A group of leading Komsomol members called the Komsomol 'A whole state within a state, with a smooth-running machine of rank and vassalage, a strict, ramified hierarchy of jobs, unwritten rules and traditions.'[12]

Most damning of all was a report by Victor Graivoronsky, First Secretary of Moscow's Gagarin District Komsomol Committee, in *Moskovsky komsomolets* in April 1990. He termed the Komsomol apparat the 'System' whose core constituted 'more than a 100 000-strong apparatus (one functionary to every 250 ordinary Komsomol members) on whose maintenance is spent the astronomical sum of 400 million rubles'. Graivoronsky detailed the extensive material privileges of the 'System': over 1300 people in the apparat of the Komsomol Central Committee received an average salary of between 350 and 820 rubles a month (at a time when the average pay of young workers was 130 rubles a month). But salaries were not the chief perquisite.

There were the

cars and special polyclinics, the rest homes and sanatoriums, the state dachas, trips abroad and offices, and the three-room apartments given to all Komsomol Central Committee functionaries for half the year. All this, including the half million rubles allocated under the 'remedial' label for strenuous work, creates a powerful stimulus for lower-ranking officials of the various apparatuses to rise to the higher apparatus, it binds them much more strongly than any satisfaction from simply telling the truth.[13]

Significantly the biggest bone of contention at the 1990 Komsomol Congress, and one that raised the hackles most visibly, was the proposed tax on Komsomol property – a rise from 35 per cent to 55 per cent. It enflamed passions so much that some delegates proposed a picket of the USSR Supreme Soviet. The new tax, it was claimed, could lead to the closing of over 400 000 youth enterprises.[14]

What has been apparent over recent years is the alacrity with which the

Central Committee apparatus has begun . . . to acquire cost-accounting centres and associations. Between August 1989 and August 1990, it set up some 20 subsidiary structures with staffs of nearly 500 people and foundation funds of hundreds of millions of rubles. This is where the old Komsomol *nomenklatura* has shifted its employment.

(Graivoronsky, 'Kuda letyat milliony'.)

The new-found economic enterprise on the part of the Komsomol led to the establishment of 'youth scientific centres', the Youth Bank, the Association of Training Cooperatives and a host of other enterprises. All of them found a guaranteed source of income from the Komsomol coffers. For example, the Komsomol Central Committee invested 750 million rubles in the Youth Bank.

Naturally, it is presented as yet another magnificent step in improving the lot of young people. In fact, all profits from the Bank go to the Komsomol Central Committee; the same applies to profits from publishing activity, the commercial enterprises and membership fees in hard currency from joint foreign institutions.[15]

Of late there has been a mad rush to jump onto the commercial bandwagon, 'using young people's property with which to do so'.[16] What is interesting is the facility with which yesterday's Stalinists have become today's businessmen, fired by the same self-assurance that it is all for the good of young people! A major reason for erstwhile Komsomol structures and officials turning themselves into thriving business corporations is that, until 1989, Komsomol commerical organizations, like the youth scientific centres, were practically the only institutions permitted to transfer credit into ready cash; revenues were virtually tax-exempt.

One of the most distasteful aspects of this new spirit of enterprise is the lack of scruple shown by Komsomol businessmen in their striving for profit. It is the Komsomol that organized the first beauty contests in 1988 and that planned to stage bullfighting in Moscow's Lenin Stadium in 1990. It is Komsomol newspapers and journals that in the latter years of *perestroika* have begun to feature scantily-clad or naked young women in sexually provocative poses. As *Moscow News* has said, 'most of the clubs that show trashy videos round the clock are owned by the Komsomol. Most of the erotic art exhibitions and beauty contests are run by the "Komsomol economy" '.[17]

A price had to be paid by the 'System' for being permitted to carry on its money-making enterprises.

> The System must have guarantees for existing from other, more powerful Systems in the form of the state, the CPSU, the Trade Union Council, etc. A price has to be paid in loyalty. In exchange come guarantees in all manner of resolutions on strengthening Komsomol monopoly rights on economic enterprises, entry into prestigious universities and institutes, employment in certain professions (the Foreign Ministry, KGB, etc.). In gratitude, the agencies and leaders of the Komsomol always observed the rules of the game, not poking their noses into politics, getting on with youth communist education as laid down by the current Party leadership . . . The juniors of the System assist the elders to preserve the image.[18]

In the wake of the attempted coup of 19–21 August 1991, much of the Komsomol's formal property (educational institutions, printing works, administrative buildings) has been sequestered; other Komsomol enterprises swiftly switched patrons and began to operate on a self-financing basis. Thus, while the Centre for Youth Research was shut down, the neighbouring Institute for Youth Studies (recently the Higher Komsomol School) continued its work under the Ministry of Labour. Several Komsomol functionaries moved into commercial business, while others found a home in other 'non-political' youth organizations, such as the Committee on Soviet Youth Organizations. Some Komsomol periodicals changed their names: for example *Molodoi Kommunist* is now *Perspektivy*, others have long been democratic 'flagships': *Komsomolskaya pravda, Moskovsky komsomolets* and *Sobesednik*.

YOUTH AND PERESTROIKA

Disillusionment with the Komsomol and the Soviet past has produced in some young people a frustration, bitterness and alienation from the older generation and society. Among others, however, the democratic changes of the past few years have presented opportunities for genuine participation in social change, self-expression, defence of democratic gains and pushing back the frontiers. Often students have been in the vanguard of the latter just as they were in Western Europe in 1968 and Eastern Europe in 1989.

It was students of school and college who forced the authorities to remove compulsory communist studies from the curriculum of all educational institutions (History of the CPSU, Marxism-Leninism, Political Economy). They have helped to de-ideologize and demilitarize schools and colleges by making the authorities remove the Octobrists, Pioneers, Komsomol and pre-conscription training units. They have engineered the democratic election of faculty heads and college principals. And they have halted the use of cheap student labour for harvesting and construction brigades.

The most successful example of student action was that of Kiev University students in October 1990. Two years previously, Ukrainian students had formed their first independent student organization, 'Gromada', which agitated for the universal use of Ukrainian in all educational institutions in the Ukraine, and the independence of the Ukraine. In December 1989, the Ukrainian Student Union (USU) came into being, one of the first fully independent student unions in the entire country. While 'Gromada' remained primarily nationalist, the USU campaigned mainly for student rights (higher grants, radical changes in social science teaching and a boycott of university military faculties). Other Ukrainian student associations appeared: the Democratic Student Union and the Student Fraternity. These three organizations openly acknowledged their debt to Chinese, Czechoslovak and Bulgarian students for the tactics they employed.[19]

From 2 to 17 October 1990 the students occupied Kiev's Revolution Square, where the Ukrainian Parliament is housed, and they declared a hunger strike. They called for the resignation of the Prime Minister of the Ukraine (which they achieved), the dissolution of parliament and the holding of new elections on a multi-party basis (also achieved); further they wanted a new law on the nationalization of Party and Komsomol property (later achieved) and on the option for conscripts to serve in their own republic (granted). One press correspondent summed up the action of the Kiev students as follows: 'For the first time in the nation's history, young people have acted as the main political opposition to a system that seemed invincible just a few years ago.'[20]

The success of the Ukrainian students inspired similar actions elsewhere. Thus the newly-formed Moscow Student Union and the student 'Echo' group staged a 24-hour hunger strike on Red Square coinciding with a meeting in late October 1990 between President Gorbachev and official student leaders. Their demands were also political: resignation of the central government, nationalization of Party and Komsomol property and the abolition of conscription. Out of this Moscow-based student organization came the establishment on 1 August 1991 of a countrywide student strike committee – the first in Russian and Soviet history. The immediate demands of the committee are for an alternative form of conscription for students, the right to conscientious objection and far-reaching reforms of the armed forces.[21]

It is largely students who have been active in forming 'non-political' children's and youth organizations as alternatives to the Young Pioneers. Moscow students, for example, staged the first congress of the Russian Scout Movement in Moscow in November 1990 and organized Scout camps in the Crimea during the summer of 1991; some 300 young people attended the camps of an organization founded in Russia back in 1909 but proscribed by the Soviet regime in 1924.[22]

Students are not alone in acting for progress and defence of democracy. It was particularly ex-conscripts, many in their battle fatigues and the blue-and-white striped paratrooper vests, who formed the self-defence units protecting the Russian Parliament during the coup. Two of the three young defenders who were killed were decorated veterans of the Afghan war. The reforms of recent years have also brought into being a plethora of independent youth groups. Such is the pace of change that it is difficult to grasp that they have only been lawful since May 1986; no youth organization could legally exist without Party permission prior to then. Of course informal youth groups have been around for much of Soviet history: the Scouts, YMCA, Sokol, Poteshnye and various religious groups in the 1920s; the poetry, guitar and jazz clubs, debating societies and *stilyagi* of the 1960s, the rock groups and sports fans of the 1970s, and the vigilantes (the 'cleansers' or 'purifiers') of the early 1980s.

As *perestroika* matured, however, several observers noted a distinct change of mood and tactics that brought a new wave of informal groupings which was much stronger and more irresistible than previous ones. The upsurge engendered many groups and methods that were novel to Soviet society. The 'informals' were learning they could not only fight each other, but they could also learn from one another, exchange information and organize concerted action. Major cities witnessed an unlikely alliance of punks, hippies, skinheads and heavy metal fans, organized to oppose self-righteous vigilante groups. The informals also became increasingly political as they found officialdom on the retreat, unable to resort to its old repressive measures owing to *perestroika* and *glasnost*. In this uncertain period, from the 'May events' of 1987 when mass protest demonstrations took place, open clashes became regular occurrences in the big cities, involving hippies, rockers and neo-fascist groups.

Bans on demonstrations (such as that imposed by Moscow City Council on 23 August 1987) gave rise to new tactics: petitioning and direct action. This led to the blossoming of ecological and heritage protection movements. According to *Kommunist*, the country had a single youth nature protection unit in 1960; by 1970 there were 11, by 1978 57, by 1985 96 and in 1987 as many as 121.[23] The number is probably double that in 1992.

Among specifically political groups, the 1980s spawned a large number of previously unheard-of groups impatient with the distortion of socialist ideals, of Marxism, Leninism, and Russian and Soviet history. There appeared the Young Marxists, Young Leninists, Genuine Revolutionaries, the Internationalists, the Young Bakuninists, the Young Bukharinists, the Alliance (Anarchists), the Democratic Socialists, Eurocommunists, Young Trotskyists, even Young Stalinists. As an example, the Nostalgics (*Nostalgisty*) come together on the basis of moral, aesthetic and political interest in the past; they dress in the manner of their preferred period and associate themselves with its music, literature and political values, so there are Nostalgics of the 1920s (subdivided into advocates of New Economic Policy and War Communism), the 1930s, 1940s and so on. At the other end of the political spectrum are the Optimists, who focus attention on contemporary domestic and international problems; they oppose consumerism, drug and alcohol abuse and profiteering, regarding them as a brake on social progress. Being 'highly intelligent and politicized', they organize themselves into various 'think tanks' and exclude women on the grounds that women are insufficiently intellectual. Pacifists are to be found in various groupings, particularly the hippy movement, but as a separate group they campaign for peace, unilateral disarmament and renunciation of nuclear testing; they also oppose conscription. The Anarchists subdivide into several groups: anarcho-communists, anarcho-individualists and anarcho-syndicalists. The Confederation of Anarcho-Syndicalists, which claims 500 activists in 30 cities and publishes *Obshchina*, *Volya* and *Zdravy mysl*, espouses

Gandhian-type non-violence in its campaign for the demilitarization of society, decentralization and the transition from technocratic to ecological thinking.[24]

Such largely socialist-oriented informal associations have tended to fade into the background in the early 1990s under pressure of events, particularly in the aftermath of the coup. With the Soviet communist model in disrepute and East European socialism in disarray, the popular mood would seem to be predominantly anti-socialist or apolitical. Only 20 per cent of young people polled in 1989 believed in socialism, and as few as 8.4 per cent felt that the future belonged to communism.[25] It would be an illusion to think that all young people, or even a majority, are interested in politics. Not more than 15 per cent of young people are at all politically active.[26] At best, the 'silent majority' reads newspapers, watches television and observes the 'political game' from the sidelines – some with distrust, some with distaste, some with indifference. Some young people are drawn to oriental philosophies, but the most discernible trend is towards a resurgence in religious faith, mostly that of Russian Orthodoxy in European Russia and Islam in the Muslim areas of the country. One survey showed that as many as 55 per cent of young people in seven urban centres declared their belief in God.[27]

Another important tendency is the rise of a consumerist-hedonistic ideology. With mounting lack of confidence in authority and disillusionment with Soviet life generally, perhaps it is natural that many young people should look to Western youth culture with its rock music, trends and fashions. Thus have appeared punks and heavy metal fans, hippies and rockers, skinheads and breakdance fans. But if the new liberalization has created legal opportunities for liberals and Western-oriented youngsters, it has also produced an ultra-patriotic, conservative backlash from some young people determined to combat liberalization itself, just as the Black Hundreds and other right-wing groups did in the 1905 Revolution. In the last few years a motley assortment of youths in and around urban conurbations have been forming their own clandestine vigilante groups to fight what they perceive as anti-social behaviour.

The borderline between 'noble' vigilante groups (which contend with corruption, bureaucracy and officials who abuse their position) and gangs of 'patriotic' thugs is thin and mobile. While the common foe would seem to be 'people harmful to society', the perception of 'villainy' differs, as do aims and methods. The Rambo-style youth cult known as the 'lyubery' have more ambitious objectives relating to society as a whole and they espouse violence in pursuit of their mission. Their victims are largely Westernized youth, and sometimes Westerners themselves. The 'lyubery' impose a strict discipline upon members, requiring initiation tests of neophytes (like beating up punks) and they possess a hierarchical structure, with leaders who are sometimes older ex-servicemen, especially those who have served in Afghanistan – the so-called Afgantsy.

The name 'lyubery' comes from the Moscow industrial suburb of Lyubertsy, some 12 miles south-east of the capital; its teenage gangs have been terrorizing neighbouring urban centres for years. Today they are joined by other 'hurrah-patriots' like the 'Russian Knights' from Khimki, the 'Bolsheviks' (!) from Bolshevo, the Beryozka gang which mugs foreign-currency clients of the Beryozka stores, the Remont gang whose aim is to 'repair' the damaged psychology of young people whom they regard as insufficiently patriotic – hippies, punks, Nazis and heavy metal fans. Other cities have the Furagi, named after the old-fashioned caps they wear; these are valiant fighters against all Western and imported fads. Irkutsk has its Kufayechniki, who wear prison-type jackets and mete out rough justice to anyone who takes their displeasure. The Striguny of Volgograd crop the heads of young women suspected of having contacts with Westerners. More recently the 'cleansers' have had new recruits from a variety of *ulichnye* gangs that patrol urban centres. They include Nabat, Mukhomor, Appache and the Black Hundreds. On the whole, members of such streets gangs come from a low educational background or are runaways who find their 'courage' in glue-sniffing, drugs or home-made alcohol; some live in the (central heating) basements of apartment blocks.[28]

Many cities are plagued with teenage gangs, especially on housing estates, many of which are said to be 'no-go' areas for young 'outsiders' and the representatives of law and order. The gang problem 'exploded' in the early years of *perestroika*, so that already by 1987 a journalist could write:

> the scope of mindless action is vast; it encompasses a variety of activities: from skirmishing to full-blown battles . . . drug-taking, gambling for huge stakes and hostility between rival youth gangs. This is an entire generation of young people from the age of ten to 30; it amounts to tens of millions of people.[29]

The rash of senseless cruelty extends back to children as young as eight or nine, and is portrayed in many contemporary films, such as Roman Bykov's *Chuchelo* ('Scarecrow') in which a schoolgirl is burned to death by her classmates while grown-ups turn a blind eye to her plight.

A survey of various informal youth gangs by Leningrad sociologists in late 1989 made some startling revelations. First of all, the gangs were composed mainly of under–16s, 70 per cent boys, 30 per cent girls. As many as 52 per cent said they had fights regularly with other gangs, usually to defend 'their territory' and sometimes to harass ethnic groups from other republics (Russians and Ukrainians in the Baltic, Moldavia and Central Asia; Central Asians, Siberians and Transcaucasians in the Slav and Baltic areas; Europeans (by Tatars) in Kazan, the Tatar capital – and vice versa). Virtually all of them accepted violence as the only way to resolve conflict, and fewer than a quarter were prepared to take part in socially useful activities. Some 70 per cent admitted that all gang members drank heavily (spirits) and 46 per cent said 'free love' existed within the gang.[30]

Such gangs parcel off their cities into zones which each gang patrols, giving them appropriate names: 20th Precinct, Hillview, Filth, Footwear Store and so on. The distinguishing 'badge' of gang members is often a knitted 'pompom' hat of a particular colour (known as 'tea pots'). The police are often powerless to intervene or gather information on ringleaders, coming up against a wall of silence. A more recent name such gangs give themselves is *motalki* (somewhat equivalent to 'drop-outs').

Much research was done on Kazan gangs after the public had been shocked in the mid–1980s to read newspaper reports of teenage street battles which had left a number of dead and hundreds of injured. Kazan gangs use all manner of home-made and stolen weapons, from guns to grenades and Molotov cocktails. According to recent police figures, the city has 68 terrorist teenage gangs, a fifth of which are fully armed, and 80 per cent are said to have forced under-age girls into sex. The gangs also run protection rackets, forcing parents to pay (from 100 to 300 rubles) so that their children will not be harmed. Interestingly enough, some gangs consist entirely of girls, who mug lone men and specialize in robbery.[31] It is no exaggeration to say that much of the city of Kazan lives in as much fear of teenage gangs as Chicago did of its adult gangsters in the 1920s. As with Chicago, the situation is exacerbated by the racial admix, Kazan being roughly equally divided into native Tatars and Slav immigrants.

The worsening economic situation has driven many of these gangs into the arms of the adult mafia, which often arranges comfortable jobs for the teenagers – in bars, sports clubs and video salons; the mafia thereby inveigles disaffected and prospectless youngsters into its various drug, prostitution and protection rackets. The desperate need for money, the pervasive anti-social sentiments, the yawning generation gap and the disintegration of the family (not to mention the Union) are all contributing to the escalating gang warfare and its accompanying racial clashes.

The extremists who are causing the older generation most concern are those professing Fascist sympathies. Although the extreme right is active in society and exhibits plainly racist, neo-fascist tendencies (in such organizations as Pamyat, Patriot, Rodina, Otchiznya, Otechestva, Molodaya Rossiya and Rus) and is ever eager to exploit young people as 'storm-troopers', the young 'fashiki' generally differ from their nominal counterparts in the West. In a totalitarian society some young people react in a totalitarian way: extremes breed extremes. A 1989 youth survey showed that 10 per cent of young people considered the use of force necessary to achieve democracy![32] Frustrated aggression among young people may well be channelled into the various nationalist parties and armies that could expand in the immediate future. The bloody ethnic clashes of recent years have actually been 'youth actions' insofar as 90 per cent of their participants were young people. There lies the gravest danger to budding democracy.

To sum up, in a relatively brief period, independent youth groups have constituted a movement embracing most young people. To be an 'informal' is more prestigious than not to be one. The groups are extraordinarily diverse: some are of a subcultural nature (hippies, black marketeers, gangs, neo-fascists), others are eager to display civic initiative, like the environmentalists and the various charity groups; yet others organize themselves around their favourite music or art or sport. Despite the diverse names, interests and causes, however, most exist in the form of relatively small clubs of like-minded members, embracing no more than 100–150 people. The small, parochial and transitional character of the vast majority testifies that no real mass youth, let alone political, movement exists in the country today. None of the informal groups can claim to reflect or defend the interests of a substantial number of young people. None yet come close to replacing the disgraced Komsomol.

The reason for this may well be that for years young people were in a state of social anaemia, debarred from displaying any initiative. They therefore lost the habit of self-organization. Even now, when history is in the making, young people in their overwhelming majority exempt themselves from all important political and social movements. The lack of a mass youth organization to replace the Komsomol is all the more paradoxical in that the many problems concerning young people's social status and their position in the labour market and consumption sphere are bound to become more acute in the immediate future. In other words, young people are confronted by the need to move from small informal groups to a youth movement for their own legal defence and protection.

THE FUTURE

Young people may be estranged from the old system, yet surveys show that they do not yet believe in establishing a new economic order. When asked, however, if they would prefer to work abroad, 16.4 per cent of 1600 young people said they would take a permanent job abroad and 65.8 per cent said they would work for a short time 'to see what it was like' – some 82 per cent were prepared to take the first chance to leave the country and live abroad, if only temporarily.[33] It is evident that the West could only accept a small proportion of these 50 million people, but such is the sad verdict of the younger generation on their own society, which could well face a 'brain drain' of enormous proportions, the loss of the best-qualified personnel and the most enterprising young people. Even 23 per cent of 600 12–14-year-olds, surveyed in 1991 at their Crimean summer camp, Artek, voiced their desire to leave the country.[34]

The economic and political processes are set against a background of deteriorating living standards that are particularly affecting young people. What can a young person think of *perestroika* if his or her monthly wage is a mere 130 rubles when the official 'social minimum' – that is, 'poverty level' – is 283 rubles?[35] What can a student think if his or her monthly grant is only 40–45 rubles? What can a young married couple think with an average monthly income of 220 rubles? How can young people think of building a new society if only one in ten young workers has a separate apartment, and if seven out of ten live in a hostel strictly divided by the sexes, or have to rent a room?[36] Of 4000 young people surveyed in 1989, 42 per cent said they were disappointed in *perestroika* and only 22.3 per cent expected things to improve in the near future.[37] Even among 12–14-year-olds, a mere 22 per cent trust their political leaders.[38] So there is much pessimism about the future, much lack of faith in politicians.

Some young people are searching for new values, new constructive goals based on human rather than class values. But there is another part of the younger generation which is growing impatient with the sluggish pace of change and the deepening crisis; this section of youth looks to negative, destructive solutions, thereby reinforcing their own sense of anomie and alienation from society.

The future is unpredictable; some believe the country is on the brink of civil war or, perhaps, several civil wars. The course would seem to lie in the militant nationalism of some republic leaders, the unstable mix of ethnic groups within the future sovereign states, the populism of certain politicians, perhaps even yet the intrigues of old Party cadres, the military and KGB. Yet the principal danger might well come from an unexpected source: disaffected young people. It is unexpected because, in their preoccupation with global politics, neither the politicians nor the public seem to realize how explosive the youth situation is, especially when faced with a possible unemployment figure of some 25 million within the next five years. It could even be that young people will become the gravediggers of democracy. On the other hand, there are those young people who believe that, while *perestroika* was 'a revolution of people in their forties', the repulsion of the coup heralded the start of a genuine youth revolution.[39] We shall see. One thing is clear: the constant feature of youth is that, unlike other social categories, it does not last forever.

NOTES AND REFRENCES

1. Igor Ilynsky, 'Perestroika sostoitsya yesli', *Molodoi kommunist*, 1987, no. 12, p. 15.
2. See Igor Ilynsky, 'Soviet youth: past and present', in Jim Riordan (ed.), *Soviet Social Reality in the Mirror of Glasnost*, Macmillan, London 1991, p 33.
3. Yevgeny Tsetlin was 18 when he took office in 1918, Oscar Ryvkin 19 in 1918, Lazar Shatskin 17 in 1919, Pyotr Smorodin 25 in 1922, Nikolai Chaplin 22 in 1924, Alexander Milchakov 25 in 1928 and Alexander Kosarev 26 in 1929. See Riordan, 'The Komsomol in crisis', *Coexistence*, 1989, no. 26, pp. 7–30.
4. Tsetlin, Ryvkin, Shatskin, Smorodin, Chaplin and Kosarev were all shot; Milchakov spent 14 years in a Magadan labour camp.
5. See 'Arax interval', *Soviet Weekly*, 14 November 1987, p. 13; Boris Kagarlitsky, 'The intelligentsia and the changes', *New Left Review*, July/August 1987, no. 164, p. 16
6. See Victoria Semyonova, 'Changing attitudes to deviant behaviour', in Jim Riordan (ed.), *Soviet Social Reality in the Mirror of Glasnost*, p. 158.
7. See N. Popov, 'Krizis doveriya – krizis vlasti', *Ogonyok*, 1990, no. 7, p. 3; *Argumenty i fakty*, 1990, no. 7, p. 6; *Dossier 'Vybory–90'*, Moscow, 1990, p. 7.
8. *Materialy XXI-ovo syezda VLKSM* Moscow, 1990, p. 194.
9. See *Organizatsionno-ustavnye voprosy komsomolskoi raboty*, Moscow, 1987, p 59.
10. See *Argumenty i fakty*, March 1991, no. 12, p. 8; and *Soviet Weekly*, 3 October 1991, p. 4.
11. Maria Pastukhova, 'Dengi my otrabatyvayem', *Sobesednik*, 1990, no. 6, p. 3.
12. S. Anokhin, V. Graivoronsky, V. Lepekhin, P. Romanov and M. Sotnikov, *Ocherednoi krizis ili tupik (polemicheskie zametki o komsomole)*, Moscow, 1989, p. 1.

13. V. Graivoronsky, 'Kuda letyat milliony', *Moskovsky komsomolets*, 13 April 1990, p. 1.
14. 'Trudnosti s parlamentom', *Moskovsky komsomolets*, 13 April 1990, p. 1.
15. Graivoronsky, 'Kuda letyat milliony'.
16. Ibid.
17. Yelena Tokareva, 'XXI syezd komsomola', *Moskovskie novosti*, 1990, no. 16, p. 4.
18. Graivoronsky, 'Kuda letyat milliony'.
19. Yuri Petrus, 'Golodovka: posledneye sredstvo?', *Perspektivy*, 1991, no. 2, p. 15.
20. V. Savichev, 'Studenty i politika', *Argumenty i fakty*, 1990, no. 49, p. 7.
21. Ibid. See also 'Student protest shakes Ukraine MPs', *Soviet Weekly*, 8 November 1990, p. 7.
22. Personal communication. See also 'Scouts get prepared', *Moscow News*, 15–21 June 1990, p. 2. For a history of the Russian Scout movement, see Jim Riordan, 'The Russian Boy Scouts', *History Today*, October 1988, pp. 48–52.
23. *Kommunist*, 1988, no. 9, p. 95.
24. See D. V. Olshansky, *Neformaly: gruppovoi portret v interiere*, Moscow, 1990, pp 63–5. On the Confederation of Anarcho-Syndicalists, see *Argumenty i fakty*, 3–9 March 1990, no. 9, p. 8.
25. See Tatiana Zaslavskaya, quoted in I. Savvateyeva, 'A national nervous breakdown', *Soviet Weekly*, 29 November 1990, p. 14.
26. Ilynsky, 'Soviet youth: past and present', p. 37.
27. Zaslavskaya, 'A national nervous breakdown'.
28. Olshansky, *Neformaly*, pp. 45–54.
29. A. Radov, 'Bezdelniki ponevole,' *Komsomolskaya pravda*, 11 March 1987, p. 2.
30. N. Kofyrin, 'Kto ukhodit v neformaly', *Argumenty i fakty*, 31 March–6 April 1990, no. 13, p. 1.
31. Olshansky, *Neformaly*, pp. 53–4.
32. Ilynsky, 'Soviet youth', p. 37.
33. Ilynsky, 'Soviet youth', p. 34; see also Yuri Bogomolov and L. Dobrynina, 'Kto uyedet iz SSSR', *Argumenty i fakty*, 1991, no. 29, p. 5.
34. A. Zhavoronkov, 'Deti: dengi, politika i t. d.', *Argumenty i fakty*, 1991, no. 29, p. 7.
35. See *Argumenty i fakty*, 1991, no. 3. p. 3.
36. Ilynsky, 'Soviet youth', p. 35.
37. See Marina Mulina, 'Verit li molodyozh v sotsializm?', *Sobesednik*, 1990, no. 42, p. 3; 'Perestroika: chto vperedi?', *Sobesednik*, 1989, no. 43, p. 3.
38. See Zhavoronkov, 'Deti'.
39. See Politsovet Dvizheniya za demokraticheskie reformy, 'Obrashchenie k molodyozhi', *Moskovsky komsomolets* 3 September 1991, p. 1.

10. *Perestroika* and Female Politicization

Genia Browning and Armorer Wason

The position of women in what was the USSR has always been marked by ambiguity. On the one hand, women had legal equality; on the other, the roles of paid worker, unpaid housewife, mother and active citizen weighed on women as a double, for many a treble, burden. The communist ideology of sexual equality supported by legislation, combined with systemic needs, ensured that some 90 per cent of women of working age were members of the paid labour force. It also meant that a significantly higher proportion of women had further and higher education and they entered the professions to a greater extent than women generally did in the West. Women were also evident in what have been perceived as traditionally male areas of work – science and engineering. In attitude Soviet women, especially those in the professions, took paid work as a right, had experience as union, political and social activists and displayed a self-confidence often lacking in women elsewhere. State child care provision was extensive. There was little public exploitation of female sexuality and sexual offences appeared to be less prevalent than in other industrial societies.

However these advances were not gained at the expense of male expectations. Women were over-represented in the labour-intensive, undermechanized industries and remained noticeably absent from the upper levels in all fields, and virtually non-existent in political power. Within the family the expansion of female roles was not reflected in an expansion of male roles. Parenthood was synonymous with motherhood, homemaking remained a female responsibility and biologism lurked unhindered in Soviet ideologies. The specificity of female needs was, in the main, ignored.

Perestroika marked a change in women's position, and once again the situation was ambiguous. Unemployment emerged as a threatening phenomenon particularly likely to discriminate against women. It was accompanied by ideologies which brought biologism to the fore. The shorter working day and week, proposed under Brezhnev, was put into effect with *perestroika*. Support came from many women themselves, exhausted by the treadmill of continuing conflicts between work and family. Now, with the cost-cutting needs of economic transition, social welfare provision such as child care is less likely to be provided by employers.[1]

There has been much speculation on the effects a changing economy will have, and is already having, on women.[2] There has been less discussion of how political change is affecting women. Low representation in the decision-making bodies and poor avenues for articulation of interest generally meant women were the objects of Party and state policies. There was little means by which women could recognize issues of common interest, let alone ensure that they appeared on the political agendas. This chapter questions whether *perestroika* introduced change in this area as in others.

The official line of the CPSU was that the new conditions in society enabled women to have an enhanced political role.[3] This was not a view supported by women. According to Galina Sillaste, describing a poll conducted by the Academy of Social Sciences in 1990 on women's public attitudes, 62 per cent said women were not playing a more active part in public life, and half of these thought participation had actually dropped.[4] Certainly, in terms of formal representation within state, government and Party structures, female numbers fell severely. Sillaste referred to this as 'a paradox'.[5] But it was not the only one. A second paradox was that, whilst statistically women were less represented in formal political structures, politicization, in the sense of women's awareness of their exclusion and their organization, has increased. There have been two significant developments: firstly, explicit recognition of male control and secondly, action by women themselves. It will therefore be argued that, despite the fall in female representation, the changing society afforded women political space and the opportunity to engage in a radically new kind of informal political activity.

We begin by considering female representation in the political structures and official attitudes, as expressed by the CPSU, to female participation. The significance of such attitudes is that they represented the barriers confronting women wanting fundamental change. We question the extent to which the CPSU was undergoing its own *perestroika* and consider the political outlook for women post-*perestroika*. We then look at the emergence of women's politicization and the formation of women's independent organizations. We do so by focusing on two almost concurrent events: the meeting of the Secretariat

of the CPSU Central Committee, 26 March 1991, which was dedicated
to the 'woman question', and the First Independent Women's Forum,
which took place from 29 to 31 March.

FORMAL POLITICAL PARTICIPATION

Perestroika brought no radical reconstruction of mainstream attitudes
or theoretical analysis on the 'woman question'. However the CPSU
did address the issue and by early 1991 some change in approach was
evident. From a Western perspective, some of this was more progressive than the policy of the political formations challenging for power
in the post-*perestroika* period. The first practical measures were
adopted at the 27th Congress – to reorientate the Soviet Women's
Committee (SWC) and to breathe new life into the *zhensovety*
(women's councils).[6] In March 1991, before the August coup, the
Secretariat had considered the proposals of the Central Committee's
Standing Commission on Questions of Women and Children, and
issued a resolution 'On the basic direction of CPSU work with women
and the women's movement'.[7]

Before *perestroika*, formal female representation within the CPSU,
the government bodies and the trades unions showed a consistent and
steady rise.[8] Yet a pattern continued – the greater the level of power,
the lower the participation of women. Thus, within the CPSU, women
were most represented in the primary party organizations and least
on the All-Union Central Committee. Control by the *nomenklatura*
system meant numbers represented policy, a policy which paid reference to formal equality. A woman in the leading decision-making
body marked major political change. During the Khrushchev period,
Ekaterina Furtseva was elected a candidate member of the Presidium
(1956–7). Similarly with the advent of *perestroika*, Alexandra Biryukova was adopted as a candidate member on the Politburo, replaced
by Galina Semenova at the 28th CPSU Congress. But such restrictive
use of *nomenklatura* meant little change in women's general participation and indicated the limits of Party policy on sexual equality.[9]
Furthermore Semenova's promotion took place at a time when the
power of the Politburo was being eroded.

It was always evident that the quality of female participation significantly differed from male participation. Women on the Central Committee had less powerful bases than males, and their political timespan
was shorter.[10] Given the nature of representation, how did its fall
actually affect women? In general, fewer women did not mean higher
quality. Women themselves criticized as ineffectual those nominated

through the *zhensovety* for selection by the Soviet Women's Committee to the 75 seats allocated on the Congress of People's Deputies.[11] Female functionaries of the CPSU were dismissed as not 'representing the female soul'.[12] It is this entrenched pattern of female insignificance which the political culture has inherited.

Despite the block of 75 seats, the proportion of female deputies virtually halved during *perestroika*. By 1991 there was just one woman on the Presidium of the Supreme Soviet; one in the Cabinet of Ministers. Only 18 per cent of Supreme Soviet deputies were women. In the Supreme Soviet of the RSFSR, the figure was a low as 5.6 per cent, and 5 per cent on average in the other republics. Within the CPSU, female secretaries on the Central Committees, the *krais* and *oblast* committees fell to 6.5 per cent and an all-time low of 4.3 per cent at *gorkom* and *raikom* level.[13] In Leningrad women had their lowest representation ever with only 4.8 per cent of *obkom* members and less than 10 per cent of the *Lensovet*.[14] Only three women headed *oblast* committees – all in Central Asian republics: Uzbekistan, Kyrgyzstan and Turkmenia. In 125 Republic Central Committees, *krai* and *oblast* committee secretaries, there was not a single woman.[15] The 344 female delegates to the 28th CPSU Congress represented just 7.3 per cent of the total, the lowest since the war.[16] Furthermore, by March 1991, 73 per cent of women who had left the CPSU said they had had enough of politics and rejected the idea of further political participation.[17]

CPSU RESPONSE TO THIS SITUATION

The CPSU response to this situation, encapsulated in a resolution of the March Secretariat of 1991,[18] is a useful measure of the extent of change undergone in its thinking on female participation. Prior consultation with activists from women's groups, such as the 'Committee of soldiers' mothers' and 'Nadezhda', indicated at least partial recognition of women's alternative organizations.[19] The rationale cited for addressing the issue of female participation was 'democratization'. In this context there was concern to defend the rights of individual Party members, to give women freedom to choose motherhood, professional and public activity,[20] and to utilize the specificity of women's 'humanizing' influence to establish a humane society.[21]

Despite these proposals, and a sense that the issue of female participation could not be postponed,[22] subsequent events forcibly underlined how out of step the CPSU was with reality.[23] Even without the demise of the CPSU the proposals were likely to remain passive, for two main reasons. Firstly, there was little development in the concept of gender roles. Whereas individuals like Rakhimova pointed out that the psychology of the leadership and the organization of Party committees meant women were unlikely to be promoted speedily,[24] no plans to re-educate male party members were adopted. The old paradigm of how to help women combine the roles of motherhood, professional and social activity, still remained. Posing the problem in this form prevented it from being resolved.

Secondly, CPSU perception of women's organizations, in essence, remained unreconstructed. There was careful recognition of the plethora of women's groups, references to pluralism, and the need for women both to initiate policy and to engage actively in resolving their own problems.[25] But references were grudging and the fear evoked by independent women's groups was tangible. Mention was made of the 'negative tendencies' of some groups and the 'emotional' influence of other parties and organizations. The concept of separatist women's politics was still condemned.[26] The CPSU continued to perceive its role as 'doing something for women', rather than allowing women to develop their own political space to set an agenda. In that sense the party's leading role syndrome was still evident. It is this failure to grasp the significance of emergent women's activism which illustrates how far the CPSU was from understanding the civil society which was developing.

POST-*PERESTROIKA*

Is female representation likely to improve in the immediate post-*perestroika* period? A survey conducted by the Soviet Women's Committee to ascertain attitudes and political programmes on women's issues suggested that other parties would be less likely to campaign for women's rights than the CPSU. The Liberal Democratic Party favoured the return of women to the family. The Democratic Party of Russia replied that it would deal with the issues when it was in power.[27] But this no longer represents the full picture. Women have been creating their own organizations and, in so doing, politicizing themselves.[28] Increasingly a number of women are not waiting for political parties to sort out their gender policies. The issues of male dominance of political decision making, and of women as political objects, is high on their agenda.[29] These women's groups are as yet a tiny sector of the embryonic civil society, but their existence posits a potential challenge to the present gender nature of politics and could raise the questions of female representation and women's issues onto the political agenda.

WOMEN'S ORGANIZATIONS

Although involving a minority of women, the new groups represent a broad spectrum, from 'openly feminist groups to narrowly professional ones, from organizations devoted to struggle for peace and human survival, to leagues of women voters'.[30] Female political activity, as described by Sillaste, was already developing in a variety of directions during *perestroika* – as members and supporters of political parties, movements, associations, unions, clubs, and committees, and women-only organizations and a women-only party.[31] This phenomenon marked a qualitative change from previous female activity and was a direct outcome of *perestroika* and *glasnost*.

Official women's organizations have not been entirely immune to these changes. The *zhensovety* were the official women's groups entrusted with raising women's political consciousness. These were the groups favoured by the CPSU, supported by Gorbachev and relaunched at the 27th (CPSU) Congress. Since 1989, *zhensovety* nationally have been answerable to the Soviet Women's Committee. This was intended to raise their effectiveness, but they have yet to make their mark. Although over 300 000 are claimed, many exist just in name.[32] The proposals from the Commission on Women and Children and the Secretariat resolution gave them only passing reference. Party committees were taken to task for paying them insufficient attention and asked to help 'strengthen their authority' in the workplace and living areas.[33] A poll on membership and attitude to official women's organizations gives 6 per cent as active members and 29 per cent as supporting the *zhensovety*.[34] Sillaste suggested *zhensovety* appeared to be closer to women's interests and to their everyday needs than the 'centrally imposed mechanical structure' of the women's commissions.[35] In fact under a third of the women questioned supported the *zhensovety* and, as with the other official organizations, over half (52 per cent) had no comment. Sillaste accepted that the *zhensovety* were 'too removed from politics and the major problems of public life'.[36] This opinion is echoed widely, *zhensovety* being characterized as 'distributors of food' rather than raisers of women's political consciousness.[37] Women have created other organizations partly as a rejection of *zhensovety*.

Although the *zhensovety* carry a double burden of ineffectuality and being perceived as officially imposed,[38] their 'independent' status, that is their lack of formal relationship to other bodies such as committees of the CPSU and soviets, potentially provided them with an opportunity for self-transformation. This 'independence' and their structure as women-only groups, has led to a few *zhensovety* taking an independent stance.[39] One of the outstanding examples has been that of the Central Aerodynamic Institute in Moscow. Its members began in 1989 by nominating their own alternative candidates for selection to the Congress of People's Deputies, and have since transformed themselves into a 'sociopolitical, civic women's association'.[40] Olga Bessolova, their chair, was an active and supportive participant of the Independent Women's Forum. The potential 'independence' of *zhensovety* is illustrated by the action of a workplace *zhensovet* in Dubna which defied the town *zhensovet* by hosting the forum.[41]

THE INDEPENDENT WOMEN'S FORUM

Three days after the discussion of the CC Secretariat resolution, on 29–31 March 1991, the first Independent Women's Forum was held at Dubna in Moscow Region. We suggest that the significance of this event lies not in the numbers of women who participated but in the way it was organized. The organizers sought to break with the political forms of the old regime. 'The major problem,' said Natasha Filippova in her plenary address, 'is that social movements consistently reproduce social structures, hierarchical structures. We need to start something new.'[42] The organizers aimed to make the Forum accessible to women active in informal, grassroots organizations, to reach women they did not know and to welcome a pluralism of views. This section aims to examine the extent to which they succeeded, and the degree of politicization of the women who attended.

How successful were the organizers in reaching beyond their own circles? About 200 women (and a small number of men) attended from 48 organizations and 25 Soviet towns and cities. In all, 36 women came from outside the cities and regions of Moscow and Leningrad. Most came from Russia. Six women came from Sverdlovsk, others attended from such cities as Vladivostok, Tomsk, Kemerovo and Murmansk. A few women attended from Lithuania, the Ukraine, Kazakhstan and Georgia. A total of 26 women from eight other countries were present as observers. A report on the Forum was published by the Institute of the Far East of the Soviet Academy of Sciences.[43] Information about the Forum participants was compiled by the Centre for Gender Studies.[44]

The Forum was advertised in the newspaper *Business Woman*, the

Moscow newspaper *Kuranty* and the Leningrad-based *Chas Pik*, and on two radio programmes: 'Sovremennitsa' and 'Molodezhny kanal'. Advertisements headlined 'Democracy without Women is not Democracy' invited applications from representatives of any women's group or organization, and from any people interested in the issues of the women's movement.[45] The organizers sought to break with elitist tradition in issuing no invitations. Applications received before a closing date were accepted on a first come, first served basis. Expecting an official invitation, the Soviet Women's Committee telephoned after all places had been allocated. The organizers' policy of granting no special favours meant their only option was to gatecrash.

The Forum was planned by an organizing committee that identified themselves in advertisements as representatives of different women's organizations and women working on the theory and practice of the women's and feminist movement. They proposed that the conference cover themes of women's rights, women as consumer objects, 'from the emancipation of women to the emancipation of the individual', the image of women in the media, women and the market, problems and prospects for the women's movement, and 'language, women and power – a feminist critique of totalitarian power'.[46]

The organizing committee was drawn mainly from SAFO, the Free Association of Feminist Organizations, a network of informal women's groups; the Centre for Gender Studies at the Academy of Sciences' Institute of Social and Economic Problems of the Population; and the *zhensovet* at the Joint Institute for Nuclear Research at Dubna. Commitment to independent activism led to a decision not to hold the Forum under the auspices of any one organization.

SAFO is a small-scale network of individual women and women's groups, based mainly in Moscow, which espouses a feminism very recognizable to Western feminists. Its main aim is to raise awareness of negative social attitudes to women. It includes Olga Lipovskaya, who produces the journal, *Women's Reading*, originally hand-typed, in Leningrad, and Tatiana Klimienkova from the Institute of Philosophy of the Academy of Sciences, who gives public talks on the oppression of women. SAFO members organized a small but successful protest demonstration against moves to petition for a ban on abortion,[47] and added a feminist voice to demonstrations against the Lithuanian crackdown in January 1991, with placards reading: 'We won't let you use women's silence.'[48] They were among the women who refused to leave the White House barricades during the August coup when asked to do so by Eltsin and his defence committee.[49]

The Centre for Gender Studies was set up within the Institute for

Social and Economic Problems of the Population of the USSR in 1990. Anastasiya Posadskaya, the director, together with Natalia Zakharova and Natalia Rimachevskaya, initially challenged orthodox thinking on women's position in 1989, drawing on large-scale social surveys of male and female behaviour and attitudes to propose that 'privileges' accorded mothers be made available to fathers and the creation of incentives for enterprises that employ higher proportions of parents.[50] They have undertaken long-term socioeconomic research at the Kamaz truck construction plant on women in the transfer to the market economy and are energetic in seeking to influence government policy on women. They were joined by the organizers of a Woman and Democracy Fund, among them Liudmila Sherova from the Moscow City Council office that liaises with informal organizations,[51] and by Olga Voronina from the Institute of Philosophy.

The Forum was conceived as a 'show of strength' for women social activists and women's organizations in the growing women's movement.[52] The organizing committee's stated aim was to promote mutual exchange of information. They felt that this would make possible a 'horizontal' unity of organizations and individual women without any 'formal' or 'informal' diktat from above. The conference report states that the organizing committee considered that it should not put forward principles, platforms or other forms of structure.[53] A second implicit aim, however, was to offer women a chance to consider a feminist perspective, as reflected in the plenary papers. Many women attended the Forum who may never before have heard feminist ideas expressed positively.

The organizers were treading a delicate path in setting a feminist agenda while at the same time seeking not to alienate the many women who believe that 'emancipation' has led to their problems. Perhaps this was possible because women are now organizing themselves, independently of a commitment to feminism, in response to the decreased participation of women in politics, growing unemployment and a sense of the need to do something in the face of the crisis in the country. It is a truism that the experience of activism generates greater awareness and a broadening of agendas, and it is perhaps an indication of the way this politicization is developing that the agenda was altered during the course of the Forum to include an unscheduled discussion of rape, a subject never publicly addressed in many years of discussing 'the women question'.

The range of groups attending the Forum is some evidence of the organizers' success in attempting to welcome difference of opinion. Some of the groups subscribed to traditional notions of women's contribution. One group called itself 'Beauty will Change the World', another 'The Love Association'. Others, which one might have expected to be traditional, were not. One single mothers' group bore the name 'Only Mothers – Who is to Blame?'[54]

Many women and groups came with a specifically political purpose.[55] Though no elected deputies attended, several women who had sought election participated. These included Olga Bessolova and Larisa Kuznetsova, mentioned above, and Kaluga executive committee lawyer Liubov Mikhailova, who set up 'NOZhI', 'An Independent Organization: Women's Initiative', when she failed to become a candidate for the regional soviet. Several women attended to represent women workers. Rimma Sharifulina came on behalf of the 'women workers' movement' within the Independence Trade-Union Workers' Association. A member of a Kuzbass striking miners' committee, Natalia Saptsina, was vocal about the needs of women miners and the need for male miners' leaders to find constructive forms of political discourse.

Sherova reported that, from what she had learnt at Mossoviet, people active in mainstream politics were wary of the Dubna Forum: the Communist Party in Mossoviet had decided not to take part and some of the democratic organizations decided not to send representatives, or told them to come, but not to identify where they were from.[56] No-one disputed the need for women to be located in political life. In her inaugural plenary paper, 'Woman as Object and Subject of Changes in the Present Epoch', Posadskaya argued that even the most progressive policies to be proposed under *perestroika* are still put forward *for* women rather than *by* them.[57] And without an independent women's movement there can be no broad-based backing for progressive policies, such as those put forward in 'A State Programme for Improving the Position of Women and the Protection of the Family, Motherhood and Children'.[58]

Valentina Konstantinova from the Centre for Gender Studies also emphasized the importance of an informal women's movement which would create opportunities for raising the level of women's consciousness, bring into practice the idea of a civil society, and work for women to take part in political decision making on an equal footing with men. She argued that democracy was a key to the emancipation of women, that women politicians be put forward with an awareness not just of general human values and democratic ideals, but of the existence of discrimination against women and a readiness to work to dismantle it.[59]

Liudmila Sherova described her study of women in the democratic movement.[60] There is a difference in the representation of women in the sociopolitical (*obshchestvenno-politicheskiye*) and the voluntary (*obshchestvenniye*) organizations. Though women form just 2–3 per cent of the leadership bodies and leadership posts in the former, 20 per cent of the coordinators of the latter are women.[61] Of 194 coordinators, 38 were women; 20 of the organizations were political, seven set up to defend particular rights, seven ecological and four cultural. Sherova believes it was the democratic nature of internal relations and the absence of quotas and formalities in these organizations that made it possible for women to take these key roles.

There was great variety in the degree of interest and awareness which groups expressed in democratic process and self-organization. At one end of the spectrum 'NieZhDI', acronym for the 'Independent Women's Democratic Initiative', was described as 'an organization of a new type', 'an independent women's voice, a network of autonomous women's groups and organizations linked by a commitment to prioritize the solution of women's problems and democratic reforms'.[62] Similarly the 'party', 'A Search for a Radical Women's Initiative', advocates the need for consciousness-raising and non-hierarchical structures.[63] By contrast, Vera Kurilchenko started her own 'United Women's Party' with an advertisement in *Rabotnitsa* asking women to write and describe their problems. She was deluged by letters and claims her party has 2000 members.[64] It is supported by Alexander Nevzorov, the controversial presenter of Leningrad television's '600 Seconds'. Kurilchenko was wary of the feminist organizers of the forum. At a subsequent meeting of the United Women's Party in Leningrad feminists were accused of links with the CIA and KGB and asked to leave.[65]

A number of strategies were put forward by different groups as to how women might gain political influence. The International (*Mezhnatsionalny*) Coordinating Centre for the Defence of Women's Rights in Social and Political Activity advocated organizing to select and prepare women for top political posts.[66] One of the few men at the conference, E. Pilshchikov, has argued the case for this in *Pravda*.[67]

There was also some discussion of working in the new political parties with the aim of including women's issues in their agendas. In her plenary paper Sherova examined policies proposed by sociopolitical organizations.[68] Of the 30 documents she looked at, 15 did not mention 'the woman question'. In most of the others women are mentioned only in their role as mothers, mothers of large families, single mothers and so on. Women are viewed as objects, and appeals are made to liberate, defend and protect her as mother, continuer of the species and keeper of the hearth. Only in four manifestos are women seen as a subject of activity. The Estonian Popular Front states that women should choose their own social role. The Interfront organization based in Latvia declares that it should be possible for parents, not just mothers, not to work. The only Russian organization to demand recognition of equal rights for women is the Committee for the Liberation of Russia.

Posadskaya advocated a number of forms for the women's movement. Primarily she recommended autonomous, informal groups where women can talk about their problems and be heard, and which will then be able to publicize their opinions.[69] There was some recognition that groups needed to develop organically, independently of each other. Olga Bessolova described the experience of her women's political group, Prologue, asserting that it was essential to go through stages of self-development to develop political experience and resources.Not all women were attracted to the idea of building small, independent groups of women. One might surmise that the value of developing a new grassroots politics to counter relations of subordination and domination was less appealing to women who had not made the connection with their own oppression. The context of political and economic crisis lent an urgency to calls for more obvious action. In subsequent discussions many called for women to 'consolidate'. One woman suggested that women should consolidate so as to execute a stabilizing role in social processes. Others favoured consolidation in favour of 'national harmony', 'the preservation of the family', or 'renewed union'. E. Gromova proposed that groups unite to realize the UN Convention, signed by the USSR in 1981, to remove all forms of discrimination against women.

Olga Bessolova opposed these suggestions, maintaining that there are not, at the present moment, constructive policies around which real consolidation can take place. In her opinion the existing groups are currently engaged in a process of defining what they are against, a necessary and important stage, but one which does not make for effective consolidation.[70] Certainly the focus at the Forum was on strategies for political participation rather than on developing policies. It was generally agreed that some kind of structure was necessary for women's groups to exchange information and coordinate and support the activity of groups around the country and a group of women agreed to meet to attempt to organize this.[71]

The Dubna Forum was attended by a relatively small number of women, but the level of organization and discussion points to increasing politicization among women. Events since the Forum would tend to support this. Women played a significant role in the August 1991 coup. According to eye-witnesses there were at times more women than men present at the White House on the first day of the emergency.[72] Outside Russia, women have begun to take 'direct action' to protest against what they perceive to be rigid nationalism. Moldavian, Russian, Ukrainian and Jewish women from several towns around Tiraspol in Moldavia organized to disrupt train services for several weeks.[73]

CONCLUSION

Perestroika failed to reconstruct the elites to include female representation. The CPSU began to address the issue, but offered too little, too late. Its Secretariat on women suggests the CPSU was undergoing change, but trailed behind the thinking of many individuals, both within and outside the Party. Its resolution indicated the limits of its concept of democratization at that time. This was most marked in its attitude to the emergence of women's political independence. Women's groups were viewed with suspicion, rather than welcomed as harbingers of civil society. The CPSU retained for itself, with limited modification, the belief that it knew best for women. Successors to the CPSU so far appear to be less, not more, enlightened on the need to address the question of gender.

The period of *perestroika* and *glasnost*, despite this, did initiate change for women. The space it afforded enabled women to voice their concerns and begin to seek with others the means for their resolution. Individual women have been projected into the political, indeed international, arena for the first time in decades. Although these remain isolated examples and do not represent general female politicization, there is a growing realization among some women that they can enter the political arena, and do so on their own initiative. The collapse of the omnipotence of the CPSU led these women to realize that not only are there other avenues for political expression, but that the totalitarianism of maleness can, and must, be challenged.

As the Dubna Forum illustrated, the range of groups is diverse. Many embrace what Shreeves refers to as a 'specifically feminine world view'.[74] There are those who determine to prepare women for political leadership and others who reject 'equality'.[75] Those groups which might challenge male dominance of power are as yet too unstable and too inexperienced. Yet there were those at the Forum who recognized the importance of the process by which women would come to intervene effectively in the political arena.

Politicized women are not a factor to be dismissed. There are now women who have tasted the headiness of discovery, of making their own decisions. Their experiences during the period of *glasnost* have provided expectations for a more democratic society. Whatever their focus of concern, the significance of women's organizations is their identification of oppression, the effect that has on the women involved, and its influence on other women.

Konstantinova maintains that a changing attitude to women, and to their political activity, is the 'litmus paper' of a pluralist political system, and that development of a civil society needs independent women's groups,[76] as a channel for women to articulate their agendas. The emergence of women's groups, however small, however seemingly unrepresentative, is necessary to ensure that women's issues not only return to the political agenda, but that, this time, women have their pressure groups and their representatives in the political power structures to ensure that they do so effectively.

NOTES AND REFERENCES

1. Andrea Stevenson Sanjian, 'Social Problems, Political Issues: Marriage and Divorce in the USSR', *Soviet Studies*, 1991, vol. 43, no. 4, p. 645. Price reform increased the cost of baby foods by 200 per cent and of children's goods by 195 per cent. For families with children, social benefits increased by an average of 60–80 per cent. *Izvestia*, 20 March 1991, p. 3, trans. 'Price Reform, What Pain? What Gain?', *CDSP* vol. XLIII, no. 12, pp. 1–5.
2. The issue has been taken up sharply by the Soviet Women's Committee. See, for example, interview with Fedulova, *Izvestia*, 6 August 1991 referred to by Sarah Ashwin, 'Development of Feminism in the *Perestroika* Era', in *Report on the USSR*, RFE/RL Research Institute, 30 August 1991, p. 23.
3. Galina Sillaste, 'Zhenshchina v politicheskoi zhizni', *Kommunist*, 1991, 8, p. 9.
4. Rosamund Shreeves, 'Mothers against the Draft: Women's Activism in the USSR', *Radio Liberty Research*, 21 September 1990, vol. 2, no. 38, p. 7. The poll, 'Zhenshchiny i demokratiya', was conducted by the Academy of Social Sciences TsK KPSS, amongst 2667 women in ten union and autonomous republics: Sillaste, *Kommunist*, p. 9.
5. *Kommunist*, p. 9. Sillaste is Dr Philosophy of Science, professor, assistant head of Department of Sociology, Academy of Social Sciences and advisor to CC CPSU commission on women and children.
6. The *zhensovety* have been widespread throughout the USSR since the mid–1950s. See Genia Browning, *Women and Politics in the USSR, Consciousness Raising and Soviet Women's Groups*, Wheatsheaf, Sussex/St Martin's, New York, 1987.
7. 'Partiya i zhenskoe dvizhenie: novye podkhody', *Izvestia* Tsk KPSS, June 1991, 6 (317) pp. 25–39.
8. Browning, *Women and Politics*, pp. 25–6.
9. Nor did Furtseva or Biryukova address the question of female representation, despite Biryukova previously having worked on the Women's Commissions. See Alexandra Biryukova, *Komissiya po rabote sredi zhenshchin pri FZMK, Profizdat, 1979*, Moscow.
10. Browning, *Women and Politics*, pp. 27–32.
11. Meeting with committee members of Ivanovo gorod zhensovet, Ivanovo, November 1989.

12. Larisa Vasileva, 'Post Congress Reflections', *CDSP*, 1989, vol. 41, no. 25, pp. 33–4.
13. Sillaste, *Kommunist*, p. 9.
14. E. I. Kalinina, *Izvestia Tsk KPSS*, p. 36.
15. *Izvestia Tsk KPSS*, p. 28.
16. Ibid.
17. Sillaste, *Izvestia Tsk KPSS*, p. 39.
18. The three-hour discussion included contributions from a number of women invited to the meeting.
19. The Committee reformed in June 1990 as an All-Union committee, 'Materinskoe serdtse', was formed by mothers to campaign for their son's release from the armed forces. '*Nadezhda*' dealt with Soviet POW's in Afghanistan: Shreeves, 'Mothers against the Draft', p. 6.
20. *Izvestia Tsk* KPSS, p. 25.
21. Ibid.
22. Ibid., p. 29.
23. Ibid., p. 27.
24. Ibid., p. 34. Yet this was being recognized increasingly: G. Litvinova, doctor of Law: 'the question is of changing men so that they understand the problem', in I. Viktorova, 'Ne pora li potesnitsya?', *Rabotnitsa*, 1991, 2, p. 11.
25. *Izvestia Tsk KPSS*, p. 27.
26. Ibid., p. 28.
27. Tatyana Khudyakova, *Izvestia*, 21 October, p. 23, trans. *CDSP*, 1990, vol. XLII, no. 42.
28. As Shreeves documents, groups which started as individualized concerns, such as the committees of 'mothers of soldiers' initially drawn together as 'loosely structured groups', p. 5, have become 'increasingly radicalised as they have encountered the indifference of the military authorities' (ibid.). Similarly with groups concerned with pollution: see Shreeves, 'Mothers against the Draft' fn. 21 pp. 5–6.
29. The goals of the 'Political Club' formed by Ivanova and Kuznetsova were stated as preparing women for political battle, to cultivate leaders from their ranks, help women generally to advance up the social ladder and have opportunities to enter the top echelons of power: Khudyakova, *CDSP*, 1990, p. 23.
30. Khudyakova, *CDSP*, p. 23.
31. Sillaste, *Kommunist*, p. 11.
32. *Izvestia Tsk* KPSS, p. 31. For more detailed discussion see Browning, 'The zhensovety Revisited', in Mary Buckley (ed.), *Perestroika and Soviet Women*, Cambridge University Press, Cambridge, forthcoming.
33. *Izvestia Tsk KPSS*, pp. 28, 31.
34. Sillaste, *Kommunist*, p. 14.
35. Ibid.
36. Ibid.
37. Valya Konstantinova, member of Institute of Gender Studies, Moscow, in Brighton, April 1991.
38. Shreeves, 'Mothers against the Draft', p. 7.
39. Sillaste, *Kommunist*, p. 15.
40. Nina Belyaeva, 'Feminism in the USSR', *Soviet Women, Canadian Studies*, Winter 1989, vol. 10, no. 4, p. 19.
41. Conversation with Konstantinova, April 1991.
42. Natasha Filippova, SAFO, member of organizing committee.
43. 'Itogovy otchet o rabote i nezavisimoi zhenskogo foruma 1991', *Pechatano-mnozhitelnaya laboratoriya Instituta Dalnego Vostoka ANSRR*. This section of the chapter is drawn from the report as well as from conversations and discussions at the forum.
44. Women's Information Network Newsheet 117218, Centre for Gender Studies, Moscow.

45. Advertisement in *Kuranty*, newspaper founded by Moscow City Council, 22 September 91.
46. Ibid.
47. *Moskovsky Komsomolets*, 5 March 1991, p. 1.
48. Personal communication from Marina Regentova, SAFO.
49. Personal communication from Natasha Filippova, SAFO.
50. 'How we resolve the woman question'. *Kommunist*, 1989, no. 4.
51. Obshchestvenny tsentr Mossoveta.
52. 'Itogovy otchet', p. 2.
53. Ibid.
54. Women's Information Network newsheet.
55. This chapter focuses on discussion of political action at the Forum. This was one of three workshops: the second was 'Women in the Market Economy'. There were many groups of women present who have started up their own businesses, or are training women to do so. The third workshop was 'Women in Contemporary Culture', with many artists and film-makers present.
56. Personal communication from Liudmila Sherova.
57. 'Itogovy otchet', p. 6.
58. 'A State Programme for Improving the Position of Women and the Protection of the Family, Motherhood and Childhood', Institute of Socio-Economic Problems of the Population of the Academy of Sciences and Goskomtrud, USSR, 1991.
59. Referred to in 'Itogovy otchet', p. 8.
60. Ibid.
61. *Samodeyatelniye obshchestvenniye organizatsii SSSR*, 1988, Moscow, ch. 1.
62. 'Itogovy otchet', p. 6.
63. Information sheet presented at the conference.
64. Conversation with Kurilchenko at the conference.
65. Personal communication with Marina Regentova, SAFO.
66. Information sheet presented at conference.
67. 'Zhenshchina – prezident, ili Igra, kotoraya stoit svech', *Pravda*, 9 December 1990.
68. *Samodeyatelniye obshchestvenniye organizatsii SSSR*, 1988, Moscow, ch. 1.
69. 'Itogovy otchet', p. 7.
70. Ibid., p. 9.
71. Ibid., p. 10.
72. Personal communication with Marina Regentova, SAFO.
73. Personal communication from A. Posadskaya.
74. Shreeves, 'Mothers against the Draft', p. 7. Members of groups such as the 'New Feminist Forum' (formed in Sochi, 4 November 1990) tend to profess the belief that a woman's politics will produce a more humane, more peaceful, 'softer' approach. This possibility remains to be proved, not only in the USSR: Viktorova, 'Ne pora li potesnitsya?', pp. 10–11. Professor Sobakin cited two female people's deputies, Starovoitova and Koriarina, as, on the contrary, giving an impression of hardness(ibid.); it is interesting to speculate that the attitude to a 'feminine' politics was in part engendered by the CPSU with its ideology of biologism.
75. In using the Dubna Forum as an indicator of women's politicization, we have not addressed the full range of groups, including those who consider that women should return to the home.
76. Konstantinova, London, April 1991.

PART III

New Inequalities

11. The New Business Elite

Olga Kryshtanovskaya

The Soviet Union is in transition from a command to a market economy which is bringing into being a new social class of entrepreneurs, business people or bourgeoisie. Such people existed in the past, but their activity was illegal; now they have emerged from the underground, they can register officially and millionaire clubs have even been formed.

DEFINITION

Before 1987 the term 'business elite' did not apply to Soviet conditions. It was only after the USSR parliament passed a law on cooperatives and other similar laws that the group of legal entrepreneurs began to grow rapidly; we may define its most successful and economically influential section as the 'business elite'. In selecting criteria to define this group we were faced with two alternatives: first, to include in the group all directors and managers of the country's leading economic enterprises. In this case, however, our sample would cover all ministers and managers of the largest state factories – that is, the *nomenklatura*, the old state elite formed by the old regime. In the new circumstances, however, *nomenklatura* status is no longer significant; economic indicators are becoming more important and the centre of public affairs is shifting from the political to the economic domain. The second alternative was to use as our key indicator the aggregate size of finance capital or a person's other assets – that is, personal wealth. This seemed to be a more relevant indicator, given the move to a market economy.

We therefore define the business elite as a group of individuals possessing large fortunes derived from the private economic sector, or those individuals who control, own or co-own private companies worth millions of rubles and having significant impact on the market.

DETERMINING THE SIZE AND STRUCTURE OF THE ELITE

We did not know either the size or the professional structure of the business elite. The business community still partly operates clandestinely, insofar as some business people are afraid of having to pay extortion money to racketeers on the one hand, and of arbitrary action against them by government bureaucrats, on the other. We therefore followed the following sampling strategy.

First, we included those individuals who openly admitted to owning millions of rubles as capital. In the spring of 1991 a group of 13 entrepreneurs set up a millionaires' club in Moscow, so it was easy to identify these members of the club. Then, through press information, we made a list of people who had publicly admitted to owning assets worth millions of rubles. This group is fairly well known and easy to identify.

Second, we drew up a list of the most successful private companies and then tried to obtain information on their directors, contriving thereby to trace a group of entrepreneurs who, although remaining in the shadows, could be identified as controlling powerful companies. We were helped in this by obtaining from the media lists of their largest advertisers.

Finally, we used specialist interviews to pinpoint wealth. Our specialists were people close to business circles; they were able to persuade some millionaires to provide the names of others who were said to own millions of rubles.

Although our sample cannot be regarded as representative, it does enable us to define the major types of Soviet millionaire. Altogether we conducted 100 anonymous interviews; only 7 per cent of our potential respondents refused to be interviewed.

SAMPLE CHARACTERISTICS

The respondents included in the sample represented the following business spheres:

- commercial banks – 9 individuals,
- stock exchanges – 21,
- joint ventures – 10,
- cooperatives – 23,
- joint stock companies – 5,
- private publishers – 6,
- showbusiness companies – 12,

- farming companies – 6,
- top managers of business associations – 8.

The average age of the 100 was relatively low – 36 years. As many as 70 per cent have had a higher education and 7.5 per cent possessed higher academic degrees; 86.5 per cent came from an intellectual background. All were male. A further indicator of social background is that a mere 2.5 per cent were born in the countryside; 53 per cent were born in Moscow and 72 per cent were married.

LIVING STANDARDS

It was not possible to establish exactly what the income level of those in our sample was. One millionaire assessed his average hourly income at 2593 rubles; others told us that an hour of their work was worth as much as 10 000 rubles. It is hardly surprising, therefore, that the millionaires have a different conception of poverty than do ordinary people. On the whole, poverty to them begins at 450 rubles a month, compared to the average monthly earned income of 255 rubles (1991). In the opinion of our sample, the average (normal) living standard begins at some 6800 rubles a month; a wealthy person is one whose monthly income exceeds 30 000 rubles.

The pattern of expenditure for our group is roughly as follows: 85 per cent is invested in business development; they spend 3300 rubles a month on food and 2500 rubles on entertainment. Understandably, married millionaires spend more on personal needs than do the single individuals; on average they 'give to the wife' about 8000 rubles a month.

It would seem that all the Moscow business people are 'workaholics', with their average working day lasting 13 hours; some work as long as 16 or 18 hours a day.

INTERESTS AND LEISURE TIME

The structure of leisure time was approximately as follows:

- 58 per cent was spent within the family,
- 38 per cent was spent with friends,
- 36 per cent was spent on reading,
- 28 per cent was spent on watching television or home videos,
- 28 per cent was spent on sport.

A quarter of those interviewed did nothing in their leisure time, or just slept. An indication of devotion to work is that one in three said he had no time for a vacation at all; 40 per cent of the sample holidayed in the USSR and 25 per cent went abroad.

As many as 53 per cent of the sample admitted to having mistresses, although very few stated an interest in women. Drinking parties featured in their lives at least once a week, usually at the weekends, and they tended to eat at restaurants every other day (it should be noted in passing that most Soviet people cannot afford to go to restaurants: the monthly salary of an ordinary employee would hardly be sufficient to pay for dinner with wine at a Moscow restaurant). In line with the above statistics on drinking parties and restaurants, it will hardly come as a surprise to learn that only 15 per cent of the millionaires do not drink or smoke, the remainder drinking frequently – six days a week.

In terms of general demeanour and beliefs, the millionaires are surprisingly conventional, even conservative. For example, 62 per cent said they believed in God and as many as 95 per cent subscribed to the concept of romantic love. It would be hard to distinguish them from the man in the street, for they tend to dress and look like most other Soviet people. Several of the Soviet millionaires have no car and as many as a quarter complain of cramped housing conditions. It is perhaps indicative that the USSR is the only country in the world where one can find a millionaire whose cherished dream is to have an apartment of his own.

SOCIAL BACKGROUND

Our biographical studies of the Moscow business elite enable us to differentiate groups according to social background. There follow some typical career histories.

Mr A. A., 37 years old, a graduate of the Plekhanov Economics Institute; worked as a Komsomol secretary at a research institute, then Komsomol instructor and a Party official, ending up as Second Secretary to his local Party Committee. He then went into business and is currently chairman of a financial and industrial concern.

Mr G. B., 23 years old, went to university but was sent down for poor attendance; up to 1987, he was engaged in black marketeering while working as a street sweeper. This followed a spell in the armed forces as a conscript and employment in a sports goods store. After 1987 he was employed in several cooperative ventures and then, in 1990, he started out in his own private business. He estimates his assets at some 10 million rubles.

Mr M. N., 53 years old, no higher education, first 'made money' during the Brezhnev period which he regards as the 'golden age' for shadow economy business – though he has spent seven years in prison. A couple of years ago he set up a small private venture with his brother and cousin, making pies and other pastries.

Mr V. S., 40 years old, took two degrees and has a PhD in the history of art; a specialist in art and an antique collector. Originally employed at the USSR Academy of Sciences and then at a museum. His business career commenced in 1988 in publishing, and he quickly made a fortune out of religious literature and books on sex, such as *How to be a Sexy Woman*.

These four case histories give some indication of the diverse age and social backgrounds of the new business elite. At the initial stage of the Soviet market, in 1987–8, business people tended to come from the two extreme poles of social hierarchy: *nomenklatura* and the 'underworld'.

Nomenklatura business people

These made up 12 per cent of our sample. All have had a successful Party or Komsomol career. The old elite made an initial attempt to enter business legally back in 1987, when each district Party committee in Moscow set up what were called Centres for Youth Scientific and Technical Creativity. Their activity was coordinated by a Council which was itself monitored within the CPSU Central Committee by none other than Egor Ligachev.

High-ranking Komsomol officials were put in charge of the centres, their main work being as 'middlemen' converting into cash the funds they received from various organizations through clearing operations. They made their profit by taking a percentage of the cash conversion for their intermediary services. This Komsomol economy enjoyed certain tax privileges, paying its patrons, the Komsomol Central Committee and the CPSU, a mere 5 per cent of the profit.

The *nomenklatura* business, which was extremely profitable and easy to operate owing to its powerful patrons, developed rapidly, so that today, when privatization is being undertaken, it has absolute monopoly over certain spheres of business activity, such as private banking and insurance, international tourism, computer sales and the video business. Before the attempted coup of August 1991, as many as 126 new concerns, 54 companies and 1500 associations came into being with the right to use state and Party property. Before the formal privatization process had got under way, half of state property had

been handed over to the privileged 'affiliated companies' set up by
the old power structure.[1]

This process was concealed from the public. The fact that we were
able to interview only a dozen *nomenklatura* millionaires veils the
actual scope of the *nomenklatura* business elite. Their companies normally have their offices directly within what were then the buildings
of the local or city Party and Komsomol committees, and their officials
are recruited from the so-called 'cleared' personnel – that is, those
from a *nomenklatura* background.

The Parvenu millionaires

This type of successful entrepreneur comes mainly from all manner of
failures – people who failed in their own trades or those who have
no trade at all. It falls into two major age groups: the 30–40-year-olds
and the 20–30-year-olds. The former consists primarily of university
graduates who failed in their careers or who were dissatisfied with
their jobs and living standards. Only 10 per cent went into a business
related to their qualifications (for example, as doctors or engineers);
the rest made a complete break with their past trades and jobs.

The younger group had no time to learn a trade; they are, as the
old song says, 'a generation of nightwatchmen and yard sweepers'.
Most went into business early, sometimes at 15 or 16, often profiteering while at school by selling or reselling imported electronic equipment or fashionable clothing. Inasmuch as 'parasites' used to be pros-
ecuted, they had to find a job, often working as nightwatchmen, yard
sweepers and the like – jobs leaving enough time for business activities.
Today they can engage in business legally.

In a similar category are the shadow economy dealers, the under-
cover millionaires who made their fortunes in the Brezhnev era. They
owned 'underground' shops, manufactured the same products as legal
factories from 'saved resources' and 'materials' excluded from official
end-of-year accounting. Most of these millionaires have criminal and
prison records, yet they now occupy a prominent position in the
economy, owing to their invaluable business experience.

THE WAY TO SUCCESS

The most profitable business spheres, according to our respondents,
are trade (75 per cent), banking (20 per cent), stock exchange (18 per
cent) and publishing (15 per cent). Most respondents believed that
1991 was an excellent year for making money ('as good as 1988');

some say that they needed no more than four months to make a million. Some brokers maintain that, given favourable conditions, they could make a million in a single week. On the other hand, those involved in making consumer goods put the length of time necessary to make the first million at between six and eight months.

Despite the existing opportunities to make 'a fast buck', as many as 90 per cent of the respondents would wish to see Western-type market relations in the country. Most believe that the introduction of the market economy is an irreversible process. At the same time, 53 per cent of the millionaires felt legally insecure, fearing that their companies could be liquidated by government agencies at any time. If that were to happen, 43 per cent said they would emigrate to the West, 24 per cent would change their business sphere and 16 per cent openly admit they would revert to the shadow economy (as many as 40 per cent had already experienced such activities in the past).

A sizable number of respondents would be willing to engage in profitable business that is still illegal, such as gambling and pornography: 38 per cent would open gambling establishments and 18 per cent would peddle pornography. Some (13 per cent) said they would open brothels, should the opportunity arise. There was one form of illegal activity that 99 per cent of respondents condemned: dealing in drugs. These attitudes clearly reflect the early stages of business activity in the country, retaining the conventional Soviet attitudes to circumventing the law and uncertainty about the current legal status of business. At the same time there is an evident unwillingness to engage in business that goes beyond conventional morality, particularly in drug trafficking.

THE LAW AND BUSINESS

To our question as to whether one can be successful in business without breaking the law, 51 per cent of respondents replied in the negative. We have a situation in which business can have a lawful existence, yet be tinged with elements of criminality. There are several reasons for this. First, the country is in transition from a planned to a free market economy; the pace of change is outstripping existing legislation. The various parliaments and city councils just cannot keep up with the rapidly changing situation. For example, stock exchanges were permitted in 1990, yet the law regulating their operations was still being elaborated in late 1991. As a consequence, the exchanges possess quite a few fiscal and other privileges, and their activities are so profitable that in just one year as many as 400 stock exchanges have opened in the Russian Republic. For the moment, even though they are unregulated by law, these spheres of business are considered to be highly profitable, encompassing banking, consulting, auditing and various information and communication systems.

Nonetheless there are serious hindrances to doing business. For a start, 90 per cent of respondents stressed that they cannot conduct their activities without giving bribes. The principal bribe-taker is government agencies which extort bribes from would-be business people from the very start of their operation – that is, from the moment they try to register. The major bribe-takers are as follows:

- local councils (63 per cent of entrepreneurs have had to bribe such officials);
- revenue-controlling agencies (58 per cent);
- customs and foreign trade organizations (48 per cent);
- the various councils of people's deputies (48 per cent);
- the police (35 per cent);
- the courts and the Procurator's Office (25 per cent);
- Communist Party officials (23 per cent);
- KGB officials (8 per cent).

One interviewee told us,

> Unfortunately, the old bribe-takers are being replaced by a new generation. In Brezhnev's time the bribe-takers not only took bribes, they undertook certain obligations to you so as to speed things up. Nowadays, officials come and go so rapidly that they take your money and don't keep their word. And then there are the indirect bribes: a local council may agree to register your business on condition you pay for the building of three children's play areas or for school computers. It has an aura of charity about it, but it is yet another form of extortion.

This situation led the 13 largest stock-jobbers, headed by Konstantin Borovoi, President of the Russian Stock Exchange, to declare, 'We've had enough of this pervasive corruption. A whole army of government parasites extorts money from business people through bribes and other payments for so-called intermediary services; this is too heavy a burden on developing business.'[2]

Racketeering is thus engaged in by both criminal bands and government agencies, pursuing the single goal of making money out of embryonic and semi-legal Soviet business. Most respondents had suffered from such racketeers, which explains their unwillingness to be interviewed openly. A total of 87 per cent agreed only to an anonymous interview. To protect themselves from racketeers, 15 per cent of the millionaires have bodyguards. In some cases, to escape their persecutors, the millionaires have had to flee to the West and direct their company activities by fax or telephone.

It is apparent that the business community may fall foul of the law while being innocent, but it would be wrong to imagine that all business people are without sin themselves. As many as 40 per cent had once engaged in illegal profiteering (usually reselling contraband goods), 22.5 per cent had been before the courts and one in four has close friends in the criminal underworld. Some brokers confess that they try to employ only former shadow-economy dealers since, in their view, they are the most experienced and reliable business associates.

BOURGEOIS ETHICS

The protestant ethic is not easily applicable to Soviet conditions, particularly because value systems differ radically according to age group. The Soviet system appears to have given the over–40s (even the over–30s) a sense of romantic idealism which is rarely found in the younger generation. Millionaires of the older generation said that their most cherished desires were 'to do something for Russia, something to make my descendants feel proud of their country'; to help people in Russia to live without fear; and to revive the traditions of Russian entrepreneurs. A surprisingly high proportion (58 per cent) of the entrepreneurs are antagonistic towards foreign aid and believe that the mission of resuscitating the national economy should be left to native entrepreneurs. Respondents frequently emphasized that Gorbachev's loans will only tighten the noose around the necks of future generations. When asked what they would recommend to Western businessmen who wish to invest in the Soviet economy, one in four replied that they should take their money elsewhere: 'they would be mad to invest in Russia'.

The younger generation of under–30s is far more pragmatic and, for the most part, Western-oriented. But all respondents valued such personal qualities as honesty and reliability; they are often nostalgic for the traditions of the old Russian merchants, who sealed their deals 'by word of honour'. They insist that commercial activity must be fully legitimated: for 73 years propaganda had depicted business in an utterly negative light. They are aware that business people were unpopular even at the time of the New Economic Policy; today successful entrepreneurs are often looked upon by the public as profiteers, making fortunes out of people's misfortune. As many as 51.3 per cent of the millionaires mention this negative reputation and try to conceal their activity and wealth from public gaze. The popular attitude towards business appears to be based on the notion that all business-men come from the shadow economy and can do the country no good.

Money per se does not seem to mean a great deal to Soviet business people. Their hierarchy of values puts family first (58 per cent), health second (53 per cent) and work third (48 per cent). Money comes only sixth. When asked what the principal motive behind their activity was, 65 per cent of respondents put first 'the chance to exercise their abilities', 45 per cent gave preference to 'the chance to be independent of society' and 28 per cent (mainly those in the 20–30 age band) favoured 'becoming wealthy'.

Donations to charity featured fairly high on the list of priorities. Some 88 per cent of respondents said their companies were giving money to old people's homes, schools, residential schools for the underprivileged, homes for the disabled and maternity hospitals. How-ever there is often more to charitable activity than meets the eye. Sometimes charity is used to mask profit or an indirect bribe to municipal authorities. For example, when its profit rose sharply, the Association of Small Businesses established a charitable fund to sup-port small enterprises; in fact, the fund functioned as a bank for a limited number of entrepreneurs.

POLITICAL ATTITUDES

Private business is already becoming politically important. Thus Mikhail Khodorovsky, Manager of Menatep, the largest of the Soviet commercial banks, is currently adviser to the Russian Prime Minister. Other businessmen are directly involved in politics through sponsor-ship of political programmes or charity funds. For the Russian presi-dential elections, the business elite is intending to put forward its own candidate.

Our research discovered that only the older generation of business people has any serious interest in politics, with the 'new wave' of younger businessmen indifferent to politics and more interested in horse racing, sport and rock stars. The older an entrepreneur, the higher tends to be his cultural level and the greater the interest he shows in politics. In order to study the political attitudes of respon-dents we used two different criteria: their self-estimation and an analy-sis of their reading and political interests. The survey was completed in 1991 before the attempted coup).

According to self-estimation, business people regard themselves as democrats (23 per cent), then communists (8 per cent) and anti-communists (8 per cent). An analysis of reading interests reveals that the most popular periodicals come from the democratic press – *Moscow News* and *Nezavisimaya gazeta* – though the most popular paper, regarded as obligatory reading, is *Kommersant*. Political leaders received the following rating:

Positive	Negative
Sobchak (33%)	Pavlov (33%)
Eltsin (20%)	Polozkov (23%)
Tarasov (10%)	Ryzhkov (13%)
Gorbachev (10%)	Gorbachev (10%)

As we see, democrats come top of positive attitudes. This is hardly surprising since, if conservative communists were to take power, that would spell the end of the market, and business would once more become a criminal activity. By far the majority had no self-defined political position.

VIEWS OF THE FUTURE

Generally speaking, the millionaires forecast that 1992 would see an increase in entrepreneurial influence on politics. The business community was already strong enough to establish its own lobby. To achieve the complete victory of market relations, however, the millionaires needed to have access to legislative bodies. As mentioned above, some are considering putting up their own nominee for presidency at the next elections. The main issue on the economic agenda in the nearest future, in their view, is the tension between the *nomenklatura* and genuine business people.

NOTES AND REFERENCES

1. *Izvestia*, 29 June 1991, p. 1.
2. *Moskovskaya pravda*, 31 July 1991, p. 3.

12. Poverty and Underprivileged Groups

Alastair McAuley

Even before the coup of August 1991, the USSR was in deep economic crisis. The system of central planning had largely collapsed before a market mechanism could be put in place. The ruble was no longer really acceptable either as a store of value or as a medium of exchange. The country was in the grip of severe inflation, made worse by government policy and nationalist rivalries. Enterprises were forced to resort to primitive barter to acquire inputs – and goods for their employees to consume. Inevitably aggregate output was falling. In the wake of the virtual collapse of central power after August, these processes have been accentuated. As a result, living standards have plunged, deepening the deprivation experienced by many Soviet households and threatening new groups with poverty. The plight of the Soviet poor – new and old – is the subject of this chapter.

The chapter begins with a report on recent Soviet estimates of the so-called minimum material security budget or poverty level. There is also a report on the numbers with incomes below the various poverty lines and an attempt is made to identify them socially. The second section deals with Soviet social policy and the social security system: an attempt is made to show how it helps and how it has failed the poor. Much of this material draws on published Soviet statistics and on the work of economists and sociologists. Inevitably it is concerned with the situation in the late 1980s – or earlier. The next section attempts to compensate for this; focusing upon the impact of *perestroika* on poverty and making use of somewhat more journalistic sources. The chapter ends with a summary of the argument and a brief conclusion.

SOVIET CONCEPTIONS OF POVERTY

There is significant disagreement in the USSR about the extent of poverty and about how much it had increased under Gorbachev. In

196

part this reflects methodological differences between groups of specialists, and between specialists and the general public. In part it reflects the difficulty of making sense of a confusing and rapidly-changing situation.

Responsibility for anti-poverty policy has been vested in Goskomtrud and its predecessors. As a result, its research institute, NIITruda, has carried out the investigations upon which the official or implicit poverty level has been based. This work has been based upon the so-called normative approach, according to which levels of consumption of all goods and services needed to reach a particular standard are specified by a panel of experts. (The standard prescribed in the Soviet case was that needed for the reproduction of simple labour.) The specified amounts of goods and services are then priced and this determines the poverty line or the minimum material security budget (hereafter mms budget).[1]

In 1988 the mms budget was valued at 78 rubles a month per capita when all supplies were purchased at state retail prices. When allowance was made for the fact that some goods might only be found on the kolkhoz market (and at higher prices), this figure rose to 85.80 rubles a month. Goskomstat is reported as claiming that, when allowance is made for tobacco and alcohol consumption, the poverty line rises to 92.30 rubles a month.[2]

It is not clear how these estimates should be adjusted to allow for the inflation that occurred in 1989–90. There are various estimates of the increase in the retail price index, including and excluding adjustments for hidden inflation, for the more rapid increase of prices on the kolkhoz market and so on. But the information needed to construct a statistically reliable cost of living index is not available. Goskomstat reports, however, that retail prices increased by 7.5 per cent in 1989 and by 19 per cent in 1990.[3] These estimates are on the conservative side, but they allow us to produce heuristic estimates of the poverty line in 1989 and 1990 (92–9 rubles a month and 109–18 rubles a month, respectively). The implications of the April 1991 price increases are dealt with later.[4]

There are certain problems with these estimates of the poverty line in the Soviet Union. Most important, perhaps, is the meaning to be attached to a ruble figure in circumstances where markets do not clear. Faced by widespread shortages, families may not be able to buy the goods and services prescribed by experts. At best they may be able to substitute more expensive alternatives; at worst, they may be forced to go without. Further, where one works and whom one knows can be important as well. An increasing proportion of scarce goods such as meat is available on ration or through one's place of work. Rationing schemes are administered by cities and amounts allowed differ. Equally some enterprise managers are more successful than others in obtaining the requisite supplies. None of these factors can be reflected in a single All-Union poverty line.

Second, it is probably not possible to specify a poverty line in the abstract. One needs some idea of what it will be used for. Often it is used to determine who will receive assistance under the government's social policy. Then it is no use specifying a level such that a majority of the population lives in poverty. The poverty line must bear some relation to the availability of resources. If it is to help those most in need, it should be fairly conservative. This has not always been true of Soviet estimates.

Third, the USSR is a large and culturally diverse country. It probably does not make a great deal of sense to talk about a single poverty line for the country as a whole. But at the present time there is no satisfactory framework within which to analyse geographical differences in poverty or the cost of living. The determination of a poverty line is only the first step in an analysis of the extent of poverty in any country. It must be complemented by estimates of the number of people whose incomes fall below the poverty line. Speaking in the Supreme Soviet in the summer of 1989, Nikolai Ryzhkov claimed that there were some 40 million people living in poverty in the USSR. This amounts to some 14 per cent of the population. This figure has been repeated by other analysts.[5] It refers to the number of persons living in families with a per capita money income of less than 78 rubles a month in 1988.

We can go behind this figure. In the last five years or so Goskomstat has published regular estimates of the distribution of the population by per capita income. These allow us to derive more detailed estimates of the extent of poverty in the USSR. There are two problems with Goskomstat's figures: first, they refer to total income, whereas the poverty line definitions given in the last section referred to money income;[6] it is thought that total income defined in this way is likely to exceed money income by less than 10 per cent. Second, they are derived from the family budget survey, which is thought to suffer from upward bias.[7]

The most recent figures given by Goskomstat are shown in Table 12.1, where the distribution above 125 rubles a month has been collapsed. Three conclusions can be drawn from these figures. First, there are substantial numbers of individuals with per capita incomes well below the poverty line. In 1988 there were more than 8 million with incomes below 50 rubles a month and a further 20 million or more with less than 70 rubles. In 1989 the figures were still 7.9 million and 19 million.

Table 12.1   Distribution of the population by per capita total income
in 1988 and 1989

Per capita total income (rubles per month)	Million persons	
	1988	1989
– 50	8.3	7.9
50.1– 75.0	27.7	23.8
75.1–100.0	44.7	39.2
100.1–125.0	50.2	46.3
125.1–	154.6	169.5
All	285.5	286.7

Source: *Narodnoe khoziaystvo SSSR v 1988g*, Moscow, 1989, p. 92; *Narodnoe khoziaystvo SSSR v 1989g*, Moscow, 1990, p. 89.

Second, if we use the alternative definitions of the poverty line, for example those derived from average incomes, the numbers in poverty rise. In 1988 it is estimated that more than 54 million people had a per capita income of less than 85 rubles a month and 66 million had less than 92 rubles a month. This is almost a quarter of the population. Third, the numbers whose incomes fall below the equivalent poverty lines in 1989 (83 rubles, 92 rubles and 99 rubles, respectively) have risen. On the narrowest definition, there were 44 million people below the poverty line, or 15 per cent of the population. On the most generous interpretation the number of poor rose to 69 million.

Goskomstat have also published distributions of the population of individual republics by per capita income. This allows one to explore the geographical distribution of poverty in the USSR. Some relevant figures are given in Table 12.2. In calculating them we have defined poverty as 60 per cent of mean income. Two distributions are given: the first defines poverty according to All-Union mean income, the second uses the mean income in each republic to calculate its own poverty line.

According to the first definition, the poverty line was equal to 88 rubles per month. At this level there were some 59 million people living in poverty. Roughly a third of these lived in the RSFSR, another third lived in Central Asia and the remainder were to be found in the other republics. Looked at another way, the population of the four

Table 12.2   Geographical distribution of the poor, USSR, 1988

	Share of total population (per cent)	Poverty line defined by reference to:			
		All Union mean income (millions per cent)		Mean income in republics (millions per cent)	
RSFSR	51	19.2	32	26.1	50
Ukraine, Belorussia, Moldavia	23	10.8	19	10.8	20
Baltic states	3	0.6	1	1.3	2
Transcaucasus	6	5.4	9	3.6	6
Kazakhstan	6	4.3	7	3.5	7
Central Asia	11	18.6	32	7.3	15
USSR	100	59.1	100	52.6	100

Source: Calculated from *Narodnoe khoziaystvo SSSR v 1988g*, Moscow, 1989, pp. 19, 94.

Central Asian republics was 33 million in 1988; of these no less than 18.6 million (or 57 per cent) had per capita incomes of less than 88 rubles a month. In Tajikistan the proportion was as high as 70 per cent.

Poverty on this scale has a different meaning to that underlying the derivation of poverty lines given above. It is difficult to know what might be meant by the marginalization of two-thirds or three-quarters of the population of a given area. For that reason the exercise was repeated using implicit republican poverty lines. The results are given in the fourth and fifth columns of the table. Poverty lines varied from 110 rubles a month for Estonia to 49 rubles in Tajikistan. For the USSR as a whole, approximately 53 million people were below the poverty line. Of these, half lived in the RSFSR and only 15 per cent in Central Asia. (More generally one can infer that inequality is greatest in those regions where the share of the poor exceeds the share in total population: Kazakhstan and Central Asia.) These two approaches to the definition of poverty have substantially different implications for anti-poverty policy.

Now we turn to a different question: who are these poor families? Sociologists have identified four groups who are particularly likely to suffer from poverty. First, there are pensioners – particularly those on minimum pension who live alone. Second, there are incomplete families; these are more prevalent in Slav areas and the Baltic states, where the divorce rate is higher. Third, there are large families (in Soviet circumstances those with more than two children are considered large). These are more prevalent in Central Asia. Finally, there are those who work in low-wage sectors – light and food industry, health, education and culture. Of course these groups may overlap.

THE SOVIET SAFETY NET

Soviet families have access to an extensive system of cash transfers designed to provide financial assistance in most of the circumstances in which they suffer temporary or permanent loss of earnings. In addition there are various welfare benefits, free and subsidized services that are intended to contribute to household real income. In this section we describe these programmes and ask how well they function as a safety net.

In 1989 the Soviet authorities spent some 187 billion rubles on these transfers and benefits; this amounted to a third of personal money income, or 29 per cent of net material product. In addition the government spent a further 100 billion rubles subsidizing the prices of consumers' goods.[8] Approximately 54 per cent of social consumption expenditure was distributed in the form of cash transfers. Their share has been rising throughout the post-war period. In part this has been a consequence of demographic change, such as increases in the numbers of old people entitled to pensions. It has also been a consequence of past attempts to solve specific social problems.[9] Similarly the cost of consumer subsidies has risen rapidly over the past decade or so. As a result the resources available for services such as health care and education have been squeezed. This helps to account for the decline in quality of service from which they have suffered over the last few years.[10]

Pensions accounted for almost three-fifths of all cash transfers in 1989 (or almost three-quarters if we exclude holiday pay). But, as was argued in the previous section, many pensioners are below the poverty line. A new pension scheme was approved in 1990 and will come into operation in 1992, but, at present, entitlement to support is still governed by laws passed in the Khrushchev period. These suffer from a number of weaknesses.

First, there are different schemes for state employees and kolkhozniki; the latter were treated much less favourably. This distinction will disappear under the new system. Second, neither scheme included any mechanisms for the automatic upgrading of pensions to reflect increases in the cost of living or average earnings. What has tended to happen is that, when the minimum pension has been raised, those previously below the new figure have had their pension raised to the minimum. As a result there is significant bunching at the minimum pension; this group consists disproportionately of the most elderly.

Further, when the Khrushchevite law was adopted in 1956, it allowed for a fourfold differentiation of pensions, reflecting inequality in previous earnings. But increases in the nominal minimum pension and a failure to raise the maximum have resulted in a compression of the distribution. These difficulties, too should be resolved by the new law.

In 1988 average earnings in the USSR were 219.8 rubles a month, only 2.5–2.8 times the poverty line. This suggests that the Soviet Union is a relatively low wage economy; it is difficult to support a family on the earnings of a single wage-earner. On the one hand, this helps to explain the very high female labour force participation rates achieved in the USSR. It also underlines the importance of child allowances and other such transfers in the family budget.

Child allowances are paid to women with four or more children; they are paid monthly from the child's first until its fifth birthday. Mothers receive a lump-sum payment on the birth of their third and subsequent children. Both lump-sum payments and monthly allowances increase with birth order. The system in its present form was introduced immediately after the Second World War; benefit levels have failed to keep pace with increases in money incomes. At the present time, the bulk of expenditure under this programme goes to the Central Asian republics. In addition to this programme of child allowances, single mothers receive a monthly payment – until the child's sixteenth birthday. Employed women are entitled to full pay while on maternity leave; if they choose to remain at home after the end of their maternity leave they are entitled to a flat-rate benefit until the child's first birthday. Finally, since 1974, poor families (and this has meant those with a per capita income of less than 50 rubles a month) have been entitled to a payment of 12 rubles a month for all children under eight years of age.[11]

Given the socialist commitment to full employment, there has been little provision made for the unemployed, and there have been few of them. But the situation is changing and both government and specialists assume that a market economy will result in substantial unemployment. A first attempt to provide for the unemployed was made in 1988, when a law was passed providing for the payment of one month's wages to those made redundant. Those undergoing retraining were to be entitled to up to three months on previous average earnings.[12] In late 1990 these provisions were extended.

These cash transfers have been supplemented by the provision of subsidized or free services and by a range of other subsidies. These programmes have not always achieved their aims. For example, although medical care has been made available free to the whole population, the authorities have been unwilling or unable to commit sufficient resources to the sector to ensure that demand was satisfied. Similarly the justification for subsidizing the price of consumer goods such as meat was to make them affordable by ordinary and poor families. The problem is that such a policy also reduces the prices paid by more affluent families, who tend to benefit more since they consume more![13] Here, too, the problems of the poor are compounded by the state's failure to expand supply sufficiently to make sure that markets clear at the subsidized prices.

The Soviet government redistributed a substantial proportion of national income in pursuit of its social policy goals. But, as was argued in the opening section, it has not been able to eliminate poverty. In part this is because the elimination of poverty has not been a primary policy goal. Rather, many of the programmes introduced under Stalin or Khrushchev were intended to underpin the so-called socialist distribution principle: from each according to his ability, to each according to his labour. This penalized those whose labour market links were weak. Moreover administration of policy has been inflexible: benefits have not been differentiated to take account of circumstances. The value of payments has been changed only at infrequent intervals, and so on. This may have been owing to the fact that the Soviet bureaucracy had too many other problems to deal with; or because social policy enjoyed too low a priority.

THE IMPACT OF *PERESTROIKA*

Perestroika, or rather the more general economic crisis that the USSR is experiencing, has affected the position of the poor in three ways. First, there has been a significant increase in the rate of inflation; second, there appear to have been changes in the government's approach to social security; and third, the commitment to introduce a market economy has increased the risk of unemployment. All three of these increase the population's sense of insecurity; all three have consequences to which the poor are particularly vulnerable. These issues are explored in this section.

The collapse of central planning and the rise of localism has resulted in breakdown of the country's retail trade system. There has been an enormous increase in the rate of inflation, hidden as well as open. Cheaper varieties of many goods, primarily bought by the poor, have disappeared from the shops; families have had to resort to collective farm markets to satisfy their needs.

Soviet official statistics on changes in the cost of living are often misleading and there is not the space here to discuss the relative merits of alternative estimates. In general terms, however, under Khrushchev and Brezhnev prices increased moderately – but at an accelerating rate. Since 1985 inflation has been much more rapid. It has also continued to accelerate. One estimate of changes in the Soviet price level between January 1990 and April 1991 brings this out clearly:[14]

1990					1991	
January	March	June	September	December	March	April
100.0	101.0	102.5	106.3	110.4	130.7	209.1

The prospect of hyperinflation in the immediate future is very real.

These increases in prices have been accompanied by increases in wages and in other sources of money income. For example, in 1988 average earnings in the state sector were 219.8 rubles a month;[15] by the fourth quarter of 1990, they had risen to 309 rubles a month.[16] But such increases have not fully compensated families for inflation; indeed they cannot. Since real GNP appears to have been falling since the beginning of 1990, it is almost inevitable that the living standards of some groups must fall.

In general the groups who suffer least during a period of rapid inflation are those whose market power allows them to renegotiate wage contracts at frequent intervals and those whose wealth is invested in real assets. Those who suffer most are those whose incomes are fixed in nominal terms. In the Soviet context, the former probably include skilled workers and those already involved with the second economy. The latter include most of the vulnerable groups identified above, whose income depends to a greater or lesser extent upon cash transfers from state social consumption funds. In practice, however, many of these groups do not appear to have suffered the expected collapse in their standard of living in the first quarter of 1991. In this period, while nominal wages and salaries increased by 11 per cent, population money income went up by almost a quarter.[17] This was a consequence, in part, of the payment of compensation for increases in official prices. (Of course, since this compensation increased the budget deficit, it is likely to lead to more rapid inflation in the future.)

Reformers in the former USSR emphasized the need to abandon central planning and to introduce markets. President Gorbachev and successive Prime Ministers appear to have accepted much of the reformist argument. But a market economy implies an active price mechanism. This in turn means that relative prices should reflect relative costs. It also adds to the importance of price stability. Both of these requirements impose additional constraints on the government's freedom to pursue *socialist* economic policies; in the short term at least, they also threaten the living standards of the poor.

Stabilization requires that the increase in the money supply be slowed down or halted. This will involve the imposition of hard budget constraints on state enterprises; it also involves the imposition or reimposition of fiscal discipline on the state. The spiralling budget deficit must be cut, if not eliminated. The authorities have already reduced the availability of central funding for investment; they have reduced their commitment to the defence sector – relatively, if not absolutely. They have also turned their attention to the state's extensive social programmes. At present the emphasis appears to be on reducing the cost to the budget of consumer subsidies. This was the rationale behind the increases in state retail prices in April 1991.

The steep price rises of April 1991 also go some way towards achieving the second objective of policy: relating prices to relative costs. But the new prices are still unsatisfactory: they have not been set at market-clearing levels, nor is it clear how large a supply response they will elicit, if any. The price rises were substantial, however, and had a significant impact on the cost of living. They have also had an impact on perceived living standards, despite the payment of partial compensation. Estimates of the scale of the increase vary. The Ministry of Finance claimed that the cost of purchasing the same basket of goods as in March 1991 increased by 49 per cent.[19] Others suggest it was higher: L. Pronina suggested that the cost of purchasing the 1989 consumption basket increased by 64 per cent for state employees and 66 per cent for pensioners.[20] N. Kirichenko claims that the cost of living increased by 213 per cent for those at or near the poverty line; it increased by 250 per cent for those with average incomes.[21] Insofar as substitution is possible, all these estimates will overstate the fall in real consumption.

Soviet consumers were to have been compensated for 85 per cent of the increase in prices.[22] In actual fact the degree of compensation was substantially less. First, some of the elements included in the compensation calculation by the Ministry of Finance should not be there. Furthermore it is not clear whether the budget deficit will benefit from the new policy: the Ministry appears to have spent all the savings.[23] Secondly, not all Soviet citizens received the compensation payments to which they were entitled. In particular some firms have been unable to pay their employees the additional 60 rubles a month they were supposed to.

Finally there is the question of unemployment. There are no accurate estimates of the level or growth of unemployment in the USSR; there is even still substantial disagreement about what the concept means. One report, by Goskomtrud, claimed that, at the end of 1989, there were two million people unemployed; that is, not working and actively seeking a job.[24] Others suggest that the figure is twice or even four times this.[25] In much of the country, unemployment has been frictional and of short duration; only in Central Asia has there been substantial structural and long-term joblessness.

It has been suggested that structural change and market-induced improvements in efficiency will lead to the shake-out of some 13–19 million workers over the next five or ten years. These will add to existing sources of unemployment, as will any collapse in economic activity occasioned by hyperinflation. But little of this unemployment has yet materialized.

CONCLUSION

There has always been poverty in the USSR; there have always been households whose claims on resources have been insufficient to allow them to participate fully in the life of the society. It is not possible, however, to give an unambiguous answer to the question: how many? The answer to this question depends upon the reason for asking. On the one hand, one may be interested in the numbers who are unable to enjoy the material benefits of a late twentieth-century European lifestyle, in which case one would choose a poverty line based on international consumption standards. Alternatively, one may wish to focus upon those households whose claims on resources are so limited that their members run a serious risk of suffering from malnutrition. Here one would specify a more modest poverty line; but one would expect the state to provide a much more reliable safety net to help this group. Poverty analysts in the USSR, just like those in other countries, disagree over which of these two approaches to poverty should be adopted. They disagree, therefore, about the scale of poverty in the Soviet Union.

There is a fair measure of agreement, however, that *perestroika* and the economic crisis with which it is associated have made the situation worse. Inflation is a tax that everyone has to pay. All Soviet households will have experienced a measure of disillusion as increases in nominal incomes have not been translated into equivalent increases in their standard of living. This has created a great deal of resentment towards the authorities, but it does not yet seem to have crystallized into a *political* commitment that anti-inflationary policy should be given overriding priority.

Rapid inflation and the collapse of the traditional retail distribution system have intensified the deprivation experienced by many of the existing poor. Those who have survived on fixed incomes in the past, who do not have a cushion of substantial savings upon which to rely and who do not have meaningful access to the alternative distribution channels that have proliferated in the last five years or so, are particularly likely to have suffered. They will almost certainly have been joined by other households; again, those without reserves, or whose main breadwinner has few market-relevant skills or works in a small enterprise are most at risk.

Who are these new Soviet poor? Who are the losers from inflation and from the reorganization of economic administration that is promised by *perestroika*? Some of them will be socially indistinguishable from the existing poor: pensioners, incomplete families and so on. Many of these depend upon the social security system for part or all of their income. They will fall below the poverty line if their social welfare benefits fail to keep up with the cost of living.

There are other groups, however, whose economic status has been undermined or is threatened by reform. Crisis and the economic disruptions of the past two or three years have led to a sharp fall in the level of investment in the USSR. This poses a threat to the viability of enterprises producing capital goods, that is to heavy industry. This threat will be increased if reform and a new detente lead to continuing reductions in weapons procurement. The position of those in the so-called military – industrial complex will be undermined. At present and in the foreseeable future, those most at risk from the run-down or closure of so-called smokestack industry will be the middle-aged and the semi-skilled. They have few transferable skills; their age and educational background mean that frequently it is not profitable to invest in retraining for them. They will find it difficult to obtain alternative employment. They will form much of the long-term unemployed of the future. I believe that the bulk of this group will be male – although others have suggested that women may be particularly vulnerable. Another social group whose economic position has been undermined by uncertainty is the young. There is already concern about the difficulties in finding work experienced by unqualified school-leavers.

Reform and the introduction of a market economy are intended to lead to substantial structural change. The Soviet economy is to become more similar to the advanced industrial economies of Western Europe. If this occurs it will create other sources of poverty and insecurity.

Growth in the services sector will result in the creation of a substantial number of low-tech and 'no-tech' jobs. If Western experience is relevant, wages will be low and security of employment minimal. Many of these jobs will be taken, I believe, by women displaced from traditional sectors. Their lot will not improve, but at least they will avoid the stigma of long-term unemployment.

It is clear that present safety-net provisions do not eliminate the risk of poverty for all Soviet households. If they were to remain unchanged, one could expect a significant increase in deprivation. But stability is not to be expected. Of itself, the switch to a market economy would require a change of strategy in the field of social security policy: free provision and the maintenance of widespread consumer subsidies, which distort relative prices and subvert rational choice, would be scaled down, if not abandoned. They would probably be replaced by a system of more selectively aimed benefits.[26] But the resources available for social policy purposes are likely to be limited, especially if the All-Union government commits itself to a stabilization programme and attempts to bring down the rate of inflation. It is unlikely that future social security programmes will provide sufficient protection against poverty.

The trade unions were opposed to *perestroika*, as was much of the CPSU apparat, but they have not focused upon this consequence. They have not set out to organize the poor. Thus poverty is not yet a 'political' issue. This is because the existing poor are to be found primarily among marginal social groups. Their links with the existing political system are limited. The unions (and the Party) have traditionally seen their support as being concentrated among workers in heavy industry. If and when these groups suffer long-term unemployment and poverty, this situation may begin to change.

On the other hand, there is much more candour about poverty and anti-poverty policy than there was under Brezhnev or earlier. Many specialists appear to have been influenced by Western discussions: for them social justice involves a radical recasting of the traditional socialist welfare project. This academic concern may also be translated into political commitment and even action.

NOTES

1. A. McAuley, *Economic Welfare and Inequality in the Soviet Union*, Allen and Unwin, London, 1979, ch. 4.
2. A. V. Kormilkin, 'O bednosti' – ne v poslednii raz', *EKO*, no. 7, 1990, pp. 63–4.
3. *PlanEcon Report*, Washington DC; vol. vii, no. 17, p. 3.
4. An alternative approach to the definition of a poverty line, (reportedly favoured

by the ILO – see Kormilkin, 'O bednosti', p. 60) is to take two-thirds or three-fifths of average income. For the USSR in 1988, this implies a poverty line of 88–98 rubles a month. (*Narodnoe Khoziaystvo SSSR v 1988g*, Moscow, 1989).

For 1989, the poverty line was between 93 and 103 rubles a month per capita (*Narodnoe Khoziaystvo SSSR v 1989g* Moscow, 1990, pp. 33, 87). More disputably, it is claimed that money income increased by 24.9 per cent in 1990 (*PlanEcon Report*, Washington DC, vol. vii, no. 17, p. 3). This yields an approximate poverty line of 115–28 rubles a month.

5. See, for example, N. M. Rimashevskaia and A. A. Rimashevskii, *Ravenstvo ili spravedlivost*, Finansy i Statistika, Moscow, 1991.

6. Total income is defined as: 'the sum of monetary receipts in the form of wages, pensions, stipends allowances etc., receipts in cash and kind (expressed in money terms) from kolkhozy, the value of the net output of subsidiary agricultural activities valued in state-cooperative retail prices . . . Total income does not include the value of free education, free medical care, housing subsidies and so on *Narodnoe Khoziaystvo SSSR v 1989g*, Moscow, 1990, (p. 87). This differs from definitions used in earlier years where these latter elements of social consumption were included (see A. McAuley, *Economic Welfare and Inequality in the Soviet Union*, ch. 1).

7. The family budget survey is based on a sample of 90 000 households; but the sample is thought to be biased. It contains too many affluent households. Again the upward bias in mean income is not thought to exceed 10 per cent; it is not clear how the variance is affected (M. V. Alexeev and C. G. Gaddy, 'Trends in Wage and Income Distribution under Gorbachev: analysis of new Soviet data', Berkeley-Duke Occasional Papers on the Second Economy in the USSR, no. 25, mimeo, February, 1991).

8. G. Ofer, 'Budget Deficit, Market Disequilibrium and Soviet Economic Reforms', *Soviet Economy*, April, 1989, Vol. 5, no 2, p. 155.

9. A. McAuley, *Economic Welfare and Inequality in the Soviet Union*, Allen and Unwin, London, 1979, ch. 11.

10. A. McAuley, 'Social Policy', in A. Brown and M. Kaser (eds), *Soviet Policy for the 1980s*, Macmillan, London, 1982, pp. 154–6.

11. A. McAuley, 'The Welfare State in the USSR', in T. Wilson and D. Wilson (eds), *The State and Social Welfare*, Longman, London, 1991, p. 202.

12. 'Ob obespechenii effektivnoi zaniatosti naselenia', *Izvestia*, 20 January 1988.

13. A. V. Kormilkin, 'O bednosti – ne v poslednii raz', *EKO*, no. 7, 1990, p. 57.

14. *PlanEcon Report*, Washington DC; vol. vii, no. 17, p. 8.

15. *Narodnoe khoziaystvo SSSR v 1989g* 1990, Moscow, p. 76.

16. *PlanEcon Report*, Washington DC; vol. vii, no. 17, p. 3.

17. Ibid., p. 2.

18. See S. M. Nikitin, 'Inflatsia', *EKO*, 1990, no. 6, pp. 3–13, reprinted as 'Inflation', in *Problems of Economics*, April 1991, p. 60–9.

19. *Izvestia*, 29 April 1991.

20. *Argumenty i fakty*, 1991, Moscow, no. 16.

21. Ibid., no. 23.

22. *Izvestia*, 29 April 1991.

23. A. McAuley, 'Komu poydet kompensatsia', *Nezavisimaia gazeta*, 7 May 1991.

24. S. Marnie, 'Employment and the Reallocation of Labour in the USSR', paper given at the IV World Congress of Slavists, Harrogate, July 1990.

25. V. Busygin, 'Skol'ko zhe ikh lishennykh raboty v SSSR', *EKO*, 1990, no. 6, pp. 14–22, reprinted as 'How Many People are Deprived of Work in the USSR?', *Problems of Economics*, April 1991, pp. 70–6.

26 'Mery sotsialnoi zashchity v usloviakh rynka: proekt Goskomtruda', *Izvestia*, 8 August 1990.

13. Housing Reform and Social Conflict

Greg Andrusz

One of the great paradigmatic shifts being perpetrated in the Soviet Union in the field of housing – and being replicated in other social policy areas – is the move from regarding the provision of shelter to citizens as one of the state's principal objectives to seeing housing as a commodity which the citizen must acquire in the market place. It is widely recognized, even outside the circle of housing specialists, that housing reforms in the Soviet Union are integral to the macro economic stabilization of the national economy. Not only do housing subsidies constitute a major burden on the central government's budget, but present policies act as serious constraints on labour mobility and the mobilization of household savings. Hence housing reform is closely connected to radical transformations of the financial system, legal framework and laws governing property ownership. The restructuring of the economic and housing systems is linked by the need to move away from the combination of low cash wages and heavily subsidized housing. In policy terms, the reduction in government revenue and expenditure requires that greater assistance be given to household financed and self-build housing programmes.

Historically, societies in transition to capitalism have witnessed a 'fissuring' of the social structure and a rupturing of the traditional value system which legitimized it. This generated tensions and heightened social conflict. The deep and intense conflicts associated with this transition are visible in the production, distribution, acquisition and consumption of housing. Attitudes produced by paternalistic Soviet-type societies – where accommodation is granted (as a benefice) rather than purchased – are seen as conducive to 'begging, dependency and neglect of the home'. Such traits are accompanied by a swelling bureaucracy, whose functionaries in a situation of housing shortage are capricious in their judgements and corrupt in their allocation policies.[1]

As Durkheim observed, all sociological research is in a sense comparative; so is policy formulation. The period since the mid–1960s has witnessed the further evolution of international organizations within Europe, such as the United Nation's Economic Commission for Europe, whose secretariats bring together civil servants and specialists from member states. As transnational think-tanks, they have served as important forums for debating new policy initiatives of common concern. Even before *perestroika*, delegates to their seminars and symposia from the Soviet 'hackocratia', with their origins in the *nomenklatura*, were being supplemented (rather than wholly supplanted) by younger specialists. Both the feeble and the quick of mind were influenced by the similarity of some of the housing problems experienced by the Soviet Union; by the range of alternatives available to deal with them; and by the costs and benefits of different problem-solving approaches.

Above all they were brought face to face with a rejection in much of Western Europe of the post-war concensus on the necessity of planning and state intervention in spheres of social life, such as housing, which until recently had been the sacrosanct domain of the caring state.[2] It was this criticism of Maynard Keynes which presaged the revolt against Karl Marx. So, even before the advent of *perestroika*, there were calls for 'more detailed studies' on housing issues. By 1976 the Soviet delegate to one such symposium, after stating the ideological norm that the dominant role of the state as provider of urban accommodation 'will remain the case in the foreseeable future', went on to add that 'interest in the development of cooperative and individual housing construction changes as personal prosperity rises and this is true whatever the country'. In other words, 15 years ago, a rational technocratic and bureaucratic solution was, to borrow a phrase, pushing itself forward as an iron law of necessity.

This chapter begins by reviewing the structure of housing ownership and selected statistics to demonstrate the extent of its being a 'problem'. This is followed by a commentary on recent legislation in this sector. Two policy areas of particular interest, rent and privatization, are analysed. The chapter ends with a look at the way in which the housing shortage and current policies – in housing and more generally – can generate social conflict, followed by a brief conclusion.

THE STRUCTURE OF HOUSE OWNERSHIP

In the past the study of Soviet housing legislation provided an indication of the central government's thinking on policy. Legal textbooks and commentaries on housing law dealt with the management and distribution of housing, eviction and tenants' rights in terms of the type of tenure classification. In 1991 the four tenure categories which had emerged by 1924 continued to be the pillars of house ownership: (1) local soviet (municipal housing); (2) state ministries, enterprises and trade unions ('departmental sector'); (3) house-building cooperatives; and (4) individual home ownership.[3] Although subletting has been legally permitted, private housing built or acquired specifically for renting has not been tolerated since 1937.

Nationwide, from 1960 until 1988, the state sector (publicly rented) grew at the expense of the private sector (owner-occupier). As late as the mid–1980s government officials continued to declare that the trend towards greater state prominence would continue. In 1990 the housing stock was divided between the state (55 per cent), the private sector (39 per cent) and cooperatives (4 per cent). Property belonging to the state was divided amongst local soviets (23 per cent), firms, ministries (29 per cent) and social organizations (3 per cent).[4]

Enterprises and ministries remain the main commissioners of new construction and the main allocators of newly constructed housing.[5] Their concern to control the construction process has been directly related to their manpower requirements. Paradoxically enterprises with good house-building records experience greater labour turnover, since the worker when provided with shelter no longer feels constrained to remain with the employer.

On the other hand, enterprises building less suffer from an unstable workforce, since those on the housing waiting list have a strong incentive to find an employer where the waiting time might be shorter. Such a system gives rise to a quasi-housing market in which the individual 'shops around' for accommodation on the basis, not of his actual spending power, but of his marketable skills. Another attribute of the housing system, even more widespread and generalized in the control which it exercises over the population, is the residential permit (*propiska*). This plays a pivotal role in preventing real residential choice and in impeding geographical and occupational mobility.

STATISTICS: THE MAGNITUDE OF THE PROBLEM

In 1986 the 27th Party Congress pledged that the government would provide each household with a separate flat or house by the year 2000. In doing so it acknowledged both the enormous shortage and the importance of overcoming this shortage as part of a programme of reform.

In order for the government to reach its objective, 40 million new flats and individual houses would have to be erected in the 15-year period 1986–2000, thereby doubling the housing stock. But even this utopian goal had to be revised *upwards* in 1988 when the foremost housing research institute in the Soviet Union concluded that 2.8 billion square meters would have to be constructed in order to provide an average of 19.5 square metres of overall living space per person, in average-sized flats of 66 square metres. It was deemed that, at this level of need satisfaction, housing would no longer have an adverse affect on infant mortality, birth and death rates and morbidity generally.[6]

The state will inevitably have to play its role in helping to achieve these targets, but it recognizes that it will have to share this responsibility. Accordingly it has estimated that over the period 1991–5 investment by collective farms in house building will have to decline from 7.2 per cent to 5.9 per cent, with substantial increases in cooperative and individual construction, from 18.3 per cent to 40.3 per cent.[7] The enterprise social development fund must increase its share from 22.9 per cent to 31.8 per cent and social organizations from 1.4 per cent to 1.5 per cent.[8] This means a considerable shift in responsibility from the state: its capital investment in the housing sector will *decline* from 50.2 per cent to 20.5 per cent.[9]

In 1990, in the country at large, 14.3 million families and individuals (23 per cent of all urban families) were on housing waiting lists. This figure rises to 33 per cent in Moldavia, 32 per cent in Turkmenia, 28 per cent in Belorussia and 25 per cent in Russia.[10] These figures are best seen as 'orientational', in that they point towards the magnitude of the problem, which is probably underestimated. A variety of factors, including cultural norms, keep people off the waiting list register. In fact waiting lists are *closed* after the (low) minimum living space norm per person has been attained.[11] Therefore the figure of 23 per cent queueing for accommodation underestimates the actual number of households who would like to be placed on the waiting list to receive better accommodation.

Of the 14.3 million in the queue, 13 per cent live in communal (shared) accommodation, 14 per cent in hostels and 4 per cent in properties scheduled for demolition. The 1989 Population and Housing Census revealed that 17 per cent of urban households in self-contained accommodation and 16 per cent of those in communal flats had 7–9 square metres of dwelling space per person, with no fewer than 4.5 million having less than 5 square metres per person.[12]

According to one Soviet housing specialist, planners omit to consider as in need of housing individuals in the 20–30-year-old age range, since they already have homes with their families. This means that the demand for housing is seriously and consistently underestimated.[13] He concluded that by the year 2000 the country will have 119 million households, in contrast to Gosplan's estimate of 97 million. So, instead of the projected 40 million new homes which are to be provided in the period 1986–2000, the figure should be 54 million. Despite this revised calculation, by 1989 house building plans were not being fulfilled and people were beginning to doubt whether the 1986 goal was achievable. Because of the current economic and political chaos the rate of construction had been declining in Moscow since 1989, and had only begun to recover towards the end of the first half of 1991. Small wonder then that, in July 1991, the Minister of Construction told an interviewer that the latter should forget the pledge to provide each Muscovite family with its own separate flat.[14]

Considerable intra-republican disparities in housing standards continue to persist. For instance, in the three Baltic Republics the average per capita living space was 17.4 square metres in 1988, while it stood at 11.4 square metres in the Central Asian republics and Azerbaijan. Even greater differences are found in the countryside. Despite the fact that the housing situation of Estonians has been above the national average, in 1989–90 housing output fell to one-half of that achieved annually in 1981–7. Inflation has forced construction costs higher, so that prices of newly-built housing units will be 220 per cent higher in 1991 than in 1987. This increase is partly explained by the fact that from 1991, new housing construction will not receive direct subventions from the central state budget.

Long waiting lists, poor housing, considerable regional differences in provision, ambitious construction targets and falling building rates compel reform of housing policy.

LEGISLATIVE REFORM

Following the initial legislation in 1962, house-building cooperatives began to play a role in meeting housing demand. By the early 1980s, voices could be heard suggesting that, given the general rise in the level of income and savings, a larger proportion of the population might be expected to use their own resources to finance house building.

There was also a second, long-term trend in housing policy. Since 1957 decrees had been passed on the need to transfer accommodation owned and controlled by industry and institutions into the jurisdiction of the local soviets. This was regarded as a 'technically rational' way to improve the management and maintenance of the state housing stock, and thereby to reduce the high and escalating costs of housing in the national budget. The general trend towards decentralization and the greater autonomy being accorded to local soviets *may* lead to a concentration of housing in the hands of municipal authorities, thus fulfilling a 35-year-old government objective.

However the concentration of the bulk of state accommodation in the hands of local soviets itself probably represents a transitional phase: the 1988 Decree of Cooperatives (see below) is clearly designed to encourage the establishment of housing associations and housing trusts, similar to those found elsewhere in Western Europe. These will be smaller, self-managing tenants' and residents' associations.

Secondly, continuing budgetary conflicts between the central government and local soviets might see a reduction in the central government subsidy to housing which may not be compensated by an increase in spending from local budgets.[15] Thirdly, in the largest cities which are subdivided into constituencies (*raiony*), conflicts already exist between the city soviet and *raion* soviet over the distribution and use of budgetary revenues. Fourthly, individual republics and settlements are, at present, pursuing their independent courses with their own timetables on the privatization of state-owned accommodation. Lastly, because rent is a component in the local soviet's revenue, the size of rental charges will fluctuate between local governments.

Three important housing decrees were published in February, March and December 1988 and all marked, in the consistency of their prime objectives, a major change in policy direction. The first of them came in the decree of February 1988 entitled 'On Measures to Accelerate the Development of Individual Housing Construction'. At the beginning of the year it represented the most radical of all post-war government promulgations on housing policy. It stated that much greater reliance would have to be placed on the population using its own labour, income and savings to provide accommodation. Savings deposits were an obvious target for the government, and in a period of open inflation and economic insecurity it also makes sense for citizens to invest in property. In comparison with 1985, when individuals erected 16.3 million square metres of living space (14.4 per cent of all housing construction), by 1995 the figure should be 60 million. By the end of the century, 'housing erected by the population' will comprise 29.3 per cent of all accommodation built and 19.7 per cent of that erected in urban areas. This compares with 17.1 and 8.8 per cent, respectively in 1988. The new 'legislation' thus signals a reversal of the long-term decline of the 'private sector'.

Banks are allowed to make credit available to enterprises intending

to start or expand production of building and decorating materials and
to make advances of up to 20 000 rubles, repayable over 25 years in
towns and 50 years in the countryside. The decree increased the size
of the loan from 3000 rubles and extended the repayment period from
10 years. The same favourable terms are to be granted to people
wishing to purchase individual homes – an important requirement for
the furtherance of an open housing market.

The development of a housing market was enhanced by allowing
enterprises and organizations to sell houses to their workers if the
latter pay them 'no less' than 40–50 per cent of the value of the house
over a period of 25–50 years, depending on the location. This was the
nearest the Soviet Union ever came to the UK policy of selling council
housing.[16]

Secondly, insofar as 'encouraging the population to use its resources'
to expand the supply of housing has in recent years been directed at
least as much to the house-building cooperative as to the owner-
occupied sector, it was to be expected that the increased benefits
accruing to the latter would soon be accompanied by amendments to
legislation governing cooperatives. This duly occurred in March 1988
in the decree 'On Measures to Accelerate the Development of Housing
Cooperatives'.

The decree stated that housing cooperatives would become 'one of
the main ways for expanding housing construction . . . so that by 1995
they will contribute no less than two to three times more than at
present, to the overall volume of housing construction'. In the period
1996–2000 this could mean cooperatives contributing 20–30 per cent
to new building in towns, compared with 9.5 per cent in 1988. The
legislation defines two types of cooperative, one of which is for the
purchase of older and newly-erected buildings from the state at a huge
discount, with the purchaser having to pay 'not less than 20–25 per
cent of the property's assessed value'. This was symptomatic of the
shift towards acceptance of the principle that at least part of the state
housing stock may legitimately be privatized.

Thirdly, in December 1988, the logic of these developments culmi-
nated in the acceptance of proposals to allow local soviets and enterprises to transfer dwellings controlled by them into private ownership.
Since then the local soviets have been attempting to decide on their
sales policy and set the rules for service and maintenance charges for
individuals who want to buy their flats.

The prescription preferred by many housing specialists is a future
housing system comprised of a municipal sector – which would provide
low-cost housing for low-income families – and owner-occupier,

cooperative and privately rented sectors. Following practices in a number of other European countries, the owner-occupier and privately rented tenures are regarded as sources for profitable capital investment, while cooperatives will, like British housing associations, enable households on average incomes to satisfy their housing needs at a 'reasonable' level of expenditure.[17]

The acuteness of the housing situation, within an ever-deteriorating economic and political environment, the failure of production forecasts to be translated into reality and the slowness in implementation of the above decrees, prompted Gorbachev to issue a presidential edict (*Ukaz*) in May 1990, 'On new approaches to the solution of the housing problem in the country and measures for their practical implementation'.[18] The edict requires an 'expansion in the sources of finance by drawing upon state, leasing and cooperative enterprises, public companies, voluntary organizations, bank loans and personal savings'. This is to be accompanied by building houses for sale with low monthly repayments spread out over a long period and by the establishment of a network of commercial banks, building cooperatives and firms dealing with the sale and renting of accommodation.

In this 'regulated market' phase, which places emphasis on solving the housing problem principally through private individuals (and cooperatives) and work collectives, the state's role is to concentrate on actually increasing the aid that it gives to a whole range of disadvantaged social groups. For example, the Ukaz recommended that young families should be helped to build their own homes and housing complexes, cooperatives and hostels for young adults and young families. The extensive reliance placed on self-build by young people is still attractive, for, although the heroic period of the metaphoric building of socialism has passed, the concrete construction of one's home is for many of them the only way in which they can acquire a place of their own.

The principal aim, as stated in the edict, is to create a housing market in which every individual may freely acquire a flat or house through purchase or leasing in the public or private sectors. The next two sections examine the debate over and problems presented by this policy.

RENT

In order to ensure access of low-income groups to accommodation, rents for most of the period have been maintained at very low levels and have been unrelated to household income and ability to pay.

Rents have therefore not covered the costs of production. Moreover rental income did not influence the supply of new construction, which depended solely on budgetary allocation. Since there are other demands on the budget, the government has sought to minimize expenditure in this sector by erecting low-cost dwelling units. Unfortunately low cost has been purchased at the expense of quality, which has meant that buildings quickly fall into disrepair and require renovation. In the absence of adequate maintenance, they become dilapidated and generate demands for new accommodation.

Since the basic tariff for calculating rent has not changed since 1928, rents have long since ceased to bear any relationship to costs – either of construction or of maintenance. The average urban industrial family continues to spend 2.8 per cent of its monthly income on accommodation.[19] However, a breakdown of this figure shows that, in higher-income groups, 10–12 per cent of the family budget is spent on accommodation, while it can absorb up to 25 per cent of a pensioner's total budget.[20] The 13–16 kopeks per square metre rent which is charged at present cannot possibly cover running and maintenance costs, which are constantly increasing. Yet, despite the low level of public sector rents, in 1989 arrears amounted to 307.9 million rubles (that is, 13.7 per cent of total rents for that year).

A paper prepared in 1985 for the UN Economic and Social Council of the Economic Commission for Europe (ECE) referred to the principal features of Soviet housing policy as being: (1) the constitutional right of citizens to accommodation: (2) a just distribution of housing space: and (3) low rents and cheap communal services. It reiterated that the right to accommodation is determined by *need*, while 'the fair distribution of housing space was ensured by the Constitution and by the State agencies which guarantee the objectivity and fairness of the order of priority in the allocation or acquisition of accommodation'. Two years earlier, a paper presented at the same forum stated that 'the stabilisation of rents is one of the USSR's most significant social achievements and is aimed at improving the workers' overall level of well-being'. The twin pillars of housing ideology have thus been fairness in access and low rents.

As already noted above, Soviet housing specialists have for a long time been exposed to debates on rent being conducted in the international arena. In 1982 the Commission's members observed that rent policy should be used deftly as an instrument of economic and social policy, with cost of construction, tenant income and dwelling quality employed as criteria for setting rent levels. A delicate defence of the 'old' was flexibly accommodating to the redefining of the welfare state taking place throughout Western Europe. Rental policy and attitudes towards private landlords had come to occupy centre stage.

In October 1990 a symposium held under the auspices of the Economic and Social Council concluded that in most East and Central European countries legislation was being drawn up to reduce rent subsidies and to increase rents to cost-covering levels. Laws were being enacted to reinstate private property, increase the responsibility and participation of individuals in meeting their housing needs and promote private housing construction for sale and rent. The Working Party on the Committee on Housing, Building and Planning concluded that 'rent policy was a matter of great concern to all ECE countries, especially those in transition to market economies' and that 'further work on rent policy should be pursued as an integral part of the new programme element on transitional problems'.[21]

The vast public rental sector in the USSR has been in crisis for many years. This is partly a consequence of the accelerating physical deterioration of the existing stock (because of poor materials and bad workmanship). This is in turn the result of the inadequacy of financial resources generated by rents – itself a consequence of an escalation in unpaid rents and low, frozen rental levels. According to the Minister of Construction, the whole built environment of the capital was an eyesore and a faceless dormitory. The dual objective of building more at a lower price meant the sacrifice of quality and visual attractiveness. In order to combat the horrendous uniformity, in future engineers and economists will be made subordinate to architects and not vice versa, as has been the practice to date. This, however, will mean a three- or four-fold increase in construction costs, which implies higher and more differentiated rental charges. Raising rents must, however, take into account those on lower incomes.[22]

The majority of formulations concerning the 'social guarantee' specify that families whose living conditions fall below the guaranteed minimum should automatically be entered on the waiting list. The actual definition of what constitutes the 'minimum' varies. According to radical reformers, the state will be spurred on to increase housing construction and improve its management and distribution if it is penalized for not meeting its pledge to the population.[23]

The freedom of republics and local governments to set rents in the public sector, budgetary constraints apart, are closely circumscribed. The ideological propaganda value that the state has hitherto reaped from its low rent policy, and the fact that at the extremely low rents already charged rent arrears are quite considerable, suggest that raising rents will be unpopular and possibly unacceptable. Following the

British example, the different republics might choose to use carrot-and-stick mechanisms to induce higher-income groups to leave the publicly rented sector: rents could be raised in order to generate income to subsidize low-income groups, whose size will grow with increasing unemployment and inflation.

Nevertheless rent reform is occurring, with households being surcharged for inhabiting living space exceeding a locally defined norm. In Lvov each person is entitled to 20 square metres of overall living space, with each additional square metre being charged at five times the top rate. The surcharge rates in Alma Ata begin to increase at a lower per capita norm and rise more steeply. Rents charged on a progressive scale are intended to encourage households to consider whether they wish to 'consume' so much space. The introduction of this policy has been accompanied by a simplified procedure enabling people to exchange larger flats for smaller ones.[24]

A reduction by two-thirds in the housing subsidy, as has been recommended by Latvia's Ministry of Finance, could see rents rising by 48 kopeks per square metre. This increase is to be accompanied by a fivefold rise in the charge for communal services, so that, taken together, the average two-roomed flat with two tenants will cost 50–60 rubles per month instead of the current 12 rubles. Such increments will cause a sharp decline in living standards of 70 per cent of the population, with the remaining 30 per cent experiencing varying degrees of difficulty. In the view of the deputy chairman of the Government's State Commission on Economic Reform, a household's outlay on accommodation should be increased gradually.[25] Finally, apart from Gorbachev's mention of the rent issue at the 27th Party Congress in 1986 – when he hinted that rents were too low – rent reform has not really figured on the housing agenda. Instead privatization has gained the 'top spot' on the reform agenda.

PRIVATIZATION

Learning from Western experience and economic theory, it is now recognized that the low rents in the public sector inhibit demand for cooperative and owner-occupier accommodation. So, if rents are raised, tenants will take refuge in the private (owner-occupied) sector. This subject is integral to discussions which have been taking place over the past three years on the privatization of state accommodation. Suggestions on the form it should take have been thoughtful, innovative and at times bizarre. Most of them fail to deal with the fact that, in the short term at least, privatization will perpetuate the inequalities already generated by the administrative allocatory system.

Privatization of housing, like the paradigmatic shift to the market in all spheres, is favoured because public ownership is seen as synonymous with 'no owner'. And, since no-one, neither tenants nor state officials, has an interest in looking after it, the accommodation quickly falls into disrepair. The change in ownership is also justified on the grounds that the present system 'prevents technological progress'. For, in order to stimulate the introduction of modern technology, corporate tax must be reduced and wages increased. Firms will then be able (and will find it advantageous) to substitute machinery for hired 'slave labour' (*rabskii trud*). Of course, if 'corporate taxation' is reduced, deductions into the social consumption fund, which embraces outlays on the maintenance of state housing, will also decrease.[26] The attraction of privatization to the sitting tenant is that the price of real estate is rising more rapidly than other prices; hence investing in property provides a higher return than comes from buying stocks and shares or receiving interest.

On 4 July 1991 the Supreme Soviet of the RSFSR ratified a new law 'On the Privatization of the Housing Stock in the RSFSR'. In principle the law envisages the free transfer of state-owned accommodation into the hands of the sitting tenant. However, if the estimated value of the property exceeds the average, the new owner must pay the difference. In the opposite case, where the property is below average (in standard and therefore in value) the state is not obliged to pay any compensation. This represents a major amendment to the original draft legislation and the submission of 'utopian socialism' to realism, for compensatory payments would have risen to 60 million rubles.

A further important restriction discussed during the drafting stage has been removed for the new legislation, namely the right to resell the property immediately after it has been purchased. This was hailed as an achievement by commercial interests who consider that the removal of the moratorium will stimulate the growth of a genuine housing market and a rapid rise in house prices.[27]

A better indicator of attitudes towards the privatization of housing can be extrapolated from sentiments towards the destatization of other forms of property. Where it concerns small workshops and businesses and retail outlets four-fifths of those interviewed expressed support for private ownership, with the remainder dividing between those against and those uncommitted. However, in the case of large factories, only 29 per cent approved or consented to their conversion to private ownership.[28]

If transposed to the sphere of housing these findings could be reinterpreted to suggest that, while individuals would support owner-occupation – and even 'small landlords' – they would be hostile to large-scale private landlordism. Such a speculative conclusion finds support in the fact that only 18 per cent of respondents believed that price rises were justifiable for goods in short supply, whereas 66 per cent thought that such goods should be distributed through ration cards. This would suggest that there is a groundswell of feeling for the present method of distributing accommodation.

The reality of privatization is in reverse proportion to the heated debate which privatization has generated. Since December 1988, when the decree permitting the sale of state-owned housing was published, only a minuscule proportion of the total stock has been sold off. Between January and September 1990, 19 300 flats (of which 65 per cent belong to local soviets and 35 per cent to enterprises) were sold, although this was four times more than for the whole of 1989. Over the whole period, from December 1988 to the end of 1990, according to different estimates, only 700–1500 flats in Moscow were 'privatized'. In Leningrad, 0.01 per cent of the city's publicly rented stock was sold off, although there had been 12 times as many applications.[29] The discrepancy between application and sale can be explained partly by bureaucratic delays and other management factors and partly by the loss of interest when applicants discovered the true (future) costs which they would be incurring with the loss of subsidy for the property's repair and maintenance. This low take-up rate might be accounted for by the fact that only 3–5 per cent of the population actually possess sufficient money to buy their accommodation outright. The rest of the population would require some form of subsidy or grant. In Leningrad where, admittedly, house prices are higher than in most other parts of the country, only 0.2–0.3 per cent of the population are able to purchase outright.[30]

Many people believe that, since state accommodation has already been paid for by tenants through their rental contributions (and because much of it is in serious need of repair), housing should simply be given to them free of charge. At the global level this position may be sustainable on the grounds that the population has paid for its accommodation through past rental payments and taxation.[31] On the other hand, at the individual household level, there are families who live in quite appalling conditions despite having paid rents and taxes over a long period, while other families who are better housed may have made smaller contributions.

The tangled issue of which households have paid what for which housing became more confused and conflict-generating after members of cooperatives began to demand that, if state tenants receive their accommodation free of charge, then those in cooperatives should also be compensated. This raises the question of who should pay so that others can receive their accommodation free of charge. The outcome of this progression is the formation of another queue: this time for the right to a free dwelling or its equivalent on the grounds of social justice!

Because a substantial proportion of state housing has in the past been allocated according to criteria which are now said to have breached the cannons of 'social justice' (a key notion in the political lexicon of *perestroika*) and because differences exist in the space standards and quality of amenity provided in different types of accommodation, the granting of state property as a gift to sitting tenants may unleash strong egalitarian impulses within the lower echelons of society and give rise to demands for the expropriation of the expropriator.[32]

The end of 1990 witnessed the convening by the recently created All-Union Association for the Housing Economy of a seminar on privatization and the management of the housing stock.[33] Participants were asked to reflect on the absence of demonstrators on the streets carrying banners demanding 'Give us Housing and We Will Repair Them Ourselves!' The question was partly rhetorical, for it focused attention on the fact that privatization, as a policy, emanates from above, not from the people themselves. A number of delegates working in the field of housing management expressed themselves against privatization. Their hostility to the government's privatization scheme could be an expression of unadulterated self-interest on the part of middle management possibly faced with a loss of status and comfortable jobs. As Zaslavskaya observed in the pre-*perestroika* days: 'The reorganization of production relations [implicit in privatization] promises a substantial narrowing and simplification in responsibilities for workers in departmental ministries.' Their economic influence could be reduced and some of their offices closed. Not surprisingly, 'such a prospect does not suit the workers who at present occupy numerous 'cosy niches' with ill-defined responsibilities but thoroughly agreeable salaries'.[34]

The privatization of housing could indeed threaten the incumbents of housing departments owning and controlling state accommodation. The private fear could combine with a more general hostility to the central government. On the other hand their lack of support for privatization may have a more altruistic or practical foundation; for instance, their fear that tenants who buy a dilapidated property will be unable to repair and maintain it because of the lack of building materials on the market. In the end the conference concluded that privatization would occur and could only condemn the haste with which the government was seeking to implement the policy.

The head of the Housing Repair Department in Novosibirsk asked in whose name privatization was occurring and who benefited from the change in ownership. The policy was manifestly designed to reduce the budget deficit and so 'the cheaper accommodation is for us, the dearer it is for them'. The writer's categories, analysis and lexicon seem remarkably like those of a (Western) Trotskyist: he is dismayed at the prospect of 'the people' paying more for housing – which will only benefit 'them' – an undefined class of bureaucracy whose vehicle is 'an active market – or more accurately, a bazaar of barefaced extortion'.[35] One housing apparatchik even considered the proposed tactic of shifting 'all the worries onto the shoulders of tenants to be wholly unjust, even more so since the subject responsible for the transfer is the state'.

In many ways the head of Sverdlovsk's housing services has expressed the dilemmas and confusion felt by the majority of Soviet citizens about the changes involved in *perestroika*. On the one hand, he wants to adopt a stance of the 'public servant' who wants to do 'what is best'; he wants *qua* functionary, to be seen as being on the side of reform. This he demonstrates by declaring himself for privatization. He points out how the manner in which accommodation is provided 'bonds' him, as it does other ordinary citizens, through various institutional devices.[36] Nonetheless the system does somehow function and it would be wrong to tamper with it and to allow the state to abdicate its responsibilities.

The principal thrust of privatization is to sell to those members of the population who have resources to invest, but this investment does not go into the creation of new accommodation. As a result the construction industry stagnates and prices in the market for a commodity in short supply continue to rise. The acute shortage, in generating speculative buying and selling, will make the price rises even steeper. The social conflicts likely to be engendered will be further exacerbated by tensions arising from the creation of antagonistic groups of owners and non-owners living in the same block of flats. Even without major open conflict, the co-existence of different categories of residents – owners and tenants – could be socially divisive.

These 'housing classes' harbour within them wide fluctuations around the average housing standard which create different living conditions and subsequent life chances.

In the attempt to devise policies which ensure that profit margins on the resale of privately owned dwellings are not excessive, people may be deterred from buying in the first place. On the other hand, if levies on profits are not introduced or are too low, buyers and sellers and various intermediaries may be charged with speculation. Protests organized against speculative activities could generate popular social conflict.

SOCIAL CONFLICT

At the heart of the economic and political changes inaugurated by *perestroika*, indeed their underlying premise, is the creation of a totally new set of property rights. The latter demand the establishment of a legal framework within which state property, leasing arrangements and cooperative and private ownership may coexist. Not only does this fatally undermine the ideological foundation of Soviet Marxism's project, but it is the basis for a reconceptualization of the relationship between class and property. Furthermore the very notion of 'private' property is almost wholly alien to the culture.[37]

The general trend in social policy is a move away from generalized to personalized subsidies. This will adversely effect privileged social groups who have not only had better access to the housing sector but have also enjoyed an unnecessary grant in the form of subsidized rents. In other words, the system of allocating state accommodation has increased rather than reduced inequality in Soviet society.[38] To some extent the operation of a second economy, through which state accommodation was exchanged, compensated for unequal access. However since the 'exchange' was a de facto purchase those in state tenancies have been able to valorize their advantage.

Rogovin represents the belief that the conversion to capitalism does not herald a new era of distributional justice. On the contrary, the first steps in the direction of the market have brought a degree of social polarization hitherto unknown in Soviet society. The poor are confronted by the recently established club for young millionaires. The huge income differences which this club exemplifies signify the existence of a bourgeoisie even prior to the legal foundation of private ownership of the means of production.[39] At the other end of the income scale are the poor. Already over one-third of the population is estimated to be living in poverty. Others consider that 'on any realistic calculation of the real average income, 50 per cent of the population are already on or below the poverty line'.[40] Homelessness is an acknowledged problem.[41]

Households falling within different income and social status categories could be so critically and adversely effected by housing reform that they might constitute the social base for conservative and nationalist organizations and political parties. The latter could, under certain circumstances, even sanction outbreaks of civil disobedience. The social base, in this instance, might combine those households being compelled (by the reform) to forfeit their existing privileged housing status with low income households who, still in the queue for better housing, might find that they will have to pay higher rents or be required to purchase in a housing market where prices are rising steeply.

Housing lies at the heart of much of the enmity felt by large sections of the population towards privilege. Radical newspapers, spawned among miners during their strikes in 1989, are full of detailed accounts of the way in which their employers – the 'Grand Khans of the Coal Mining Areas' – gave handouts to the traffic police and other high Party and government officials, including 'sanatoria for eight families, each with its own en suite facilities'.[42]

Of course people even prior to *perestroika* were aware of the life-style enjoyed by elites. The latter did their best to disguise the benefits and boons at their disposal and in the main refrained from ostentatious consumption. It was the task of academics as well as propagandists to shroud from view and banish from thoughts the existence of such privileged groups. Yet there were always cleaners, shop assistants, chauffeurs and building workers who had first-hand knowledge of their existence. *Glasnost* has allowed them to bring into the public domain of discourse what had hitherto been restricted to the private.

During the intoxicating period following the miners' strikes and protests in Siberia, new movements and slogans appeared, such as 'Building Workers of the Kuzbass Unite'. A component group of one such movement rhetorically asked: 'Who knows better than we, the construction workers, what sort of aristocratic flats they live in?'[43] The builders named the streets where blocks of flats for elites were located. The vehemence of their language expressed deep, long-held resentments:

> While workers are given rather humble, small flats with cramped kitchens, corridors and bathrooms on the outskirts of the city, *their* flats are well-designed, some even with a split-level layout and two bathrooms and are

located in the city centre. Who are these for? And why, even if they are for 'high officials', do they have to be better planned and in the centre, especially since the building regulations prohibit further building there? And why, if they are for workers, are they in the back of beyond?

The acute housing shortage meant that in one (of many) cases, blueprints to erect a block of 18 flats were redrawn to accommodate 40. The result was a 'totally incomprehensible layout' with kitchens having no windows and bathrooms being placed in the middle of the flat so that to go from one room to another meant passing through the toilet! These homes are reserved for ordinary Kemerovo residents.

Privileged social groups are not affected by the general lack of construction materials. Better properties housing the wealthy are erected one after another, with only a 12 month delay between completions. But for the 'poor outcast workers', the same construction trust had been trying for four years to find both the construction materials and a place to build housing for its own workers. The response of workers to these circumstances was to place on a residential building designated for 'aristocrats' a placard demanding that it should be allocated to the Construction Trust responsible for its erection. The article ended with the declaratory statement that the whole Kuzbass is well aware of what the miners achieved when they went on strike; perhaps the construction workers must repeat their action.[44] Criticism from the 'grass roots' has support from the intelligentsia, who point out that (highly subsidized) flats tend to be allocated according to a person's position in the status hierarchy, while leaving large sections of 'ordinary people' without homes or with accommodation of an inferior standard.[45]

The challenge to transformation – the movement towards a market system – is developing in phases. At first, *perestroika* and *glasnost* allowed people freely to discuss the new information on the country's history, its political structures and the imminent economic crisis. Anger over corruption and the perversion of 'real existing socialism' and doubts about the virtues of the egalitarian faith (and its reality) initially quelled fears and apprehensions about the changes being trumpeted by the leadership and the mass media.[46] A positive acceptance of the new economics and its institutional embodiment was, however, premised on the belief that the market system would work better and that most people would benefit from it, either by their seizing opportunities now presented or by a general upward shift in the standard of living. But this has not occurred. Over two-thirds of the population think that the movement towards the market will not offer people like themselves greater opportunities to earn more.[47]

Thus, in the second phase, a vague and pervasive feeling of uncertainty, a fear of unemployment and anxiety at the housing privatization process and the prospect of higher rents have come to prevail. Optimistic expectations are now being replaced by the anger of disillusionment at the losses suffered, the sacrifices demanded and the visibility of a rich stratum of merchants rather than manufacturers. Moreover large sections of the population believe and 'see' the principal beneficiaries of marketization to be members of cooperatives, small retailers and traders, the party *nomenklatura* and the 'mafia' – a loose term used to describe those engaged in varying levels of illegal economic activity. The outcome of these perceptions and experiences is a rise in social tension, criminal activity, alienation and increasing social conflict.

A national poll conducted in December 1990 revealed that 78 per cent of the respondents were dissatisfied with housing provision.[48] But in a question which required respondents to rank housing amongst the problems facing them ('Which problems cause you the greatest worry?') it featured as the last of their concerns.[49] This perception of problems is, in a sense, 'realistic'. After all, the majority of people do have shelter and their situation has not so far worsened for rents remain heavily subsidized. In this third phase a large proportion of the population is now demanding a retreat from the market, in the sense that they prefer that goods in short supply be rationed rather than that their distribution rely on market-determined prices.[50] Although this might even be a majority view, as a recent survey indicates, attitudes towards the distribution of housing vary and reveal a social polarization of interests.

The editorial offices of *Argumenty i fakty* have received several thousand letters from all corners of the country, all from people deeply worried about the privatization of accommodation. Three-quarters of them support the idea of privatizing the housing stock free of charge with the simultaneous introduction of a system of property taxation. The chairman of the Moscow Soviet, N. Gonchar, in commenting on these letters, divided them into three categories. The first consists of people whose living conditions are significantly below the average ('even by Soviet standards'). They are worried by the wish of the authorities to shed all responsibility for housing. A letter writer from this group spoke of 'living in animal conditions', outlined the problems of no heating or hot water each winter, the stench from rubbish heaps in the summer, and asked why the devil she needed to buy her flat, particularly since she had no money in any case. She had a simple demand: *give* us normal state flats.

Secondly there are those who have 'surplus' space, in terms of existing norms. They recognize the benefits from purchasing their accommodation, since real estate will never be so cheap in the future, but they cannot afford to buy that space at the proposed rates. A representative example was a family of three whose parents had died and whose sister had moved to 'Piter' (St Petersburg), leaving them with a four-roomed flat in the centre of Moscow in which the husband had lived all his life. They could never afford to pay for this huge surplus space, although someone else might be able to do so. (In fact, if the family were compelled to transfer or sell up, then there would be immediate purchasers.) He tentatively wondered whether the Moscow city council would examine different preferential tax systems to assist people in his situation. Members of the third group are the well-off. They are against the free transfer of housing into private ownership since they want to invest their rubles, which are rapidly declining in value, in real estate. A representative letter expressed an absolute rejection of giving accommodation away and demanded an end to the old equalizing policy where a person who has sufficient money to buy a five-roomed flat finds a neighbour who is a drunkard and has not a penny to his name. This member of the nouveau riche wanted to know how such a policy could be socially just and how it benefited Moscow.[51]

Already the physical fabric of certain districts has given rise to the social phenomenon of 'sink estates'. Researchers have responded by examining the factors that make some residential districts in large Siberian cities more attractive than others. In 1991 the Krasnoyarsk Civil Engineering Institute, following studies elsewhere, selected four sets of variables which determine the status attached to an area: the condition of the housing stock and the availability of services; the level of air pollution and landscaping; architectural and aesthetic environment; and level of criminality and the social and demographic structure of the population.[52] The material reality of run-down housing and a research interest in the subject has been accompanied by political movements. As early as 1988, tenants on the Moscow housing estate of Brateevo set up a committee to improve living conditions. It is far too soon to know whether such organizations will develop into broad-based 'social movements' to contest housing policy or whether they will more closely resemble 'community action groups' found in the UK two decades ago.

The housing shortage – a consequence of past policies – and the projected privatization programme and changes in rental charges are intricately linked to other important issues which also have potentially serious political implications. An article in the right-wing newspaper of the veterans' association provocatively asked whether the disappearance of the issue of refugees from newspapers meant that it was no longer a problem. In reply, the USSR Ministry of Internal Affairs announced that the number of refugees had grown from 608 000 at the beginning of 1991 to 676 000 by July. Other (unofficial) estimates put the number at over one million. In any event the actual number is constantly rising.[53]

The question draws attention to two serious concerns. The first is the tension arising between indigenes and immigrants (refugees) of the same ethnic group because of the pressure caused by the latter on local resources, especially housing. This has already been witnessed in the Krasnodar region, where local inhabitants have been less than welcoming to Russian refugees from the Caucasian republics. In the second case the tensions have an added dimension when the immigrants have different ethnic origins. In both instances the climate of heightened ethnic intolerance (and nationalism) is leading to major migration flows which will place an increased burden on the housing sector in the places of refugee destination.[54]

An intractable situation, exacerbated by the existing housing shortage, is compounded further when Armenian families, who are being evicted from their homes by Azeris, impatiently request that the country's deputies 'take care of its own refugees, instead of pouring millions of rubles into Afghanistan and Cuba'.[55] Taken together the problems faced by minorities and their interrelationship with communities in which they are alien have an explosive potential.

Another matter of concern to the government is the considerable disquiet among officers and soldiers returning from Eastern Europe, Cuba and elsewhere and finding accommodation difficult to obtain. They do not, however, constitute a homogenous group with a solidarity interest and the government is diverting resources to meet their needs.

Other sources of hardship, of which there must be thousands of instances, and of a less dramatic flavour than those associated with refugees from areas of ethnic conflict or returning from military service abroad, are caused by the general demobilization of soldiers. The number of letters emanating from military personnel, returning from Eastern Europe or from families of soldiers leaving regions of inter-ethnic conflict and sent to newspapers is constantly increasing. For instance, a soldier who had been sent to the Soviet-Chinese border during the 1970 Sino-Soviet dispute was released from service in 1987 on grounds of ill-health and offered accommodation in Kaluga, not in Kyrgyzstan where his family lived. The newspaper printed excerpts from correspondence with official bodies commencing in 1989. They told a bizarre tale with a sad and typical twist, when the rules on allocating accommodation were suddenly changed and he was informed that his name had only been put on the waiting list in April 1991.[56]

The editorial comment on this letter generalized the case and concluded that the return of servicemen and demobilization were 'exacerbating an already acute housing situation. In a situation where city authorities are trying to provide accommodation for their own citizens, naturally the instructions issued [from the centre] on how to deal with "newcomers" are open to very wide interpretation'. The solution prescribed was the 'introduction of a free market. However, since that still does not exist, then civilian and military building contractors must combine their resources to provide for the military.' This might of course be an expedient thing to do, but it may not be well received by the local population if they are to be deprived of resources to build accommodation for people on their waiting lists. The editorial ended by pointing out that the 'hundreds of thousands of people' affected are finding that, 'after serving in difficult and dangerous circumstances, they are without a roof over their heads'. Should there be another attempted conservative reaction – as some pundits in Moscow predict – then this might be a weapon in their armoury. However the weapon would soon be turned back on them, for they have no housing policy which could solve the chronic shortage that has suddenly become acute.

The prerequisites for social conflict are being generated not just by the fact that those who are visibly benefiting from change belong to groups with low public esteem (and therefore, by definition, unworthy of large rewards). The return of military personnel worsens the chronic housing shortage and contributes another dimension to the social cleavages. Finally, in a culture with a strong egalitarian strain which places greater priority on equality of *outcomes* as a measure of justice, rather than equal opportunity of access, the privatization of housing in tandem with increased rental charges is likely to be a major threat to the desire of the new elites to transform the society.

Underlying social tensions could be exacerbated by housing policies and 'lay a revolutionary mine under future stability',[57] a view shared by senior Russian government ministers. In a question and answer session with a member of the RSFSR Committe on Economic Reform and Ownership, the correspondent asked whether the actual and predicted price rises for accommodation, which are part of the general inflationary process in the transitional period, will, 'threaten a social explosion'. The reply was brutally clear. Surveys have shown that the majority of the population prefer that everything should remain as it is, with accommodation being provided free of charge. Unfortunately, 'the man in the street' is far from understanding, not just the complexity of 'various cause and effect linkages', but also the 'simple truth that there is no such thing as "free"; we all pay for everything out of our pockets through taxation'.[58] This poses the question, 'How can home ownership be introduced quickly without inspiring popular protest?' So, in order to satisfy 'the man in the street', the proposal of the Deputy Prime Minister of the RSFSR – which is the simplest solution – should be adopted: each individual household should be given the property that they already occupy. This would be, of course, very acceptable to those in large, well-equipped flats, but not to those in shared, communal flats.

Deliberations in the Moscow Soviet since summer 1991 on the form privatization should take were finalized in November. In essence they meet the needs of the above three groups: the weak will be protected and a progressive property tax will ensure that the rich will pay for the construction of municipal housing in the future.

CONCLUSION

> Despite the apparent attractiveness of the idea of justice, if one examines it closely, one realises that it represents the most destructive aspect of Russian psychology. In practice, 'justice' involves the desire that 'nobody should live better than I do'. . . . In general, when the average Russian sees that he is living less well than his neighbour, he will concentrate not on trying to do better for himself but rather on trying to bring his neighbour down to his own level. (A. Amalrik, *Will the Soviet Union Survive Until 1984?* Harper and Row, London, 1970, p. 33)

The high levels of overcrowding, the universally small flats and low space standards and often poor quality of external design and interior layout will not be remedied overnight by raising rents, or by selling state accommodation to sitting tenants or to cooperatives. Improvements can only be achieved by increasing the supply of accommodation. It is difficult to predict whether in the near future the current economic reforms will be able to have a positive effect on housing production. As in other advanced industrial countries, a revitalized private sector will have to coexist with a public sector. The latter will serve as a 'social guarantee' for those on low incomes unable to compete in the market. The exact nature of that public sector remains to be determined, but will certainly vary from republic to republic.

A huge demand for housing exists. Unemployment is rising and governments are reducing their budgetary expenditures. The immense trauma of change, exacerbated by what is virtually a national apostasy, has left vast numbers of people discontented, anomic and alienated. Embarking on a well-planned self-build programme could be of greater benefit to the people and government than merely the provision of good-quality accommodation. But it is not just a question of increasing the supply. The policies being advocated by reformers reflect a profoundly felt disapprobation and contempt for the way in which individuals have in the past gained access to this vital commodity, the self-contained family home. Greater wage differentials and the simultaneous removal of fringe benefits, such as closed shops and special sanatoria, are necessary concomitants of the demise of 'the distributor' in the field of housing. Rent reform and privatization will play their role as handmaidens of the bourgeois revolution and in the restructuring of the class system.

The replacement of universal subsidies by individually targetted means-tested housing benefits will attack the inequities, corruption and injustices characteristic of the current system. It is likely, however that the reforms being advocated will prompt the emergence of a pernicious petty landlordism and grander rentier. The intelligentsia is divided in its attitude to the privatization of housing. In general, the editorial position of *Kommersant* and *Moscow News* is favourable towards the march of the market. *Argumenty i fakty*, though against the administrative system, maintains a healthy scepticism on the subject of *cui bono?* privatization. Conservatism is keenly exhibited in the weekly newspaper of the nationwide organization of veterans, *Veteran*.[59]

The debates on privatization, especially the issue of whether tenants should be entitled to receive their homes and become owner-occupiers free of charge is reminiscent of the lengthy arguments preceding the Edict on Emancipation in 1861: the imposition of redemption payments on the former serfs only increased their heavy taxation burden, which they were frequently unable to meet. It was not until 1907 – after further peasant unrest – that the government took the necessary and inevitable step of abolishing the redemption payments and cancelling arrears. In retrospect, according to Richard Pipes, the radical critics of the 1861 settlement were correct, for the land should have been given to the peasants free of charge, 'not only on moral, but also on practical grounds'.[60] The parallel with the present day – in this instance, the issue at stake is the home not land – is clearly evident. No longer is it a matter of the peasants' appeal, 'We are yours but the land is ours'; rather it is a proletarian plea, 'Since we live here and have paid for – through rent and taxes – and looked after the homes which we occupy, the flats are ours.' Rental arrears too, it might be postulated, will be cancelled, as were payments arrears in 1907.

A paternalistic society which has created its own specific form of 'culture of poverty' as a widespread phenomenon coexists with a deeply ingrained egalitarian value system. These 'social facts' exert a negative influence on the marketization process. The now highly criticized Brezhnev regnum did cover a period of rising standards of living within a stable environment. Basic needs such as medical care and housing were provided virtually free of charge (at the point of delivery) and jobs and incomes were guaranteed. The transformation of state and economy that is now occurring would appear, like the 'iron laws' of the classical economists, to be 'necessary' and inevitable. But like those laws of capitalist development and the law of 'capitalist encirclement', the price of transformation has to be paid for by more sacrifices by the population. It was the issue of 'inevitability' that led the Russian *narodniki* to challenge the classical economists. It was the suffering brought by capitalism that occasioned the Bolshevik challenge. It would be strange if there were now no challenge to the sacrifices which the 'necessary' transformation demands.

NOTES AND REFERENCES

1. O. Bessonova, 'Reform of the Soviet Housing Model: Search for a Concept', in B. Turner, J. Hegedus, I. Tosics (eds), *The Reform of Housing in Eastern Europe and the Soviet Union*, Routledge, London, 1992.
2. Housing, which as a political party issue in the UK had finally received its place on the agenda of the contending parties in 1919, retained its position of prominence in all general elections until 1979. Today housing has virtually disappeared from political view (having been supplanted by health and education), re-emerging in a peripheral way over homelessness, mortgage interest rate relief and, more recently, the repossession of mortgaged houses. It is interesting to note that the privatization of housing as a controversial issue has been a percursor of current debates on the privatization of health and education, partly because of its greater visibility as a 'commodity'.
3. See G. Andrusz, *Housing and Urban Development in the USSR*, Macmillan/CREES, London, 1984; G. Andrusz, 'Housing Policy in the Soviet Union', in J. Sillince (ed.), *Housing Policies in Eastern Europe and the Soviet Union*, Routledge, London, 1990.

4. T. Boiko, 'Posmotrim v zuby "darenomu" zhilyu', *EKO*, 1991, 5, p. 40.
5. N. Kosareva, N. Ronkin and O. Pchelintsev, 'Na puti k zhilishchnoi reforme: analiz i prognoz', *Voprosy ekonomiki*, 1990, no. 8.
6. TsNIIEP zhilishcha, *General'naya skhema obespecheniya k 2000 godu kazhdoi sovetskoi sem'i otdel'noi kvartiroi ili individual'nym domom*, Moscow, 1988, p. 261.
7. In 1990, 1.8 million families had their names on the waiting list to join a housing cooperative.
8. It should be remembered that, at the beginning of 1989, 80 per cent of those on housing waiting lists were on registers for enterprise accommodation. See N. Kalinina, 'Housing and Housing Policy in the USSR', in B. Turner *et al.*, *The Reform of Housing in Eastern Europe and the Soviet Union*, Routledge, 1992.
9. T. Boiko, 'Posmotrim', p. 41.
10. Ibid., p. 40.
11. The amount of living space accepted as indicating the need for improved accommodation varies from city to city, but generally falls within the range of five to seven square metres per person.
12. T. Boiko, 'Posmotrim', p. 41. In 1990 the actual distribution of households by dwelling areas was as follows:

up to 5 square metres per person	10.6% of households
5.1–7.0	18.2
7.1–9.0	20.4
9.1–11.0	21.3
11.1–13.0	8.9
13.1–15.0	8.6
15.1 and over	11.9

See *Argumenty i fakty*, 1990, no. 7.

13. See Kolotilkin, *Argumenty i fakty*, 9 June 1989.
14. V. Resin, 'Deshevo khorosho ne byvaet', *Kuranty*, 20 July 1991, no. 136.
15. This problem is observable in Hungary following the 1990 Law on Self-Government and the 1991 Budget Act. See European Network for Housing Research, *Newsletter*, 1991, 3.
16. In answer to an inquiry on loans to individuals wishing to become owner-occupiers, the newspaper *Argumenty i fakty* explained that in 1991 the National Savings Bank (*Sberbank SSSR*) had become a commercial bank permitted to borrow and lend money. From 1 January 1991 the rate of interest charged on loans made to individuals to build, buy or repair homes is 3 per cent per annum (and 0.5 per cent for invalids and other social groups, such as those suffering the effects of Chernobyl). These loans will be over 25–30 years and cover up to 75–80 per cent of the estimated price. See *Argumenty i fakty*, June 1991, no. 27, p. 3. Interest chargeable on credit provided for other purposes, for instance buying consumer durables, is not fixed by these regulations.
17. O. Bessonova, 'Mina zamedlennogo deistviya', in *Delovaya Sibir'*, January 1991, no. 2, p. 4.
18. 'O novykh podkhodakh k resheniyu zhilishchnoi problemy v strane i merakh po ikh prakticheskoi realizatsii.'
19. *Narodnoe khoziaystvo SSSR v 1989g*, p. 88.
20. B. Kolotilkin, 'Kvartplata i koshelek', *Argumenty i fakty*, 22–6 June 1989. Analysis of statistics on payments for accommodation reveals that a tenant's annual outlay on one square metre of dwelling space is as follows: rent – 19 per cent; central heating, sewage, water and gas – 33 per cent; electricity – 18 per cent and telephone 12 per cent. See B. Kolotilkin, 'Kvartirnaya plata: khozraschet i sotsial'-naya spravedlivost', *Voprosy ekonomiki*, 1990, no. 8, pp. 91–4.
21. ECE, 12 October 1990, Annex 1.

22 V. Resin, 'Deshevo khorosho ne byvaet', *Kuranty*, 20 July 1991, no. 136. The subordination of builders to architects is not a novel idea, nor policy. In the past words were not met by deeds.

23. N. Kalinina, 'Privatising Public Housing in West and Eastern Europe', unpublished paper prepared for a panel discussion, Washington, 1990.

24. T. Boiko, 'Posmotrim', *EKO*, 1991, no. 5, p. 45.

25. Ibid. p. 46.

26. 'Kuplyu kvartiru', *Demokraticheskaya Rossiya*, 2 August 1991, no. 18.

27. R. Artemev, 'Privatizatsiya zhil'ya: bez anneksii i kontributsii', *Kommersant*, 1–8 July 1991, no. 27.

28. 'Osushchestvit' perekhod k rynke pravitel'stvo SSSR ne sposobno', *Moskovskii komsomolets*, 20 November 1990, p. 1.

29. T. Boiko, 'Posmotrim' *EKO*, 1991, no. 5, p. 42.

30. Ibid., p. 41.

31. O. E. Bessonova, 'Fenomen besplatnogo zhil'ya v SSSR', *Izvestia Sibirskogo Otdeleniya Ak.Nauk SSSR. Seriya ekonomiki i prikladnoi sotsiologii*, vypusk 3, 1988; G. D. Andrusz, 'A Note on the Financing of Housing in the Soviet Union', *Soviet Studies*, July 1990, vol. 42, no. 3.

32. O. Bessonova and O. E. Bessonova, 'Reforms of the Soviet Housing Model: Search for a Concept', in B. Turner *et al.*, (eds), *The Reform of Housing in Eastern Europe and the Soviet Union*, Routledge, 1992.

33. 'Rynochnye zhil'ya: budet li nyneshnee pokolenie sovetskikh lyudei zhit' v svoikh domakh', *Delovaya Sibir'. Rossiiskii kommercheskii ezhednevnik*, January 1991, no. 2, p. 4.

34. *The Novosibirsk Report*, reprinted in M. Yanowitch (ed.), *A Voice of Reform. Essays by Tat'iana I. Zaslavskaya*, M. E. Sharpe, London, p. 172.

35. *Delovaya Sibir'*, no. 2, January 1991.

36. 'We are tied by our flats, as by a rope, to our place of residence (though the *propiska*), to our place of work (which often is the provider of accommodation) and to many other "pillars" [*stolby*] of the system.'

37. Amongst the numerous writings supporting this statement, see R. Pipes, *Russian under the Old Regime*, Weidenfeld and Nicolson, London, 1974.

38. See, for instance, Z. Daniel, 'The Effect of Housing Allocation on Social Inequality in Hungary', *Journal of Comparative Economics*, December 1985, no. 9: I. Szelenyi, *Urban Inequalities under Socialism*, Oxford University Press, Oxford, 1983.

39. 'V poiskakh spravedlivosti', *Radikal*, 9 July 1991, no. 26, p. 6. The article is an interview with Vadim Rogovin of the Institute of Sociology who has had a long-term interest in the issue of social justice.

40. N. Kirichenko and A. Shonarov, 'Ch'ya korsina tyazhelee?', *Argumenty i fakty*, June 1991, no. 23, pp. 1–2.

41. 'Bomzh, pochemu ty takoi?', *Argumenty i fakty*, November 1991, no. 45, p. 7.

42. See, for instance, the front page lead article in *Nasha Gazeta*, 11 December 1989, no. 1. The newspaper was published by the Union of Kuzbass workers.

43. 'Dvoryanskie gnezda – rabochim', *Nasha Gazeta*, 24 April 1991, no. 10, p. 4. The article has been authorized by over 200 workers of the Construction Trust, 'Kemerovograzhdanstroi'.

44. 'Dvoryanskie gnezda – rabochim'.

45. O. Bessonova, 'Zhilishchnaya strategiya: Kak uiti ot gorodov Khrushchob', *EKO*, 1991, no. 5, pp. 53–9.

46. Changing attitudes to the 'huge earnings' of cooperatives and other quasi-private initiatives reflected this mollification.

47. VTsIOM, *Obshchestvennoe mnenie v tsifrakh*, Vypusk 9, 'Otnosheniya naseleniya k ekonomicheskoi reforme', 1991, Moscow.

48. VTsIOM, *Obshchestvennoe mnenie v tsifrakh*, 1991, no. 4: 74 per cent were also

dissatisfied with the health service and 60 per cent thought that the state paid insufficient attention to the citizens' needs.

49. Of far greater significance is the difficulty of obtaining basic needs such as soap, clothes and other consumer goods, food products, rising prices and lack of money: *Radikal*, 5–11 April 1991, no. 13.

50. In reply to the question, 'What should be done when a good disappears from the shops and it is impossible to increase its supply in the short term?' 67 per cent replied that rationing should be introduced and only 10 per cent thought that the price of that particular commodity should be allowed to rise. See *Radikal*, 5–11 April 1991, no. 13.

51. 'Khochu kupit' . . . no besplatno'. *Argumenty i fakty*, November 1991, no. 45.

52. 'Research on the Prestige Factors of Housing Environments in Cities and Towns of Siberia', *European Network for Housing Research*, 1991, no. 3, p. 10.

53. *Veteran*, July 1991, no. 29. The majority were Armenian (302 000) followed by Azeris (203 000); Meskhetin Turks added another 40 000 and Russian speakers from various republics another 40 000.

54. The growing xenophobia has many causes. Housing is one of the more obvious alongside anxieties about unemployment. One letter to *Argumenty i fakty* (July 1991, no. 29) asked: 'If we are now registering the unemployed, why are so many Vietnamese working in the Soviet Union?' In issue no. 31 of *Argumenty i fakty*, someone else inquired why Bulgarians are still employed in the Soviet Union, given the job shortage. The reply offered by the Ministry of Timber Production, the principal employer of Bulgarian workers, was that the were employed in areas where it was impossible to attract Russians.

55. A letter to the editor: 'My bezhentsy', *Izvestia* 30 April 1990.

56. 'Pogranichnik on zhe – bomzh', *Izvestia*, 18 July 1991, p. 3.

57. O. Bessonova, 'Mina zamedlennogo deistviya'.

58. 'Kuplyu kvartiru', *Demokraticheskaya Rossiya*, 2 August 1991, no. 18.

59. See, for instance, *Veteran*, July 1991, no. 29.

60. R. Pipes, *Russian under the Old Regime*, Penguin Books, Harmondsworth, 1990, p. 166.

Index

Aitmatov, Chingiz 107
Akayev, Askar 55
Akhmedov, Kh. 56
Amalrik, A. 232
Ananev, Anatolii 107
Andreyev, Valery 152
Andropov, Yuri V. 12, 101
anti-Semitism 106
Armenia
  Armenian Pan-National
    Movement 51, 54, 57
  challenge to centre 59
  deputies 50
  intelligentsia in 44
  leadership elections 51, 54, 55
  Prime Minister 57, 58
Aslonov, Kadreddin 55
Azerbaijan
  deputies 50
  employment laws 128
  housing 214
  leadership elections 53, 54, 55
  Popular Front 54
  Prime Minister 56

Bakatin, Vadim 25, 26, 38
Baklanov, Georgii 107
Balayan, Zorii 107
Baltic republics
  challenge to centre 59
  demand for independence 24
  deputies 50
  employment laws 128
  housing 214
  party politics in 48
  refusal to join CIS 60
  youth 150
  see also Estonia; Latvia; Lithuania
Belorussia
  agreement with Russia 29

Communist Party in 43
  deputies 50
  education 149
  employment laws 128
  housing waiting lists 213
  intelligentsia in 44
  leadership elections 53, 54, 55
  Popular Front 54
  Prime Minister 56, 57
  Russians in 45
  see also republics
Bessmertnykh, Aleksandr 26
Bessolova, Olga 172, 175, 177
Biryukova, Alexandra 168
Bocharov, Mikhail 57
Boldin, Valerii 26
Borovoi, Konstantin 192
Brezhnev, Leonid
  regime 3, 101, 102, 167
    bribes 192
    intra-elite conflict 16
    poverty 208
    power structure 15
    prices 203
    shadow economy 190
    standard of living 234
Bulganin, N.A. 11
Burbulis, Gennadii 32, 33, 38
bureaucracy 3–4, 11, 12–13
  CPSU control of 8–10
  employees in 6–8
  growth of 5–6
  housing 210
Burlatsky, Fedor 105, 107
Burtin, Yurii 105
Bush, George 30
business 190–91
  law and 191–3
  stock exchanges 191
business elites 185–95

239

characteristics of 186–7
definition 185–6
members
  CPSU members 189
  educational background 187
  interests and leisure time 187–8
  living standards 187
  millionaires 190, 193
  nomenklatura 189–90
  pattern of expenditure 187
  social background 187, 188–9
size and structure of 186
businessmen 69, 70, 71, 115
  bourgeois ethics 193–4
  donations to charity 194
  political attitudes of 194

Cabinet of Ministers 24, 25, 26, 27,
    34
Chairman of *see* Prime Minister
cash transfers 201–3
Central Asian republics
  child allowance in 202
  deputies 50
  employment laws 128
  housing 214
  leadership elections 54
  poverty level 199, 200
  representation of women in 42
  unemployment in 206
  youth 149, 150
  see also Kyrgyzstan; Tajikistan;
      Turkmenistan; Uzbekistan
Central Committee 8, 11
centre
  collapse of 125, 203
  definition 12
  transfer of power to republics 28,
      34
  weakening of 29
Centre for Gender Studies 172,
    173–4, 175
Chairman of Supreme Soviet,
    election of 50–55
charity, donations to 194
Chazov, Evgenii 87
Chernichenko, Yurii 107
child allowances 202
CIS *see* Commonwealth of
    Independent States

class
  business 115
  divisions 17, 18, 19
  interest 71–2
  middle class 63, 73
  structure 20
  working 115, 129–30
cliques, rule of 13
Commonwealth of Independent
    States (CIS) 25, 34, 36, 61
Communist Party of the Soviet Union
    (CPSU)
  20th Party Congress 104, 105
  27th Party Congress 168, 171, 212,
      220
  28th Party Congress 106, 168
  as agency of political cohesion and
      control 8–10
  collapse of 62
  female emancipation 169–70
  republics
    deputies 48, 49
    leadership elections 43, 54
  secretariat 9–10
Congress of People's Deputies, 24,
    50, 107
  elections to 41, 123, 124
  professional background of 94–5
  RSFSR 108
Connor, Walt 116
construction industry 224, 227
consumer goods
  access to 121
  subsidies for 202–3, 208
consumerism, youth 159
corruption 13, 16, 97, 103
  bribes 88, 192
  illegal money-making 20
  racketeering 192–3
Council of the Federation 24, 25, 26,
    27, 28, 31
Council of Ministers 9, 26
  Chairman of *see* Prime Minister
coup, August 1991 17, 18, 20, 24, 31,
    59
  effects of 55, 57, 94
  as end of Soviet socialism 127
  role of media in 109
  role of women in 173, 177–8
  trade unions and 127

USSR after 34–6

Dementei, Nikolai 53, 54, 55
Demichev, Petr 12
Democratic Party of Russia (DPR)
  63–81, 170
  age structure 74
  attitude to Union 64
  composition of 64
  congresses of 65
  date of entry into politics 75–6
  lack of ideology 77
  leadership of 78
  status factors
    educational level 70, 73
    income level 67, 70, 73
    occupational structure 69, 73
Democratic Perestroika party 63,
  76–7
Democratic Russia party 50, 72
democratization 41, 122, 169
Denisov, Igor 87–8
departmentalism 12, 13, 16
deputies 49, 50, 118–19
  ethnic background 45–8
  occupational background of 42–3,
    44
  see also Congress of People's
    Deputies
DPR *see* Democratic Party of Russia
Druk, Mircha 58–9
Durkheim, Emile 210

education
  spending on 201
  standards of 117
elections 41, 77, 123, 124
  leadership 36, 50–55
  under Stalin 118
  voting systems 45, 47
elites
  bureaucratic 13
  business *see* business elites
  closed membership 5, 15, 16, 21
  coherence and integration of 10–11
  conflict between 16
  confrontational 18, 19, 21
  consensual 13, 15, 18
  corporatist 16
  government 95

heterogeneity of 13, 19
intellectual/ideological 104
Komsomol and 153–5
lifestyle of 226
mono-organizational 3
monopolistic unitary 13
national 20, 118
open membership 15, 19
party 66–79
see also Democratic Party of
  Russia; Social Democratic Party
  of Russia
pluralistic 14–16, 17
political 3–4, 104
  evolution of 4–5
power 3, 15, 18, 20, 21
  in the republics 41–61
regional 16
segmentation of 16
self-governing 15
under Gorbachev 14–16, 17
women and 178
Eltsin, Boris 18, 21, 24, 25, 77, 128,
  195
  attitude to communism 30
  biography 39
  as Chairman of Russian
    government 32
  combining role of President/Prime
    Minister 57
  control over nuclear weapons 34
  CPSU
    ban on 33–4
    resignation from 49
  election of 30, 50, 51
  foreign relations 30–31
  reform programme 60, 114
  relationship with Gorbachev 27,
    28–31
  setting up of CIS 36
  setting up of presidential system 31
  suspension of CPSU newspapers
    111
  trade unions and 126, 127
  women and 173
Employment Centres 128
Engels, Friedrich 20
entrepreneurs 19, 45, 185, 193
  see also business; businessmen

environmental movement, growth of 96
envoys, appointment of 32–3
Estonia
  deputies 48
  family farming in 133–48
  housing 214
  leadership elections 51
  nationalism in 41
  Popular Front 57, 107
    women and 177
  poverty level 200
  Prime Minister 57
  see also Baltic republics; republics
ethnic groups 18, 118
  blocs 19
  conflicts 124
  differentiation 18
  housing 230
  representation of 45–8
Evtushenko, Evgenii 102, 106

farming 20, 133–48
Filippova, Natasha 172
Filtzer, Donald 121
Fokin, Vitold 56
Furtseva, Ekaterina 168

Gaidar, Egor T. 32, 39
Gamsakhurdia, Zviad 44, 51, 59
gangs, teenage 160–62
Georgia
  challenge to centre 59
  Communist Party in 49
  declaration of independence 59
  deputies 50
  intelligentsia 44
  leadership elections 51, 55
  Prime Minister 57, 58, 59
  refusal to join CIS 60
  representation of ethnic minorities 47
  Round Table 48, 51
  see also republics
Gidaspov, Boris 32
glasnost 92
  birth of 101–3
  women and 178
Godmanis, Ivars 57
Gonchar, N. 228

Gorbachev, Mikhail 18, 21, 195
  acceleration 122
  attempt to save Union 24–5
  biography 38
  bureaucracy, reform of 13
  Council of the Federation and 25, 28
  CPSU and 28
  creation of post of President 54
  democratization 41, 122
  'election' of 77
  glasnost, birth of 101–3
  housing, rents 220
  intellectuals and 101
  intensification 122
  loans from the West 193
  market economy 204
  meeting with George Bush 30
  move to pluralistic elites under 14–16
  professional background 94
  regime 3, 116
    devolution to republics 8
    elites 14–16, 17
    freedom for journalists 93
    housing 217
    increase of poverty under 196
  relationship with Eltsin 27, 28–31
  republics and 18, 24, 28–29, 41
  resignation of 36
  role of Prime Minister 27
  Security Council and 26
  State Council and 35
  student leaders and 157
  women's groups, support for 171
  see also coup, August 1991
Gorbunovs, Anatolijs 51
Gordon, Leonid 117
Goskomstat 127, 129, 197, 198, 199
Goskomtrud 197, 206
Gosplan, abolition of 27
Grachev, Pavel 34–5
Graivoronsky, Victor 153
Granick, David 120
Grebenshchikov, Boris 152
Gromova, E. 177
Gromyko, Andrei 12
Gugushvili, Vissarion 59
Gurevich, Leonid 108

Hanson, Philip 120
Hauslohner, Peter 120
health care 87–9, 201, 202
homelessness 226
Hough, J.F. 15–16
housing
  bureaucracy 210
  construction industry 224, 227
  demobilization of soldiers 230–31
  dwelling space 20, 213, 214, 215,
    218
  free transfer of 228–9, 233
  house-building cooperatives
    214–17
  immigrants 230
  legislative reform 214–17
  loans 215–16
  for low-income families 216,
    217–18, 233
  marketization 228
  owner-occupation 216–17
  ownership, structure of 211–12
  privatization 216, 219, 220–26, 228,
    230, 233
  property rights 225
  reform 210–37
  rent 215, 217–20
    reform 233
    subsidies 219
  right to 218
  self-build 217, 233
  'sink estates' 229
  subsidies, personalized 225
  waiting lists 213
  youth 213–14, 217

Ilyushin, Viktor 33
income 120–21, 198–9, 202
  differentials 19, 121, 127, 233
  youth 163
  see also poverty
informals 75, 76, 77, 157–8
  youth 162
intellectuals 77, 103
  dissident 77
intelligentsia 20, 69, 70, 77
  in new parliaments 43–4
  in republics 44
  sociopolitical role of 104
Interregional Deputies' Group 50

Ivans, Dainis 107
Ivashko, Vladimir 53, 54

journalists 92–4, 96, 103–13
  coup of August 1991 109
  as deputies 44
  independent periodicals 105
  response to *glasnost* 103–5
  Union of Journalists 93, 107

Kafarova, Elmira 53
Kagarlitsky, Boris 152
Kamenev, Lev V. 11
Karaev, Tamerlan 54
Karimov, Islam 53, 56
Karpinsky, Len 105
Karyakin, Yurii 105
Kazakhstan
  agreement with Russia 29
  deputies, Communist Party
    loyalists 50
  employment laws 128
  leadership elections 53, 54, 55
  nine-plus-one agreement 29
  poverty level 200
  Prime Minister 56
  representation of workers and
    peasants 43
  women in 42
Kebich, Vyachislav 55, 56
Keynes, John Maynard 211
KGB 26, 35, 38
  Komsomol and 153
  in Russia 30
Khodorovsky, Mikhail 109, 194
Khrushchev, Nikita 11
  decentralization 13
  intellectuals and 101
  regime
    ministries 12
    pensions 201
    poverty 203
    prices 203
    women 168
Kirichenko, N. 205
Kiselev, Stepan 110
Kitovani, Tengiz 59
Klimienkova, Tatiana 173
Kobets, Konstantin 33
Komsomol 152–5, 189

commercial organizations 154–5
elites and 153–5
KGB and 153
perestroika and 153
Young Pioneers 153
Konarev, Nikolai 27
Konstantinova, Valentina 175, 179
Korotich, Vitalii 107
Kosygin, A.N. 12
Kravchuk, Leonid 53
Kryuchkov, Vladimir A. 26, 38
Kudyukin, Pavel 77
Kurilchenko, Vera 176
Kurkova, Bella 108
Kuznetsova, Larisa 175
Kyrgyzstan
employment laws 128
leadership elections 53, 54, 55
Prime Minister 56
representation of workers and
peasants 43
urban migration 117
see also Central Asian republics;
republics

Labour, Party of 129
Landsbergis, Vytautus 44, 51, 58
Laptev, Ivan 119
Latvia
housing 220
Interfront 177
Latvian Popular front 51
leadership elections 51
nationalism in 41
Popular Front 57, 107
Prime Minister 57
see also Baltic republics; republics
Lauristin, Marju 107
lawyers 89–91
cooperatives 90
judges 90
Lawyers Union 90
Union of Jurists 90
Lenin, V.I. 8, 10, 101
Lewin, Moshe 64
Liberal Democratic Party 170
Ligachev, Egor 12, 106, 189
Linkova, Valentina 108
Lipovskaya, Olga 173

Lithuania
Communist Party in 49–50
declaration of independence 59
deputies 48
ethnic minorities 48
intelligentsia in 44
leadership elections 50–51
nationalism in 41
Prime Minister 58
women in 42
see also Baltic republics; republics
localism 12, 203
Lyubimov, Aleksandr 108

Makhkamov, Kakhar 53, 55, 56
Malenkov, Georgi M. 11
Manannikov, Aleksei 108
Manukian, Vazgen 57, 58
market economy 13, 17, 56, 126, 227
housing 228
introduction of 207–8
price mechanism 204–5
unemployment 202, 203
women in 174
marketization *see* market economy
Marx, Karl 211
Masaliev, Absamat 53, 54, 55
Masol, Vitaly 56
Mazurov, K. 12
media *see* journalists
Medvedev, Sergei 109
Meshchersky, Aleksandr 108
Meyer, Alfred G. 3
Mikhailova, Liubov 175
Mikoyan, Anastas 11
millionaires 190, 193
Mills, C. Wright 15
miners
strikes 1989 124–5, 226, 227
union 126–7, 129
women 175
ministries 5–6, 12
industrial 7–8
occupational background of
ministers 13–14
Mironov, Viktor 108
Mirsiadov, Shukurilla 56
Moldavia
challenge to centre 59
cooperatives in 45

deputies 45, 46, 48, 50
housing 213
leadership elections 51, 55
nationalism in 41
Popular Front 51, 58
Prime Minister 58
women in 178
see also republics
Molotov, Vyacheslav M. 11
Movsisian, V. 51
Mukusev, Vladimir 108
Muravschi, Valery 59
Mutalibov, Ayaz 53

Nabiev, Rakhmon 55
nationalism 41, 43–4, 50, 51, 230
students 156
women and 178
Nazarbayev, Nursultan 53, 56
Nazimova, Alla 117
Nevzorov, Alexander 176
Nikolsky, Boris 107
nine-plus-one agreement 28–31
Niyazov, Saparmurad 53, 54, 56
nomenklatura 115, 127, 168, 195
access to consumer goods 121
business elites and 189–90
deputy elections 43
housing 228
Novo-Ogarevo process 28–31
nuclear weapons 30, 34

Obolenskii, Aleksandr 77

Party of Labour 129
party politics, development of 48–50,
63–81
Paskar, Petr 58
Pastukhova, Maria 153
Pavlov, Valentin 26, 31, 195
pensions 200, 201
perestroika
effects of 19
ideologists of 105
impact on workers 114–32
journalism 112
Komsomol and 153
new political parties 17, 129
poverty and 203–6
professionalism and 85, 87–94, 96

trade unions and 125–7
women and 166–81
workers and 121–4
economic position 127–30
youth and 76, 156–63
Petrov, Yurii 33
physicians 87–9, 96
Pilshchikov, E. 176
Pipes, Richard 233–4
Podgorny, Nikolai V. 12
Politburo 4, 8, 11, 12–13
evolution of 9, 10–11
membership 12
RSFR 17
see also centre
Politkovsky, Aleksandr 108
Polozkov 195
Poltoranin, Mikhail 107
Popov, Garil 49, 94, 95
Posadskaya, Anastasiya 174, 175, 177
poverty 196–209
cash transfers 201–3
Goskomtrud, role of 197
homelessness 226
level 127–8, 225–6
defining 197–9
pensioners 200
youth 163
perestroika and 203–6
prices 203–5
rationing 198
Soviet conceptions of 196–200
under Khrushchev 203
under Stalin 203
welfare benefits 201–3
Pravda, Alex 115
President, elections to new post of 54
presidential representatives 32–3
prices 203–5
rise in 205
Primakov, Evgenii 25, 26
Prime Minister
post of 55–9
role of 27
private enterprise, cooperatives 45,
88
privatization 17, 19, 96
Estonia, family farming in 133–48
housing 216, 219, 220–25, 225–6,
228, 230

professionals 20
  definition 86
  education, training, certification 97
  funding of 97
  income 120
  perestroika and 85, 96
  professionalization 85–100
  status of in USSR 86–7
Pronina, L. 205
property rights 225
Prunskiene, Kazimiera 58
Pugo, Boriss 26

Rasputin, Valentin 106
republics
  assets, control over 18, 20
  Communist Party in 43
  joining CIS 36
  leadership elections 50–55
  legislature 42–3
  nationalism in 41
  organized opposition in 50
  participation in State Council 35–6
  political elites in 41–60
  popular fronts 51
  transfer of power to 28–9
Rigby, T.H. 3, 11, 13, 14
Rimachevskaya, Natalia 174
Rogovin, Vadim 225
RSFSR *see* Russia
Rumyantsev, Oleg 77
Russia
  challenge to centre 24, 59
  Committee for the Liberation of
    Russia 177
  cooperatives in 45
  deputies 45, 50
  employment laws 128
  ethnic minorities 45
  housing 213, 221, 222
  intelligentsia in 44
  leadership elections 50, 55
  nuclear weapons, veto over 30
  Politburo 17
  political parties in 17
  poverty level 199, 200
  presidential system set up in 31–4
  Prime Minister 57
  stock exchanges 192–3
  unemployment benefits 128

  women in 178
  youth 149
  see also Eltsin, Boris; republics
Russification 43–4
Rutland, Peter 129–30
Rutskoi, Aleksandr V. 39–40
Ruutel, Arnold 51
Ryavec, Karl W. 13
Ryzhkov, Nikolai 12, 27, 126, 195,
  198

Samsonov, Colonel General Viktor
  110
Saptsina, Natalia 175
Savisaar, Edgar 57
scientists, 91–2, 96
SDPR *see* Social Democratic Party of
  Russia
Security Council 24, 25–6, 32, 34
Semenova, Galina 168
Semichastny, V.E. 152
Sergeev, Aleksandr 127
Shakhrai, Sergei 33
Shaposhnikov, Evgenii 34
Sharifulina, Rimma 175
Sharkhrai, Sergei 32
Shelepin, A.N. 152
Sherova, Liudmila 174, 175–6
shestidesyatniki 105
Shevardnadze, Eduard A. 12
Shokhin, Aleksandr 32
Shreeves, Rosamund 178
Shushkevich, Stanislav 54, 55
Sigua, Tengiz 57, 59
Silaev, Ivan 38–9, 57
Sillaste, Galina 167, 171
Sklyapentokh, Vladimir 108
Snegur, Mircea 51, 59
Sobchak, Anatoly 32, 49, 94, 95, 110,
  195
Social Democratic Party of Russia
  (SDPR) 63–81
  age structure 74
  attitude to Union 64
  composition of 64
  congresses of 64–5
  date of entry into politics 75–6
  leadership of 77
  status factors
    educational level 70, 73

income level 67, 70, 73
  occupational structure 69, 73
Social Democratic Union, Leningrad
  63, 76–7
Sokolov 12
Soviet Union, break-up of 36
Stalin, Joseph 10–11, 101, 104
  regime 4, 11, 118, 203
Stankevich, Sergei B. 39
Starkov, Vladislav 108
State Council 24, 35–6
stock exchanges 191
Supreme Soviet 9, 26, 42, 50–55, 123,
  124
  Presidium of 4
  women in 169

Tajikistan
  Communist Party in 48
  deputy elections 43
  leadership elections 53, 54, 55
  nine-plus-one agreement 29
  poverty level 200
  Prime Minister 56
  urban migration 117
  women in 42
  see also Central Asian republics;
    republics
Talyzin, N.V. 12
Tarasov 195
Ter-Petrosian, Levon 44, 51, 57, 58
Tereshchenko 56
Tocqueville, Alexis de 105–6
trade unions 120, 123
  independent 126–7, 129
  official, reorganization of 124–5
  perestroika and 125, 208
Travkin, Nikolai 78
Trotsky, Leon 10
Tsaregorodtsev, Aleksei 33
Turkmenistan
  housing 213
  leadership elections 53–4
  Prime Minister 56
  representation of workers and
    peasants 43
  urban migration 117
  see also Central Asian republics
Tyutchev, Fedor 101

Ukraine
  agreement with Russia 29
  challenge to centre 60
  Communist Party in 43
  cooperatives in 45
  deputies 45, 50
  employment laws 128
  leadership elections 53, 54, 55
  Prime Minister 56
  students' organizations 156
  vote for independence 36
  women in 178
  youth, education of 149
  see also republics
unemployment 121, 128–9, 205–6
  benefit 128, 129
  financial provision for 202
  State Employment Service 128, 129
  women 128, 166, 207
  youth 207
urbanization 116–17
USSR, break-up of 36
Ustinov, Marshal Dimitri F. 12
Uzbekistan
  cooperatives in 45
  deputies 45
  leadership elections 53, 54, 55
  nine-plus-one agreement 29
  Prime Minister 56
  representation of workers and
    peasants 43
  urban migration 117
  see also Central Asian republics;
    republics

vigilantes 157, 158, 159–60
Voronina, Olga 174

welfare benefits 201–3
women
  anti-nationalist action 178
  biologism and 166
  cash transfers 202
  Centre for Gender Studies 172,
    173–4, 175
  child care and 167, 168
  Committee for the Liberation of
    Russia 177
  CPSU and 169–70
  Dubna Forum 177, 178

elites and 178
employment of 208
feminism 174
First Independent Women's Forum
  168
Free Association of Feminist
  Organizations (SAFO) 173
gender roles, concept of 170
groups 170–71
Independent Women's Democratic
  Initiative 176
Independent Women's Forum
  172–8
nationalism and 178
organizations 171–2
perestroika and 166–81
political representation of 167–9
post-*perestroika* 170–71
republic legislatures and 42–3
Soviet Women's Committee 168,
  173
unemployment 128, 166, 207
Woman and Democracy Fund 174
workers
  blue-collar 114, 115, 129
    CPSU and 118
    educational and skill levels 115
    interests of 119
    social mobility 117
    trade unions and 120
  manual 114–32
    organizations of 119
  participation 121, 123
  perestroika and 121–4, 127–30
  pre-*perestroika* 118–21
  representation of 130
  republic legislatures and 42–3
  skilled 69, 70, 71
  unemployment *see* unemployment
  white-collar 114

Yablokov, Aleksei 33
Yakovlev, Aleksandr 103, 106
Yakovlev, Egor 107
Yakovlev, Justice Minister 90
Yanaev, Gennadii 26, 109, 126
Yazov, Dmitrii 26
Young Pioneers 153
youth
  age at marriage 150
  aspirations of 16
  consumerist-hedonism 159
  defining 149–50
  education of 149–50
  future of 163–4
  groups
    informals 76, 162
    lyubery 159
    political
      Anarchists 158–9
      Fascist sympathisers 162
      Optimists 158
      pacifists 158
    teenage gangs 160–62
    vigilantes 157, 158, 159–60
  historical role of 150–52
  housing 213–14, 217
  Komsomol and 152–5
  perestroika and 156–63
  political activity 159
  poverty level 163
  student action 156–7
  subculture 79
  unemployment and 207
  Young Pioneers 153, 157

Zalygin, Sergei 107
Zaramensky, Igor 119–20
Zaslavskaya, Tatiana 223
Zinoviev, Alexander 11, 115